D0216128

Learning Resources Center
Santa Fe Community College
P.O. Box 4187
Santa Fe, New Mexico 87502

Violence,
Resistance,
and
Survival
in
the
Americas

▲ ▲ ▲

Violence, Resistance, and Survival in the Americas

▲ ▲ ▲

Native Americans and the Legacy of Conquest

Edited by
William B. Taylor
and
Franklin Pease G.Y.

Smithsonian Institution Press

Washington and London

Copyright © 1994 by Smithsonian Institution.

Chapter 7, "Maintaining the Road of Life," copyright © 1990 by Alice B. Kehoe.

The excerpts from *The Heights of Macchu Picchu* by Pablo Neruda appearing on page 274 in English translation copyright © 1966 by Nathaniel Tarn are reprinted by permission of Farrar, Straus and Giroux, Inc.

All other rights are reserved.

Copyediting by Gretchen Smith Mui.
Production editing by Rebecca Browning.
Design by Janice Wheeler.

Library of Congress Cataloging-in-Publication Data

Violence, resistance, and survival in the Americas: Native Americans and the legacy of conquest / edited by William B. Taylor and Franklin Pease G.Y.
    p. cm.
    Includes bibliographical references and index.
    ISBN 1-56098-260-8 (alk. paper)
    1. Indians—Government relations.   2. Indians—History.   3. Indians of North America—Government relations.   4. Indians—Ethnic identity.   I. Taylor, William B. II. Pease G. Y., Franklin, 1939–
    E59.G6V56   1993
    970.004'97—dc20   93-11331

British Library Cataloguing-in-Publication Data is available.

For permission to reproduce the individual illustrations appearing in this book, please correspond directly with the owners of the works as given in the illustration captions. The Smithsonian Institution Press does not retain the right to reproduce these illustrations individually or maintain a file of addresses for photo sources.

Manufactured in the United States of America.

10 9 8 7 6 5 4 3 2 1
02 01 00 99 98 97 96 95 94

∞ The paper used in this publication meets the minimum requirements of the American National Standard for Permanence of Paper for Printed Library Materials Z39.48-1984.

Contents

Violence,
Resistance,
and
Survival
in
the
Americas

▲ ▲ ▲

Introduction

The year 1992 inevitably will be known on both sides of the Atlantic Ocean as the quincentenary of the European discovery of America, an anniversary more celebrated in Spain and Portugal, more lamented and protested in Latin America, and more promoted in the United States. Whether celebrated, lamented, protested, or promoted, it cannot be ignored: Too much of the modern history of Europe and America flows too conspicuously from the consequences of Columbus's first voyage.

Violence, Resistance, and Survival in the Americas: Native Americans and the Legacy of Conquest is part of this commemoration of 1492. These essays are based on presentations by scholars who gathered in Washington, D.C., and College Park, Maryland, in May 1989 at the invitation of the Smithsonian Institution and the University of Maryland for two days of public conversation about Native Americans and Europeans in the history opened by Columbus. The presentations generally concentrated on two subjects: (1) the violence of conquest and (2) resistance and survival. The authors come to the subject of Native Americans and Columbian legacies from a variety of experiences and interests. Among us there are Native Americans, European North Americans, Mexicans, a Peruvian, and an Australian; there are historians, literary scholars, sociologists, and history-minded anthropologists. In the essays some authors focus on European perceptions (sometimes in combination with pointed criticism of Western scholarship as fully implicated in perpetuating a culture of conquest). Others focus on violence by rulers or armed resistance by subjects. Still others focus on Native American appropriations, adaptations, and long-term continuities that do not fit easily into the categories of violence and resistance. The 1989 symposium also was enriched by two presentations that were not revised for publication—one by Arturo Warman, distinguished Mexican anthropologist and then director of the Instituto Nacional Indigenista; the other by Patricia Limerick, professor of history at the University of Colorado and a leading figure in the "new" western history of the United States. Their presentations are discussed briefly with the essays in parts 1 and 3—Warman's for its contribution to the meaning of European conquest in the early colonial period; Limerick's for its twist on Native American resistance and survival in the United States today.

While the essays do not attempt to cover all periods or the gamut of encounters and the authors do not all agree on the nature and legacy of conquest in America, this volume offers more than diverging opinions and differences scattered over time and place. The essays overlap, converge, and complement one another in ways that were not altogether evident in the conquest-and-resistance arrangement of papers in 1989. They are rearranged here in a three-part, roughly chronological organization that highlights the strongest regional and conceptual connections and the theme of survival that runs through most of them. The volume moves from sixteenth-century Spanish-American encounters (part 1), to strategies of survival within great change in late colonial Mexico (part 2), to postcolonial and contemporary issues of the survival of native North Americans (part 3).

As Rolena Adorno observes in her essay, writings on the legacy of conquest recently have shifted from an emphasis on the defeat of Native Americans to an emphasis on survival. These essays reflect this trend, many of them offering long views of America and Native Americans after 1492 that range beyond the Black Legend of Spanish abuses—in which Europeans almost single-handedly made an American New World, first by destroying what they found—and tears for the conquered, which Michael Taussig and José Rabasa warn against as another form of colonial knowledge making. All these essays implicitly share a historical view of Native Americans and their knowledge as having a present and future as well as a past, whether their emphasis is on resistance and survival or violence and unequal struggles.

The essays by Franklin Pease, José Rabasa, and Rolena Adorno (part 1), are concerned with early colonial Spanish America and share with Michael Taussig's coda a concern for narrative forms, perception, cultural distance, and the violence that results when cultures collide and reform. Narrative accounts of the early history of the Spaniards' conquest of the Indians, whether written by Spaniards or Indians, become here less a literary form or objective description of events and circumstances than an expression of the narrator, a way to martial information and experience for political and moral uses.

Franklin Pease uses sixteenth-century Spanish chronicles of the conquest of Peru and his mastery of Inca history to reveal Spanish perceptions about indigenous leadership as justifications for colonization. Pease shows how the early chroniclers applied an ethical template of proper kingly conduct and Christian rights of conquest that imagined Atahualpa as an illegitimate, devious tyrant who fully deserved his execution. In the chroniclers' hands the conflict between Atahualpa and his half-brother Huáscar lost its ritual war aspect and became simply a civil war in which Huáscar, the "natural lord," was betrayed and eliminated by his bastard kinsman. In these accounts Atahualpa, by plotting the destruction of Spaniards as well as Huáscar, betrayed both. Pease finds in these sources a codification of the Conquest—an official version of the stories Spaniards told themselves and their subjects—in which chroniclers of the 1550s elaborated on the first accounts to complete the picture of the Inca lord's cruelty and treacherous ways. Atahualpa quickly came to symbolize the natural state of Inca society and the justification of Spanish rule.

José Rabasa also addresses a "culture of conquest"—the ideology of European colonizers who denounced atrocities done to Native Americans, as well as those who perpetrated them and those who have kept these European accounts alive in the twentieth century. His sources are the writings of Alvar Núñez Cabeza de Vaca, who experienced America from the periphery of Spain's colonial empire; he was shipwrecked on the Gulf Coast of Florida in 1528, wandering for years in remote borderlands to the west, and then served as royal governor during the 1540s on the isolated southern frontier of the Spanish empire in modern Argentina. Rabasa warns against celebrating Cabeza de Vaca the narrator as a subverter of the Conquest, as a forerunner of the modern exile who encountered the New World not as conqueror but as impotent, isolated intruder, unable to stop the Spanish atrocities that went on around him. In Rabasa's view Cabeza de Vaca's vision of himself and the Spanish mission was not greatly changed by his unusual experience of America. His accounts provide a familiar moral allegory of a sinful descent into American chaos and barbarism and a gratifying redemption that depended on good works, especially Christian evangelization and the peaceful domination of indigenous people. He never rejected the idea of Spanish colonization and control and repeatedly justified violent conquest on the basis of a right of Christians to evangelize heathens, the natives' cannibalism, and the treachery of "enemy" Indians. His denunciations of the Spaniards' abuses (including their fall into cannibalism during their harrowing journey in the southeastern United States) were framed as the true account of a law-abiding servant of the Crown who, not incidentally, presented himself as the exemplary *adelantado* (governor of a frontier province). His accounts systematically neglected native resistance that called into question the legitimacy of Spanish rule.

Rolena Adorno's "The Art of Survival in Early Colonial Peru" offers an Indian perspective on the first encounters and early Spanish colonization in Peru through Felipe Guaman Poma de Ayala's magnificent *El primer nueva corónica y buen gobierno* (1615). More than an illustrated chronicle of events, Guaman Poma's manuscript is an act of resistance expressed in loyal, colonial terms: an appropriation of the written word and Christian ethics for a withering critique of the practice of Spanish colonialism on its own terms and an appeal to the king of Spain for judgment and reform. It is an eloquent colonial Indian response to the culture of conquest outlined by Pease and Rabasa. In contrast to Atahualpa, whom Guaman Poma sees as defeated by the Book (that is, by his failure to accept the silent, written word of God), he embraces writing as an instrument of legal and spiritual defense against oppression by Spanish colonists and a means to advance the pretensions to authority of his class of descendants from native lords. Adorno sees Guaman Poma's spidery script and powerful drawings as a richly compelling document of Indian resistance to, appropriation of, and accommodation to colonial rule all at once. The massive document Guaman Poma produced with so much care stands more as an artifact of his will to resist than as proof of the successful resistance he intended. His report did not move the king to action and was filed away.

Arturo Warman's symposium presentation explored a different kind of violence in the transcontinental encounters that took place in sixteenth-century

Mexico—the conquest of the landscape, a war waged with plants, mammals, microbes, and mills. For Warman, America was "the most dramatic and traumatic conquest of all" because the sudden changes that followed Columbus ranged far beyond the Spaniards' overthrow of native states to enslavement, illness, hunger, and destruction of natural resources and much knowledge of their uses. Warman highlighted one intentional aspect of the Spaniards' ecological domination—the appropriation and redirection of water—to illustrate his vision of missed perceptions, deep political and ethical differences, and destruction. To the Spaniards the intricate irrigation works on terraced hillsides that watered patchworks of small, irregular, mixed-crop, labor-intensive gardens were chaotic. They needed reordering into great uniform valley fields of sugar cane and wheat nourished with water diverted from the hills. The crops from these fields would be ground into sweet juice and flour by water-driven mills. Ecological degradation was a brutal challenge to Native Americans' survival under colonial rule, but Warman also recognized that the destruction was never complete, that even today knowledge of the old irrigation systems survives in neglected places close to Mexico City and could well contribute to renewed agricultural productivity in a land of dwindling natural resources.

The essays in part 2 provide three case studies of Indian strategies of survival, adaptation, and cultural creativity in the colonial context of eighteenth-century Mexico. The first, by José Luis Mirafuentes Galván, introduces the armed resistance that the title of this volume seems to promise. His setting is the northwest frontier of Mexico during the active missionary and presidio expansion of the 1740s in the territory of the Seris. The mixed results of that expansion, the longer history of Spanish-Indian relations in the area, and the Seri responses in the 1740s exemplify an incomplete, ongoing conquest in which Indians usually had the upper hand and colonial policy tilted between broad concessions and armed repression. But Mirafuentes reveals more complicated reasons than Indian rejection of Christianity and permanent settlement for the failure of this mission initiative and the Seri resistance that grew to regional proportions in the 1750s and 1760s. Intertribal conflict, in this case between the Seri and the Pima Bajo, apparently was decisive. As one Seri observed, Christianity was good but it meant living in pueblos and inevitable death at the hands of the Pima. The Seri had no wish to commit collective suicide for Christian salvation and European civility.

For an area east of the Seri's territory in modern Chihuahua and Durango, William Merrill's "Cultural Creativity and Raiding Bands in Eighteenth-Century Northern New Spain" explores a different kind of armed resistance to the colonial presence and the emergence of a new cultural form. The resistance itself was not unusual—raiding bands had operated in northern Mexico from the time of the earliest colonial settlements (if not before) and had become increasingly common in central and western Mexico during the decades before 1810, when the War of Independence began. But the social origins of the members and the society they apparently were forming to support the raids were novel. In the early 1770s the familiar temporary bands of non-Indian and Indian raiders were swollen with apostate Tarahumara Indians, who resisted a revived colonial campaign to resettle more Tarahumaras in missions, establish new presidios, and launch punitive campaigns against Indians and others in the region who lived beyond colonial rule. The raiders gathered into several small settlements in the remote hill country under the leadership of two Apache Indians to organize their long-distance attacks on haciendas, establish more permanent settlements that practiced agriculture, and begin to form families and a political-military order. Here were new multiethnic bands in the process of becoming communities, which Merrill compares to Maroon societies of the Caribbean basin. As he explains, their resistance to colonial society was more political than cultural, apparently intending to destroy the haciendas but evincing little of the nativism mentioned by the authors in part 3.

William Taylor's essay concerns Indian communities in the settled heartland of central and western Mexico, where the indigenous population had been densest in precolonial times and where Spanish colonization and institutionalization were strongest. Through two symbols introduced by Spanish rulers—Saint James the Greater (the Spaniards' warrior patron saint) and the Indian officeholders' staffs of office—he illustrates how colonial Indians there operated with a good deal of local political initiative, struggled over local power, and protected against new demands from Spanish authorities after 1750 without directly challenging that authority or contributing much to Indian class identity. Both the patronage of Santiago's horse and the independence contained in the alcaldes' staffs of office, which were bestowed upon them by the Crown, expressed a localized Christian identity that interpreted, adjusted to, and appropriated the received beliefs and expectations of parish priests and other colonial officials. Resistance of the kind described in this essay was located well within the colonial framework, and its practitioners—unlike Merrill's raiders—were players more than counterplayers in the colonial experience. Taylor's Santiago of multivalent, local meanings challenges the Santiago often depicted as undergoing only one apparent change in the Atlantic crossing, from Matamoros (Moor slayer) to Mata-indios (Indian slayer).

The four essays of part 3 continue the discussion of Native American survival, adaptation, and cultural creativity in the United States since the early nineteenth century. Three of the four examine Native American resilience in the face of old cleavages and new pressures and uncertainties of their lives as Americans as well as Native Americans. The fourth is concerned with the continuing challenge posed to social and cultural survival by the reservation system.

Alice Kehoe's "Maintaining the Road of Life" and Duane Champagne's "Change, Continuity, and Variation in Native American Societies as a Response to Conquest" offer panoramic views of the legacy of conquest and general approaches to the study of social and cultural change and strategies of persistence. Kehoe's concept of maintaining the road of life, borrowed from a Plains Indian metaphor of life as a road travelled, suggests how many American Indian societies have been able to continue fundamental cultural ways even in the face of great obstacles, the greatest of which has been the European invasion of America and its reverberations. The essence of this road of life has been the cultivation of plants and an ethic of living with rather than dominating other forms of life. Her point is not that Plains Indian societies, among others, have remained unchanged but that they have been able to reestablish the road of life by "reformulation" in situations of accumulating crisis. Reformulation often has hinged on the appearance of a prophet who articulates the crisis, proposes changes, and is understood and followed by the group members. The Ghost Dance of 1890 and its heirs in the modern Wahpeton Dakota village of Saskatchewan, Canada, are her prime examples.

Kehoe, like several authors in part 1, uncovers a modern culture of conquest in the form of myths about Native American societies and their adjustments to European occupation, myths that legitimated European conquest and continue to justify the paternalism of the national government. She calls special attention to the myth of the vanishing primitive (in which Native Americans have a past but hardly a present or future and even in their pristine state occupied an inferior place in the order of human development) and the myth of the Ghost Dance as a momentary event that caused the Sioux outbreak at Wounded Knee in 1890 and resulted in the destruction of a spiritual vision of independence about the Plains Indians.

Champagne, in his thoughtful prolegomenon for a more historical and comparative study of institutional change and cultural survival in Native American society, would agree with Kehoe's criticism of the myth of the vanishing primitive (he would add that much scholarship on Indian assimilation and acculturation, as well as some of the emphasis on tribal factionalism, also has been misguided) and her emphasis on persistence and reformulation. She, in turn, would agree with his observations that the destruction of a culture is a rare event, that Native American creation myths have been an enduring aspect of social and political organization, and that one-dimensional ways of thinking about the legacy of conquest are inadequate. But Champagne's approach to social and cultural change focuses more on variation among tribal communities and the importance of internal institutional arrangements in accounting for resistance to change and the relative strength of collective action. Without slighting the revitalization movements central to Kehoe's essay (which he considers typical of groups with decentralized, segmented social and political institutions), Champagne is especially interested in the more enduring and extensive institutional changes that occurred during the nineteenth century among the Cherokee, Chickasaw, and Choctaw with their relatively differentiated social orders that were less tied to a cosmogonic prescription for political organization. His attention to the institutionalization of change leads him to highlight the importance of peyote religion in comparison with the Ghost Dance and to see internal conflict as perennial, not necessarily fractional or dangerous to the life of the tribal community.

For Patricia Limerick, too, Native American resistance did not end in 1890 at Wounded Knee any more than military engagement was the only form of conquest or the American West was conquered once and for all. In her symposium presentation "From Warriors to Lawyers: The Native American Rights Fund in Historical Perspective," she noted that resistance has moved from battlefields to courtrooms, specifically Indian lawyers' recent challenges to physical anthropologists over rights to the human remains that have been unearthed from Indian burial grounds and taken off to museums. Whether or not the museums and physical anthropologists in question qualify as latter-day conquerors and grave robbers, the litigation does pit the idea of Indian relics as artifacts of nature and the public domain against the civil and property rights of tribal communities. Here, as Limerick observed, the Indian lawyers have been "adapting the invaders' tools to native purposes." Her good-natured but not light-hearted presentation in the end turned the spotlight on scholarship concerning Native Americans, suggesting that where scholars fit into the legacy of conquest and why they do the work they do should be at the top of the academy's agenda.

David Reed Miller's "Definitional Violence and Plains Indian Reservation

Life" concerns the struggles over incorporating outsiders and maintaining old solidarities within and beyond reservation boundaries on the northern plains since the late nineteenth century. "Definitional violence"—the challenges to group identity, social organization, and traditional conceptions of land and community posed by changing government definitions of membership and rights—is at the heart of this discussion. While negotiated settlements were a strategy that Plains Indians adopted for their survival in the reservation setting, Miller's story is mainly one of forced overcrowding, disunity, friction over property rights, breakup of tribal lands, manipulation of tribal councils by government officials, and broken promises. The importance of this essay for the study of violence and survival in the Columbian legacy is to underscore the constraints on creative adaptation set by national and state governments. Miller concludes that the goals of Sioux and Assiniboine reservation Indians still are full participation in decisions that affect them and independent management of their own resources. Can these goals be realized? The history he recounts suggests that the outcome is largely beyond these peoples' control.

Jennie R. Joe completes part 3 with a contemporary study of tribal identity and native cultures among Yaqui and Tohono O'odham women in Tucson, Arizona. In contrast with the definitional violence of reservation history that Miller recounts, Joe's story concerns the results of a different kind of government program in the 1950s and 1960s, one that encouraged Native Americans to leave the reservations and relocate in cities. It is the one essay to focus on women and individual differences in this legacy of conquest that counterpoises Europe and America and emphasizes continuities within change. In her well-documented telling, the leading bearers of their tribes' culture in Tucson are the women who best know how the city works and how its officials think. While her study confirms the resilience of tribal identification, even in this most national kind of American community, and places women at the center of this continuity, it is not simply an account of separation and persistence. Although many of the women she studied choose to live among members of their tribe, many others live well within non-Indian urban culture and have married into non-Indian families. Some have come to define their separate identity less in tribal than national terms, as American Indians or Native Americans.

The collection of essays ends with Michael Taussig's reflection on the Columbus quincentenary as colonial knowledge making and representation. Although it complements the essays in parts 1 and 3 that note how scholars themselves are embedded in the legacy of conquest, it serves more as a coda than a conclusion to the volume because it proposes an alternative perspective. The touchstone for his healing subversion of much scholarship that speaks of the legacy of conquest is the response of his shaman friend, Santiago Mutumajoy, to the monumental manicured ruins of ancient Machu Picchu in Peru:

> There weren't any poor people here. These houses were for the rich. I've seen it before. These mountains. These stones. Exactly the same. Several times. . . . The Spanish built all this. . . . The Spanish threatened the Indians with the whip and that's how they carried these stones and set them in place.

Taussig invites his readers to be the sorcerer's apprentices, too—to learn from Mutumajoy's unsettling representation of a precolonial ruin as a colonial creation, to recognize "the strategic vacuities and switch-points . . . of our dominant discourses" and "our profound entanglement" and self-justifications in our representations of others. Taussig asks unsettling questions of his own about the meaning of context and "who benefits from studies of the poor, especially from their resistance." His concern for "abating misfortune" leads him to urge us to "wrest tradition away from conformism" and offer less objectified simplifications of the Other and Elsewhere. His technique is dialectical images of the "face of the people" that are intended to shock us into new ways of thinking—into discovery about ourselves as well as the New World—that resist "intellectual colonization."

Few of the authors in this collection would accept conquest as a satisfactory metaphor for the history of Native Americans since 1492. But if America was not just a "slaughterhouse of the gods" (Flandrau 1964:61) and if colonial and postcolonial "Indians" did not simply "shrink instinctively from the rude touch of a foreign hand," their members "silently melt[ing] away" (Prescott n.d.:34), what should replace the clash-and-displacement model? What kinds of survival have taken place since Columbus? How has survival been expressed? Two approaches in recent years that find occasional echoes in this volume are (1) an emphasis on collision, confrontation, and open resistance on the Native American side; and (2) an emphasis on continuities in Native American life while acknowledging external pressures for change. In emphasizing continuity both these approaches to survival tend to gloss over cultural and political changes that may have been profound.

Chances for the survivals presented in these essays depended not only on the various strategies, timing, and instruments of domination of the Spanish, the

English, and Americans of all kinds but also on natural resources, disease, and the social organization and cultural creativity of the descendants of native people. The great challenge for any approach to the legacy of conquest that would emphasize survival is to do justice simultaneously to complicated local changes as well as continuities and see American history more inclusively, not primarily as the repeated collision of alien worlds in which the only possible outcomes are absolute domination or liberation. Essays in all three sections explore this shifting ground of colonialism as a shared but contested culture that lies between the fixed points of surrender and liberation (Nandy 1983, 1989). While recognizing the inevitable oppositions and separations in colonial and post-colonial histories, they attend to ambiguities of domination, particularly Native Americans resorting to strategies of "pragmatic submission" (Scott 1985:315) and their appropriating the colonizers' power for their own purposes. Survival over the course of five centuries has inevitably entailed some creative use of the larger colonial or national system.

In a long view of the legacy of conquest, the categories of West and non-West or Native American and European become blurred despite legal definitions, self-identification, race prejudice, and reservations. As Ashis Nandy might say, Guaman Poma, colonial Tarahumaras and Seri, and nineteenth-century Cherokee, Iroquois, and Sioux were all participants in Westernization, not simply enemies or prostrate victims of it. Native American resistance could find its ideological grounding *within* the colonial or postcolonial order, as in Guaman Poma's appeal to Christian doctrine and royal law for his critique of Spanish colonialism, the new meanings of Santiago in *pueblos de indios* of central Mexico, the Cherokees' revised political institutions, the Native American Rights Fund lawyers' brief against physical anthropologists, or the Christian features of the Ghost Dance and peyote rituals.

Several authors in the collection invite the reader to ask whether these essays are just another way of possessing the conquered, whether they replace old myths of defeated primitives with new, more subtle ones that still reveal more about the authors than they do about their subjects. Are the authors acting as the heirs of the first conquerors even as they question the metaphor of conquest? If so, their versions of the 1492 legacy at least offer more room for Native American voices to be heard and the complications of human experience to be felt. They are not writing Native Americans out of history only as victims who suffered or as fallen heroes. What these essays celebrate is the variety of human responses and adaptations in a colonial and postcolonial history of demographic disaster, centralizing states, and the formation of larger and more integrated economies that cannot be understood simply in terms of conquest. In different ways all the authors, whether they regard the past as knowable or not, invite readers to consider the legacy of conquest as something more than a story of European agents and Indian victims.

References

Flandrau, Charles M. 1908. Reprint, 1964. *Viva Mexico!* Urbana: University of Illinois Press.

Nandy, Ashis. 1983. *The Intimate Enemy: Loss and Recovery of Self under Colonialism*. Delhi: Oxford University Press.

1989. *The Tao of Cricket: On Games of Destiny and the Destiny of Games*. London: Viking.

Prescott, William H. 1843. This ed., *History of the Conquest of Mexico and History of the Conquest of Peru*. New York: The Modern Library.

Scott, James C. 1985. *Weapons of the Weak: Everyday Forms of Peasant Resistance*. New Haven, Conn.: Yale University Press.

Part 1
Early Encounters
and the
Culture
of
Conquest
▲▲▲

Spanish and Andean Perceptions of the Other in the Conquest of the Andes

Franklin Pease G. Y.

Recent research has revealed the need to reexamine the way in which Spaniards and Andeans perceived each other. The Other thus takes on new importance and deserves greater examination. Scholars have noted that the attitude of the European in general was not open to perceiving and seeing the American. Rather, Europeans actually sought to recognize in American people and societies what their own European history allowed them to accept. By accepting a Eurocentric history as the only true history, Europeans interpreted Americans and their social organizations within a European mindset. This can be seen as far back as the writings of Christopher Columbus and certainly in the Spanish experience in the Antilles and Mexico.

I will not describe here the various perceptions of the Other throughout the Spanish occupation of America. I will treat only the central Andes, although I must point out a continuity in the uniformity of opinions and contrasts. That Europeans used their own preconceptions to see and recognize Americans is not a new idea. But they did more: They transferred categories and stereotypes of the people, from the Antilles to Mexico and from Mexico to the Andes. This transference and stereotyping occurred also with language. Early chronicles and administrative colonial documents recorded the presence of Nahuatl and even Taíno terms in the Andes. These helped the Spanish identify—in reality, recognize—new situations and objects (such as *tiánguez* for Indian markets or *cacique* for local ruler).

The case of the Inca is interesting. It was natural that he himself was identified as a king who obtained his power through an original divine mandate and transferred it through a legitimate patrilineal lineage. He thus had the right to levy taxes, expand his power by means of conquest, and govern on the basis of patrimony. As it appeared to the chroniclers, the Inca—like the king—appointed authorities, determined how the wealth produced was to be used, and granted even the most trivial rights of his subjects, such as marriage and the allocation of land. Certainly, the Inca was idolized, like the devil in the Christian conception, which gave credence to the Spaniards' perception of the Inca's status as "illegitimate" and "tyrannical."

It is important to describe here the dimensions of violence in the new hemisphere. Generally violence is described in terms of acts of war, theft, and extortion. However, many of the chronicles offer a different though congruent image: heroes—those who conquer—have to be strong and dominant. Their warrior's resolve required violence. The subsequent *rancheo* (thievery) and use of those conquered as laborers are regarded as natural consequences. Although chroniclers initially spoke about an avenging violence, they believed that the actions of those conquered provoked the violence of the Conquest. Their writings assumed that the conquistadors upheld high ideals—Christianization and the incorporation of Americans into civilization and, by extension, into history—and originally did not intend to wage war. Instead, those conquered betrayed the good intentions of the new arrivals, precipitating the "just" repression. It is thus important to describe some of the stereotypes that served as justification for the Conquest. In this essay I will discuss Andean traitors, specifically the Inca, and the identification of the Spaniards as gods.

Sixteenth-century Europeans did not view violence as an isolated phenomenon. On the contrary, they considered it a natural, inevitable, and not always dishonorable consequence of "just" wars or conquests. This applied not only to conflicts among Europeans, which were covered by a rule of law that was at times supernatural and always ethical, but also to their conquests to the extent that these served to integrate other human beings into the history of salvation and consequently saved them as well. Although this view appears to be contemporary, it derives from an old unilinear vision of history. From these and other such considerations a controversial interpretation of the violence of the Conquest could evolve, one that considers it independent of the realm of normal human behavior (normalcy having different characteristics at any given moment) and not a consequence of human acts and decisions themselves. Certainly this view would facilitate not a historical explanation of the violence but rather an explanation of history based on the violence itself. The latter is, of course, based on moral considerations that may very well be different today from those prevalent in the sixteenth century and also, specifically, in stereotyped visions of the past.[1] A historical explanation based on moral considerations, regardless of what these may be, is more a historical justification than a true explanation.

Most chronicles written by Spaniards during the sixteenth century about the Andean region explained the Andean people on the basis of a history understood to be already completed and ethically accepted. Not even authors usually considered to have challenged this view, such as Bartolomé de las Casas, would escape it completely. Thus it is important to analyze the stereotypes that helped justify the Conquest, for these, when combined with preexisting ethical explanations, transformed as a result of the march of history the portrayal of the Other—whether the conquerors or those conquered.

The Treacherous Andeans

The chronicles generally relate the betrayal of Native Americans who received the Europeans peacefully and subsequently not only repudiated them but also waged war against them. A good example of how the stereotype was designed is found in the chroniclers' descriptions of the Inca Atahualpa.

Francisco Pizarro arrived in the Andes at a moment when a transfer of power was taking place. The Inca Huayna Cápac had died, and the complex ritual that culminated in the designation of the new Inca was taking place. The Spaniards viewed the situation as a dynastic war in which those aspiring to power were fighting among themselves, not as the ritual war it was. They identified the protagonists as sons of the deceased Inca, ascribing to one of them, Huáscar, the characteristics of legitimacy and to another, Atahualpa, those of bastardy. The Spaniards justified the execution of Atahualpa because he was illegitimate, he had attempted a rebellion against the Spaniards, and he had ordered his brother Huáscar killed. In addition to rebellion, he was accused of usurpation, regicide, and fratricide. Thus, it was easy to condemn Atahualpa.

The version accusing Atahualpa of regicide and fratricide appears in the chronicle attributed to Cristóbal de Mena and also in a text whose authorship remains undetermined, although Miguel de Estete has been suggested as the possible author. Both were witnesses to the events at Cajamarca. The chronicle attributed to Mena, *La conquista del Perú*, was published in Seville in 1534; it is not known exactly when the other text was written, but it was published later.[2] In contrast, the accusation is not clearly stated in the chronicle by Francisco de Xerez, *Verdadera relación,* also published in Seville in 1534. He indicates only that "among the many messengers who came to Atabalipa, one of them who was bringing his brother as a prisoner came to tell him that when his captains learned of his imprisonment, they had already killed Cuzco [the name the first chroniclers gave to Huáscar]" (Xerez 1534:22b). Several pages earlier in the text Atahualpa had told Pizarro that he would deliver his brother to the Spaniards (Xerez 1534:21b).

The recounting attributed to Mena, on the other hand, sets forth a different version:

> . . . we learned that this cacique had captured another lord, who called himself Cuzco and who was a greater lord than he: he was his brother through his father and not his mother, and the same Cuzco who came as a prisoner learned how the Christians had captured his brother: and said if I were to see the Christians, I would be lord because I have a great desire to see them: and I know that they have come in search of me: and that Atahualpa promised them a hut of gold which I had for them: but I would give them four huts and they would not kill me like this one [Atahualpa] I think intends to do. After Atabalipa learned what his brother the Cuzco had said, he was in great fear that knowing this, the Christians would then kill him and elevate his brother the Cuzco to lord: and he ordered that they kill him immediately: and they killed him in such a way that he did not take advantage of the great fear that the governor had of Atabalipa. When he [Pizarro] learned that one of his [Atahualpa's] captains had him [Huáscar], he told [Atahualpa] not to have him killed, but to bring him there where they were. . . . (Anon. [1534] 1929:6–7)

Later on, the same author's version of Atahualpa's execution describes briefly how some of Atahualpa's other brothers arrived in Cajamarca ". . . well hidden out of fear of their brother. . . ." The next passage refers, as does Xerez's *Verdadera relación,* to the organization of an army to defeat the Spaniards.

The text presumed to be by Estete states that Pizarro had told Atahualpa he knew that

> . . . his brother arrived under arrest and had been destroyed by his [Atahualpa's] people; and that he had been told that he [Atahualpa] had ordered that wherever they found him on the way, they were to kill him; that under no circumstances should he do so because such things were a disservice to Our Lord God and would be so to the Emperor as well; that once [Huáscar] arrived, *depositions would be taken from both of them to determine whose was the lordship of the land, and he [Pizarro] would administer justice and there would be peace and harmony between them.* This was not to his [Atahualpa's] liking because, a few days later, news of his brother's death reached him and he excused himself by saying that he had not ordered his death and that those who were responsible did it on their own. . . . (*Noticia del Perú* 1918:26; emphasis added)

The description of Atahualpa's behavior is not only interesting but also closer to the relationship described by Mena and somewhat more detailed. It is also significant that the author of *Noticia del Perú* uses the name Huáscar (*Noticia* 1918:26), which was not known to and had never been mentioned by the other chroniclers who were in Cajamarca, including Xerez, Hernando Pizarro, and the author of the chronicle attributed to Mena. This could be one reason to believe that the text attributed to Estete was written at a later date; not even Pedro Sancho, a chronicler who served as Pizarro's secretary after Xerez's trip to Spain and who went with Pizarro to Cuzco mentions Huáscar's name. He is even doubtful about the name Huayna Cápac (viz. Sancho 1962).

In most of the chronicles mentioned, the basis for the description of Atahualpa's behavior as fickle and treacherous was his formation of an army to fight the Spaniards. Since cruelty (always more visible in the Other than in oneself) needed to be added, the author of *Noticia del Perú* would later recount that when Pizarro and Father Valverde admonished Atahualpa for having ordered Huáscar's murder, Atahualpa stated that

> . . . it was something that ordinarily he [Atahualpa] was used to doing to *his brothers,* for which he received no reprimand because, as he himself said, he had killed many others of them who had been followers of his brother, including one whom he saw [who was coming to him?] with a message from his brother, he had flayed him in front of him, and he drank from his brother's head garnished with gold; this he did the day of his undoing. (*Noticia del Perú* 1918:26)

Only years later, when better information was available to chroniclers, would the complete version take shape. The omission of Huáscar's execution in Xerez's *Verdadera relación* becomes interesting given that his chronicle is frequently described as unquestionably a defense of Pizarro in response to the accusations of the Sevillian anonymous text attributed to Mena (Porras Barrenechea 1937). But the subject takes on new dimensions with subsequent authors, such as Pedro de Cieza de León and Juan de Betanzos, who wrote and published their works in the 1550s. Full editions of their works have only recently become available, and only now do we have their complete versions of the events at Cajamarca.[3] Combining their works with the *Historia del descubrimiento y conquista del Perú,* by Pizarro's accountant, Agustín de Zárate, who published his work in 1555, significantly broadens the discussion of the stereotype.

The full third part of Cieza de León's *Crónica del Perú,* together with the complete version of Betanzos's *Suma y narración de los Incas,* confirms the cruelty engaged in by Atahualpa's generals and followers in Cuzco on his orders. Ciezà de León goes so far as to affirm that Atahualpa "employed great cruelty and abuses . . ." (Cieza de León 1987: vol. 3, 113), adding that those who took Huáscar prisoner to Cajamarca determined ". . . to remain loyal [to] Atabalipa and betray him [Huáscar] . . ." (Cieza de León 1987: vol. 3, 143). Later on, he specifies that it was made known to Atahualpa, held prisoner in Cajamarca, that Huáscar was near the city and his captors wished to know what Atahualpa ordered

. . . because Guáscara [*sic*] showed a great desire to be in the hands of the Christians, his [Atahualpa's] enemies. When this messenger arrived, he spoke at length with Atabalipa; since he was so *prudent and clever,* he [Atahualpa] felt that it did not suit him to have his brother come or appear before the Christians, because they held him in higher esteem *for he was the natural lord;* but he did not dare order him killed out of fear of Pizarro, who had asked about him on many occasions. And in order to find out if his death weighed on him [Pizarro] or if he was compelled to order him brought alive, *he feigned* great passion and pain, so much so that Pizarro found out and came to console him, asking him why he was so grieved. Atabalipa *pretending even more grief,* told him that he knew that he should know that at the time when he arrived at Caxamalca with the Christians, a war was being waged between his brother Guáscar and himself; and that after many battles had taken place between them, he had remained in Caxamalca, having entrusted the business of war to his captains, who had taken Huáscar prisoner and were bringing him to where he was without having touched him, and that they *had killed him on the way,* according to the news he had received, which was the reason he was so angry. . . . (Cieza de León 1987: vol. 3, 144; emphasis added)

Betanzos's brief account of this episode does not provide as much detail as Cieza de León, but it states more clearly Atahualpa's moral responsibility:

. . . it seemed to Atahualpa that if Huáscar arrived alive there in Caxamalca and those "Viracochas" were to see him [Guáscar] and similarly, he would see him [Atahualpa] prisoner, Guáscar would say to the "Viracochas" that he would give them much more gold than he and thus they would make him Lord [Huáscar] and would kill him [Atahualpa]. . . . (Betanzos 1987:280)

There is a direct relationship between this last statement by Betanzos and the one quoted previously in the anonymous work attributed to Mena. Its author had Huáscar saying that he would give more gold to the Spaniards, although he added that Pizarro himself had indicated to Atahualpa that he did not order Huáscar killed.

Thus, beginning with the 1534 versions, the text attributed to Mena, the second version of the *Noticia del Perú,* and in the 1550s in the chronicles of Cieza de León and Betanzos, emphasis was increasingly placed on the image of a lying Atahualpa, who feigned emotion to manipulate Pizarro to act as suited him. The moral condemnation of Atahualpa for Huáscar's death is announced. The stereotype of a cheating, treacherous Atahualpa becomes gradually more precise, and his cruelty is conveniently portrayed. Atahualpa's tyranny had already been indicated, but the Inca's malicious and treacherous astuteness appears more clearly in the accounts by Cieza de León and Betanzos. Huáscar, described by Cieza de León as the "natural lord," eliminated any possible aspiration by Atahualpa himself to natural lordship. Thus, Atahualpa was fratricidal and regicidal, obviously a tyrant, cheater, and traitor. He had dared to trick the Spaniards by trying to confuse Pizarro, informing him of Huáscar's death before it was true. He had thus taken advantage of Pizarro's natural goodness and generosity. His felony was obvious.

The issue of natural lordship is connected to the argument used later by Las Casas and his followers. Here Cieza de León, as did Betanzos, limits the frame of reference: He alludes to Huáscar's natural lordship but grants *before* his death a basis for the right claimed by the Spaniards to see that justice is done by killing Atahualpa and that the natural lordship is returned to an "heir" designated by Pizarro himself from among the sons of the Inca Huayna Cápac. Thus, even before the actual event Pizarro's conduct was being justified.

There is some confusion here as to who the heir was. Xerez does not indicate his name clearly and further confuses matters by calling him Atabalipa (Xerez 1534:33). The 1534 anonymous Sevillian work mentions that ". . . everyone rejoiced in the death of this *cacique;* they could not believe he was dead . . ." (1534:11). This interpretation was widely contradicted by later Andean tradition, which honors Atahualpa[4] and recalls that "the lord governor elevated the Old Cuzco's older son to the rank of lord of that land, under the condition that he and all his people remain as vassals of the emperor . . ." (1534:11). In 1550 Betanzos had more information and could affirm that the heir named was Topa Gualpa ". . . a son of Guayna Cápac . . ." (but did not indicate that he was the eldest), whose death in Jauja made possible the eventual naming of Manco Inca (Betanzos 1987:287, 290).

The version of Atahualpa's reprehensible attitude was thus definitively fixed. It is not surprising that an author such as Zárate, who got his information before the defeat of Gonzalo Pizarro, included in his *Historia* an account that was both broad and detailed. Although Zárate published only in 1555, after the death of Cieza de León in Seville in 1554 (cf. Maticorena 1955) and the possible completion of Betanzos's work in 1551, it cannot be assumed that he read them. It is well known that not even the manuscript of Betanzos's *Suma y narración* circulated in Spain, and it is doubtful that Zárate, who was having personal problems and may have been in jail, could have had access to the third, unpublished portion of Cieza de León's work, even though it had other readers in Spain at that time.[5] Nonetheless, the general argument is the same: Atahualpa is defined as a shrewd and deceptive person. However, Zárate integrates into the work a new reference to the issue of natural lordship. In Zárate's account Huáscar says before dying, "I have been lord of the land for a short time, and my brother, by whose orders I die, will be so for less time, as I am his natural lord . . ." (Zárate 1944:64). This allowed Zárate to advance the idea that the Andean people believed that Huáscar was the son of the sun, since he was able to predict the imminent death of Atahualpa.[6]

Each account confirms the stereotype defined by the standard Spanish version. Atahualpa was a shrewd, felonious, and cruel murderer, fratricidal and regicidal, even murdering children. He had usurped power to displace

Huáscar and was not, in any case, a natural lord. Thus, despite the influence of Las Casas in Cieza de León's account, the revised accounts reflect a gradually growing coherence that not only leads to a specific description of the stereotype of Atahualpa—a violent usurper and tyrant who deceived the Spaniards—but also provides the justification for the war.

Thus, the Inca fulfills accusations that had been made since the chroniclers' earliest versions about the Andean people—and even earlier about other Americans: Their natural character was treacherous. From the earliest accounts of contacts with the Andean people, the Spaniards had been victims of betrayals. This was what happened, for example, on Puná Island, before the Spaniards actually reached the Andean mainland. Its inhabitants plotted betrayal to eliminate the Spaniards, who had been received ". . . with much joy and warmth as well as with basic foodstuffs which they took out to the road, and with various musical instruments that the natives have for their entertainment . . ." (Xerez 1534:4). However, later ". . . the *cacique* had called a meeting of all the warriors, and . . . for many days now he understood nothing but the making of weapons . . ." to fight the Spaniards (Xerez 1534:4). This betrayal justified the war. This style of pointing out the warm initial welcome and its subsequent betrayal is itself a convention that can be traced back to writings of Columbus's time (see, for example, Todorov 1982). It then was generalized from the Antilles to the Andes, passing, of course, through Mexico.

The Spaniards as Gods

A second stereotype is that the Andean people identified the Spaniards as gods returning to earth. It has become commonplace to compare the accounts found in Mexico with those of the Andes, although the route of the information has not been identified. I have stated that the early chroniclers did not seem to be in a position to have enough information available to them about the Andean people. This circumstance is important when attempting to analyze this type of information.[7] This is also the reason that the first authors, who wrote during the 1530s, were cautious about the information they provided about the Andeans' perception of the Spaniards while offering stereotyped or superficial information about the inhabitants of the Andes.

The standard version is that Andean men confused the Spaniards with

Viracocha and his attendants, children, or companions, who returned to the world from the sea. The suggestion is found more clearly in the chroniclers of the early 1550s—Betanzos and Cieza de León—and became more prevalent and more complex during the first part of the seventeenth century, as in Guaman Poma's *Nueva corónica.*

Four authors present the basic elements for a standard version of the myth of Viracocha: Cieza de León (1550), Betanzos (1551), Sarmiento de Gamboa (*La historia general llamada Indica,* 1572), and Cristóbal de Molina (*Fábulas y ritos de los Incas,* 1575). All four gathered their information in Cuzco, but the latter two did so many years later. Sarmiento obtained his information during the government of the viceroy Francisco de Toledo (1569–81), who protected him and used his services.[8] Molina wrote a history, since lost, of the Incas at an earlier date than that specified; he later wrote a "summary" that has survived and contains repeated references to the lost chronicle. All other authors who provide additional information to the versions of these four chroniclers use as their sources the works previously mentioned, elaborated in an oral context, sometimes adding specific local information.

The information about Cuzco used by Cieza de León, Betanzos, Sarmiento, and Molina has frequently been considered closer to the oral tradition. Not all of it was, although in the case of Betanzos, who was married to an Andean woman and knew Quechua, the oral tradition probably did predominate. A document written by the descendants of Tupa Inca Yupanqui and containing a detailed account of the conquests of this Cuzco ruler was recently discovered. Upon its publication, Rowe noted that the information it contains could well have been used by authors such as Sarmiento de Gamboa or Padre Miguel Cabello Balboa.[9] The existence of this type of document opens up a basic line of research, since it is expected that similar texts of great importance also will be found.

Betanzos recounted that Atahualpa received

. . . three Tallanes Indian messengers, "yngas" from Tangarala, who told him: Only Lord, you should know that some white, bearded men have come to our village of Tangarala, and they bring a sort of sheep on which they come, and they walk, and they are very big, bigger than ours, there are many of them, and these people come dressed in such a manner that only the skin of the hands and of the face shows, and of this last one, only half because the other half is covered by a beard growing out of it and these people have certain bands tied around them on top of their clothes and from these bands they have hanging a certain piece of silver that resembles those sticks that women put in their looms to tighten what they weave and the length of these pieces that they bring is almost an arm's length and they said this because of the swords and the Ynga told them and these people what are their names, they said they did not know, but that they called them *Viracocha cuna which means Gods* [emphasis added] and the Ynga told them: why have you called them Viracocha; they told him that because in olden times the Contiti Viracocha, who created the people once he had made them, had gone into the water through that sea further on and that he had not returned again according to what their aged elders told them and that certain people had come and had news that in past years certain peoples of those had come to Payta in a *guambo,* which they call ship which guambo was very large and that they had turned back from there. . . . (Betanzos 1987:235)[10]

The text continues with a series of descriptions of what the Spaniards did and how they were dressed.

The Tallanes, inhabitants of the northern coast of Peru, were questioned on a second occasion by the Inca, after mention was made of the *capito,* ". . . the Inca wanting to pronounce captain . . ." (Betanzos 1987:254). Next, mention is made that despite the news, Atahualpa, whom Betanzos always calls "Ynga,"

suspecting what later was to happen to him because of the fear of what he was hearing from the messengers he wanted to leave there to go into the Chachapoyas where it's called Lebando and his people told him that it was not something he should do *until he saw what kind of people they were, whether they were gods or men like them,* and whether they did good or evil and what new thing he should do until he could see this, and his having seen it himself would determine what they should do in such a case *if they were "runaquicacha," which means destroyers of people,*[11] in which case, not being able to resist them, they would flee from them, *and if they were "Viracocha cuna allichac"* which means *benevolent gods of the people, that in that case they should not flee from them,* and as the Ynga saw this opinion of his captains, he drew back from the fear that he had taken and said that *he was happy that during his lifetime gods would come to his land* who could not keep from doing something good and then he ordered the Tallanes Indian messengers to return and tell the *great captain Viracocha* that he was pleased with their arrival. . . ." (Betanzos 1987:255; emphasis added)

This sequence in the Betanzos text may be interpreted as follows: The Tallanes Indians are the first to affirm the possibility of the Spaniards being gods, which Betanzos himself alluded to in the first part of his work (Betanzos 1987:15). The chronicler puts the rationale in the words of the Tallanes and the Inca's captains. The former choice is surprising, because the northernmost version known that speaks about Viracocha (even though it refers to a local divinity) is contained in the texts collected by Francisco de Avila in the early seventeenth century in the much more southern region of Huarochiri.[12]

Betanzos applies a broad meaning to the term *Viracocha:* ". . . they call them Viracocha cuna, which means Gods . . ."; thus, it loses the nominal individual sense and suggests a generic one. The chronicler presents a dialogue in which the speakers seek to distinguish whether the Spaniards were "'runaquiçaca,' which means destroyers of people" or "'Viracocha cuna allichac,' which means benevolent gods of the people" (Betanzos 1987:255). In fact, the dichotomy suggests that Viracocha was identified also as a benevolent rather than destructive divinity. This would cause a problem if the more modern identification of the Viracochas as harmful beings is recalled; in fact, much later they are sometimes identified with *pishtaco,* who extracts the fat from its victims (cf. Fioravanti 1987). The identification originates from the commonplace explanation, already mentioned in the chronicles, of *wira* as fat. In any case, Betanzos's argument would not support such an identification for the 1550s, since the chronicler's account leads to the conclusion that the Viracochas are benefactors of the people. At another point Betanzos's text again refers to the Spaniards as Viracochas; being in Cuzco or near it, Cuxi Yupanqui, a messenger from Atahualpa, declared that Atahualpa wished to make a new Cuzco and thus had to vacate the original one and relocate the survivors to the northern region. He then reiterates:

. . . and moreover, I inform you that since the Ynga was in the "guaca" of Guamachuco from whence I came, two Tallanes came from Tangarala and brought them news of how the Viracocha had come out of the ocean and many other Viracochas with him and it is believed that they must be the ancient Viracochas that made the people and with this news, he was flattered, and as they told him that they had left by that part, the Inca wants to return on the same route he followed to Quito and meet up with them on the way *in order to see what they say to do which is the order that [the captains] will give for his preservation.* Hearing this, the captains were astonished at such news and thinking that it was like Cuxi Yupanqui told them *that they were gods and the Maker* and that success would come to their lord from this, they were glad and gave thanks to the Maker that they call Viracocha and to the sun in the place of the Ynga. . . . (Betanzos 1987:262; emphasis added)

By recounting all this information in detail, Betanzos seems to want to correct the error of an earlier interpretation. Later on, Cinquichara, an *orejón* (notable) from Xaquixaguana who had met with Pizarro in Tangaralá and had been sent by him to Atahualpa, tells Atahualpa:

> . . . I have tried to learn what people they were in order to see if it was the Contiti Viracocha and the Viracochas who in olden times came . . . and I understood from them that they are men like us and do not make any miracles nor do they make hills or flatten them nor make people or produce rivers or springs in places where water is needed because crossing through sterile parts from here they carry water with them in jugs and gourds and the Viracocha who made the world before did everything that I have said. . . . (Betanzos 1987:264; for a similar text, see Titu Cusi Yupanqui 1985:26a)

The final image is clearer. Viracocha made the world, leveled hills, produced rivers and springs, and created people. Betanzos's version of divinity is somewhat more complex, since this divinity created people only after having arranged the heavens and the earth and sending the sun and the moon to the sky (Betanzos 1987:11). The Spaniards were not gods; they could not be identified with them nor did they fit the gods' image. The chronicler's work itself thus corrects the information presented earlier.

In chapter 2 of his work Betanzos had included the description of the creation of humans by Viracocha and his attendants. He recounts only one "miracle"—when the god makes fire pour from the sky and run down along a hillside toward the inhabitants (Betanzos 1987:14). The only one who levels hills in Cuzco mythology is Ayar Cachi with his sling; he ". . . took out his sling and placed a stone in it and shot it at a tall hill and with its blow, knocked down the hill and made a creek in it . . ." (Betanzos 1987:18). This and other unruly acts led his brothers to shut him up in a cave. Andean myths collected today attribute the ability to knock down hills, as well as the ability to produce water, to Incarri.[13]

The chronicler's account begins to broaden, providing information about how Andeans perceived the Spaniards once they realize they are not Viracochas:

> . . . I have seen that they [the Spaniards] take a liking to everything they see, and that they think it fine to take for themselves young women and golden and silver glasses and fine clothing which they remake for themselves into breastplates and whips and metal ropes which mean shackled Indians tied together who carry their

loads and the baskets which hold their belongings and wherever they go they do not leave anything they have not looted and they take it so easily as if it were their own. . . . (Betanzos 1987:164)

He adds: "It seems to me these people *must be quitas pumarangra, which means lordless people who ransack and loot . . .* " (Betanzos 1987:146; emphasis added). The same informant from Atahualpa ". . . told him I do not call them Viracocha but rather *supai cuna, which means demons* and the Ynga then asked him 'Who calls them Viracocha?' And the Indian responded *the beasts of the Yungas call them that, thinking they were gods . . .*" (Betanzos 1987:264; emphasis added). These descriptions coincide with that of "destroyers of people" attributed previously to the Spaniards[14] and could be related to the earlier phrase from the anonymous Sevillian work of 1534, which describes the Spaniards as devils (cf. note 11). The duality that Betanzos's information consistently maintains is interesting. On the one hand, Viracocha is considered to be a benevolent divinity. On the other hand, passages such as the previous one describe the Spaniards as "destroyers" and "a lordless people"; this latter notion does not coincide with the description of the invaders as Viracochas. Moreover, in his text Betanzos prefers to make the *Yungas people* responsible for identifying the Spaniards with Viracocha (*the Yungas people* are "beastial," which will remind the reader of phrases in Guaman Poma).

As Fioravanti says, one explanation for the link made between Viracocha and the Spaniards can be found in the statement by Cieza de León that Huáscar invoked Viracocha's help against Atahualpa.[15] This could explain why Huáscar's followers could have identified the Christians with that god. Although this is an intriguing line of reasoning, it does not explain why this version was not disseminated until the beginning of the 1550s, when both Cieza de Léon and Betanzos were writing. In any case, the first generation of chroniclers did not have access to sufficient information.

Thus the authors writing at the beginning of the 1550s or later established the relationship between the myth of Viracocha and the arrival of the Spaniards and disseminated this myth. Viracocha had arranged the world, positioning himself "with his back toward the sunrise" and looking westward; Collasuyu was behind him and Chinchaysuyu faced him. His assistants had carried out the arrangements in the two other regions, Antisuyu and Cuntisuyu, while Viracocha carried out his organizing task, traveling from east to west, following the path of the sun and later losing himself in the sea (Pease 1986:220–230).

The chroniclers' versions thus identified the arrival of the Spaniards with the return of Viracocha. All seem to be based on the myth collected by Cieza de León as well as by Betanzos. The Spaniards would arrive at the same spot where the god disappeared.

Once the Spaniards identified themselves with the gods or messengers from the gods, their supernatural self-categorization in accordance with their providential mission was complete. Endeavoring to plant this image in the minds of the conquered produced the impression that the Incas were especially open to the supernatural, here manifested in a false belief taught by the demons with whom they spoke. The most curious aspect of attributing to the Andeans the notion that the Spaniards were gods is that this reasoning entails an accusation of idolatry where in fact no accusation seems to figure in the known trials to extirpate Andean idolatry during the first half of the seventeenth century.

Imposing a stereotype of this kind and disseminating it among the Andean villagers could be understood as another form of violence exercised by the Conquest—convincing the natives that the new arrivals were supernatural and invincible. The consequences of this imposed image could have even resulted in the need of later indigenous authors to annul the trauma of the Conquest, as when Guaman Poma affirms that Huáscar "donated" Tawantinsuyu to the king of Spain.[16] Titu Cusi Yupanqui would reason during the 1570s that ". . . the Spaniards are a people who undoubtedly cannot be less than viracochas . . . " (1985:3). Later, however, his text sets forth another idea more in line with that in Betanzos's text:

> . . . and look, they—the Spaniards—deceive with good words and afterwards do not follow through with what they say; that thus, as you have seen, they did to me, telling me that they were children of Viracocha and showed me at the beginning a great amiability and much love and then did to me what you see, if they were children of the Viracocha as they claimed they would not have done what they did, because the Viracha [*sic*] can level hills, produce water, create hills where there are none, do no harm to anyone, and this is not what we see they have done, rather, instead of doing good to us they did bad. . . . (Titu Cusi Yupanqui 1985:26)

The images here are close to those of Betanzos—the Spaniards walk on silver feet, know how to read and write, and so forth. Certainly, this description does not correspond to Viracocha in the Cuzco myths. This may very well be an interpretation imposed by Fray Marcos García, who wrote the

Instrucción of Titu Cusi Yupanqui. However, it must be noted here that modern oral versions collected in the Andes say that Atahualpa died because he did not know how to read (Flores 1973:321). The violence of the Conquest is seen not only in acts of war, which the authors who were in Cajamarca represented clearly, but also in the design of a version showing the definitive inferiority of the conquered and justifying their defeat, in what were purported to be their own words, in accordance with their beliefs.

But there is another issue to be explored. The first Spanish evangelicals, showing a tendency that could be extended to the chroniclers, sought to identify one Andean creator-god (defining "creation" in the biblical sense only, while the corresponding Andean idea is an "ordering" of the world) that was comparable to the Christian God. The initial translations of "god" as Pachacama, Pachayachachi, Wiraqocha (Viracocha), and so forth, are thus logical. This urge to discover an Andean equivalent to God could be related to the significance that Cieza de León or Betanzos granted the myth of Cuzco origin that presents Viracocha as a maker, an orderer of the world. Possibly this imposition of a creator-god concept also figured in the first bilingual primers developed by friars of various orders in the early days of evangelical work. The Councils of Lima ordered these primers destroyed and replaced by official versions in Quechua and Aymará of the *Christian Doctrine,* printed in 1584. These no longer translated the term "God," but rather integrated it as a neologism into the Andean languages. Some chroniclers (Cieza de León, for example) were particularly critical of identifying Viracocha as an apostle of Christ, although the version was soon widespread, accepted by Cieza de León himself, that Viracocha was a white and even a bearded god. Years later, Guaman Poma would say that the Inca Viracocha was white and bearded (1615:197; 1980: vol. 1, 77), adding that ". . . he prayed often to Ticze Viracocha and they say that he wanted to burn all the idols and burials of the kingdom . . . he believed more in Ticse Viracocha . . . and believed that there was another world in other kingdoms of Viracocha, which they thus called it, which he would come to reign . . ." (1615:48; 1980: vol. 1, 38). Nevertheless, the matter of the beards requires a broader analysis, for they figure in the drawing of the sun in the Incas' "coat of arms" (Guaman Poma 1615:79; 1980: vol. 1, 56).

The Spaniards and the Andeans perceived each other differently. The Spaniards' assumption of easy communication with the Andeans is widespread throughout the early and subsequent chronicles. According to them, from the time of the landing, particularly in Cajamarca, there was fluid communication. However, the *Tragedia del fin de Atawallpa* (Lara 1957) presents a later Andean perception: The Spaniards do not talk, they only move their lips; their speech is thunderous but incomprehensible.

Europeans "recognized" in America not only the imperial Roman design of Tawantinsuyu but also the "primitive" belief that the Spaniards were gods and the negative descriptions of Atahualpa. All would serve as justification for the Conquest and would be extended as time went on, as happened with the "illegitimacy" of Atahualpa, which was later generalized to all Incas and even all Andean authorities (for example, the *curacas* or community chiefs). The stereotypes thus generated had a diverse life. Atahualpa, denigrated by the chroniclers, is celebrated as a hero in the Andean tradition, while the image of the Spaniards as Viracochas seems to have developed differently. While Betanzos discusses whether the Spaniards were "destroyers of people" or Viracocha benefactors, recent scholars note that the notion of Viracochas applies to foreigners, Spaniards in particular, and even as a negative categorization that can be generalized to any group of human strangers.

Notes

1. A stereotyped vision of the past originates in the acceptance of a fixed, standardized characterization of other people and processes in which those who hold the stereotypes assume themselves to be the only important products of the past. In the final analysis, this is ethnocentrism of a universal kind, valid not only for very different cultures—for example, Americans and Asians. The conception of the Other also includes the enemy (traditional or occasional); in that sense it is mutually applicable to the Spanish and the English, for example, who are stereotyped by each other in each's standard versions. The easiest way to define one's identity is in contrast with another.

2. The text attributed to Mena and Xerez's *Verdadera relación* were printed in Seville in 1534, when the authors had just arrived in Seville from Peru. The former was published anonymously; Raúl Porras dated it to 1535 and attributed it to Capt. Cristóbal de Mena (Porras presented his work to the Twenty-sixth International Congress of Americanists at Seville in 1935, whose proceedings were not published until 1948 [Porras 1986:601 and ff.; Porras 1937]). [Others, such as Veda, an editor of the early Peruvian chroniclers, had thought that the author could have been Xerez himself.] John H. Rowe has recently reviewed the question of the author of the Sevillian anonymous work of 1534; he reaches the conclusion that Mena could not have written it (Rowe, pers. com.).

Xerez's version was considered a response to the attacks on Pizarro by the anonymous publication of 1534; Xerez was Pizarro's secretary, and his chronicle was seen as an ardent defense of his master. His rebuttal deserves more study.

Miguel de Estete was a soldier in Cajamarca; Xerez included in his work the text Estete wrote on the trip that Hernando Pizarro made to Pachacama. When the text of the *Noticia del Perú* came to light in modern times, it was attributed to Estete on the basis of statements by Jiménez de la Espada (1879:ix); the text had previously been used as an anonymous work by Prescott. Upon its publication Larrea followed the criteria of Jiménez de la Espada (Larrea 1918). There were several men named Miguel de Estete among the first Spaniards in Peru; Larrea had assumed so (1919:8), but Porras offered more information. Porras differed from Larrea in identifying Estete after the events of Cajamarca and his return to Spain; he stated that the author of *Noticia del Perú* remained on the peninsula and did not return to Peru at least until 1550, appearing as a witness in various judicial files and personal resumés between 1535 and 1550 (Porras 1986:597–598).

It is generally believed that *Noticia del Perú* was written about the same time as the works of Hernando Pizarro, Mena, and Xerez. The *Noticia* includes certain information, however, that makes it highly improbable that it could be that early a work; rather, it corresponds to another type of information. For example, the *Noticia* is the only text mentioned that used Huáscar's name without any hesitation, while others speak about the "cacique," the "lord," or the "cuzco" (the "old Cuzco" was Huayna Capác). The only one named in these is Atahualpa. The *Noticia* also was the first to use the term "Inca"—"Inga, which means king" (1918:34)—which was not used by the other authors of the 1530s.

Another fact should be mentioned. The *Historia* by Gonzalo Fernández de Oviedo y Valdés included statements by Diego de Molina, who was in Santo Domingo en route from the Andes at the same time as Hernando Pizarro. Molina's text is not found in the initial editions of Oviedo's work, which must be considered his summary of an account that he heard from Molina. In the 1851–55 edition and in the 1959 edition of Oviedo's *Historia,* the text attributed to Molina does not appear in quotes, as does the letter of Hernando Pizarro (Oviedo 1959: vol. 5, 84–93). In Oviedo's work, Molina's testimony uses "Guascara," the same term (with identical spelling) used in the third part of Cieza de León's *Crónica del Perú,* where he mentions "Guascara" for the first time. Oviedo writes, "I do not want to waste time nor stop writing what *I heard Molina say*" (Oviedo 1959: vol. 5, 91; emphasis added). Possibly Oviedo was able to reconstruct Molina's testimony from subsequent documents. Later phrases by Oviedo would strengthen the hypothesis of an oral version by Molina.

3. The recent discovery of new manuscripts corresponding to the second and third part of Cieza de León's *Crónica del Perú,* found in the Vatican Library by Francesca Cantú, and the appearance in Spain of a complete text of the

Suma y narración de los Incas, by Juan de Betanzos, are important events in the story of Andean history. Cantú has edited Cieza de León's texts (cf. Cieza de León 1979, 1985, and 1987); Betanzos's text was published by Martín Rubio (1987).

4. The Andean version can be traced in texts collected and published in recent years. The most important of these has been *Tragedia del fin de Atawallpa,* edited by Lara (1957), of which there are different versions (cf. Meneses 1983), and other similar texts (Iriate et al. 1985; Burga 1988). The versions of the myth of Incarrí recall Atahualpa (see Arguedas 1964:228), thus distinguishing the generations before and after Atahualpa; all the known versions mention this myth.

    Atahualpa maintained his prestige among the colonial Andean population, as can be seen in other known texts. Despite pointing out his "illegitimacy," Guaman Poma describes him as Inca (1980: vol. 1, 275, 176, 277, *passim*). Paintings such as the "Execution of Don Juan Ataguallpa in Cajamarca," at the Museum of the University of Cuzco, are also known. The name Juan Atahualpa appears on a list of those imprisoned in the seventeenth century as a result of subversive movements (Pease 1982). During the uprising led by Juan Santos Atahualpa in the eastern region of the Andes, it was said in Cuzco that the Inca Atahualpa ruled in the Andes of Jauja, while his brother (that is, his first cousin) Huáscar ruled in the Paititi (Esquivel and Navia 1980: vol. 2, 277–278).

5. After Cieza de León's death in 1554, his manuscripts were passed from hand to hand among Spanish bureaucrats and official chroniclers. Ultimately, Antonio de Herrera copied them and incorporated a good part of the third volume of the *Crónica del Perú* into his well-known work; see Sáenz de Santa María (1976), Cantú (1979, 1987), and Pease (1984a, 1984b).

6. The attribution is at the very least a glaring error by Zárate. It is based on the concept, already prevalent at the time Zárate was writing, that the Inca was the son of the sun and had prophetic capabilities. Zárate left for Panama in 1545, ten years before the publication of his *Historia.* Porras believed that he wrote his work during his period of disgrace and probable imprisonment, using drafts that he had taken from Peru. In 1554 he went to England with Philip II, who ordered him to print his *Historia* (Porras 1986:217–218). Thus toward the beginning of the second half of the 1540s the idea of Huáscar's legitimacy had been clarified, having already been set forth by some of the authors of Cajamarca. The Inca was already known as the son of the sun, thus allowing Zárate to reaffirm the title with respect to Huáscar. It is necessary to study more closely the omens and other predictions among the Andean populations and compare them with those existing among the Spanish. The Andeans have a different notion of the future; for them the future must be preimagined within a cyclical conception of time.

7. It has been said that the Andean interpreters, recruited by the Spaniards on

earlier trips, made translation possible during the course of the invasion. I do not doubt they could have learned colloquial Spanish, but it would have been insufficient for fluent translation. They lived among Spaniards (ships' crews, servants, and the like) whose vocabulary could not have been particularly sophisticated. It is difficult to believe that they were able to translate a complicated language such as that used in legal-theological documents like the *Requerimento;* see Solano (1975) and Rivarola (1985, especially 14ff.). In fact, the chroniclers generally described early Spanish days in the Andes in the context of fluid dialogue between the invaders and those being invaded. However, later Andean versions, originally accepted in their oral versions, show a striking lack of communication. The versions known are those that relate to the celebrations of the Inca's death, which commemorate the death of Atahualpa in Cajamarca. When the *Tragedia del fin de Atawallpa* was published in 1957, it was dated to colonial times. It specified that while the Inca and the Andean people, including the interpreters, "talk," Pizarro and Almagro "only move their lips." At some point in the dialogue, an emissary of the Inca exclaims that it is impossible for him to decipher the enemy's language and understand his "thunderous tongue" (Lara 1957:131; cf. Iriarte et al. 1985; Burga 1988 offers new data).

8. Sarmiento de Gamboa led a wanderer's life. A cosmographer and navigator, he was persecuted by the Inquisition for witchcraft. He worked under the orders of Viceroy Toledo in a survey conducted among the elite of Cuzco. He also participated in the expedition that discovered the Solomon Islands and attempted to colonize and fortify the Magellan Straits. In 1572, during the Toledo government, he completed the second and only surviving part of his *Historia general llamada Indica.*

9. The document published by Rowe (1985) is of the utmost importance; although it deals with a bureaucratic file and is consequently translated into bureaucratic language, it gives a more specific idea of the type of information used by the chroniclers. It is an excellent primary source.

10. The image provided by the text assumes an attribution to the Other; the text is written from a European perspective, and the chronicler appears to be delighted that the Andean townspeople "called them Viracocha cuna which means Gods." Betanzos also pointed out that the swords were confused with wooden sticks used for weaving. Compare this description with the one Guaman Poma would make years later:

Atahualpa Inca and the main lords and captains and other Indians were appalled when they heard about the lifestyle of the Spaniards, they were appalled that the Christians did not sleep, or so they said because they kept vigils, and that they ate silver and gold, they as well as their horses, and that they wore silver sandals, they spoke of the bridles and horseshoes and the iron weaponry, and red plumes, and that they talked through the day and

night with their papers—"quilca"— each one with his own, and that they all
wore shrouds, their entire face covered with wool with only their eyes showing, and on their head they wore colored bowls—"arimanca and suriuayta"—
and that they had their very long penises hanging from the back, they said of
the swords, and that they were all wearing fine silver, and that they did not
have a senior lord, they all looked like brothers in their clothes and way of
speaking and conversing and dressing, and only one face seemed to be that of
a senior lord who had a dark face, and white teeth and eyes, that he alone
talked a lot with the rest; hearing this news, the Inga was appalled and said to
him: what news you bring, evil messenger; they were all shocked with the
news that had never been heard and thus Atahaulpa Inga ordered that they
provide them and their horses with the service of women; because they
laughed about the penis of the Christians, of the sword, Atagyalpa Inga ordered that the Indian women that laughed to be killed and turned around and
offered again other Indian women and service. . . . (Guaman Poma 1980: vol.
1, 276–277)

The reference to the penis is defined in Covarrubias as "the small bulb of a
child, coming from the Greek name *fons,* because it is the source from which
he urinates" (Covarrubias 1987:870b). Other texts similarly refer to the
beards as wool: ". . . and in the jaw they showed off/totally red beards,
similar/to long skeins of wool . . ." (Lara 1957:87).

11. In a passage that refers to a different messenger, the recounting in *La conquista del Perú,* attributed to Cristóbal de Mena, points out that

. . . one day before we arrived at Atabalipa's army camp, one of his messengers came and brought many cooked sheep and corn bread and corn liquor
urns as gifts. And since the governor had sent an Indian while he was traveling, this Indian was cacique of the villages in which the Christians were
spread out and were great friends of the Christians. This cacique went to Atabalipa's army camp and his guards prevented him from arriving there; they
first asked where *the messenger of the devils* [emphasis added] was coming
from, of those who had traveled through so much territory without having
been killed. . . . (1534:23)

I would like to thank Luis Rebaza for pointing out this text to me. The author's attribution emphasizes that the Andeans consider the Spaniards to be
devils. The concept of *supay,* usually translated as "demon," is discussed by
Taylor (1980).

12. The texts collected by Avila refer to Cuniraya Viracocha; cf. Taylor (1987:53
and ff.).

13. Cf. Arguedas (1964:228) and Pease (1982:215–216, 221, 227). In different contexts the Inca can make rocks move and become walls by command. He can also make water come from the subsoil and frequently figures as the grantor of corn.

14. *Supra estrager,* translated in the essay as "destroy," is defined by Covarrubias (1611) as "to ruin, erase, vandalize, decompose." The image of Viracocha is multifaceted, as has been frequently pointed out (Pease 1973; MacCormack 1988:981). The ordering divinity of the world can certainly be destructive, but the texts from Betanzos specify a benevolent image. It is important to discuss, of course, the image of Viracocha as "a black sun"; a period of the black sun would precede a new *pachacuti,* as Fioravanti, who sees the Spanish invasion as such, indicates (1987:80–81). On first analysis this interpretation is correct, but it is more important to verify a distinction between the formation or expression of the Andean belief and the design of the stereotype in the chronicles, which does not necessarily reflect the former.

15. The statement comes from Cieza de León (1985:11) and takes into account the observation (taken from Zuidema by Fioravanti) that the native population of Cuzco adored Viracocha. Huáscar's identification with the *urin* sector, affirmed in Betanzos, is interesting:

> . . . and then [Huáscar] ordered that nobody take him to be from Hanan Cuzco, because Atagualpa was from Hanan Cuzco and from the line of Ynga Yupangue, that he would not like to be from that line and that if he did come from it, then he would affirm that he did not come from it but from Hurin Cuzco, because those people from the town from which he, Guascar, was born, bore the last name Hurin Cuzco, which he, similarly, was and that from then on they should call him from Hurin Cuzco because he intended to kill Atagualpa and all his kinsmen and those from his lineage which was Hanan Cuzco, and re-make the lineage of Hurin Cuzco. . . . (1987:210, 211)

16. Guaman Poma relates, for example, that Huáscar sent his "ambassador" Martín Guaman Malqui de Ayala (obviously an ancestor of the chronicler) to meet with the "Ambassador of the Emperor and the King of Castilla" (that is, Pizarro); the two and Almagro "offered each other peace" (Guaman Poma 1980: vol. 1, 275, cf. 85, 118, *passim*; see also my prologue to Guaman Poma 1980:lxiii).

References

Anonymous (attributed to Cristóbal de Mena). [1534] 1929. *La conquista del Perú llamada la Nueua Castilla.* Facsimile edition. Introduction by J. Sinclair. New York: New York Public Library.

Arguedas, José Maria. 1964. "Puquio, una cultura en proceso de cambios." In *Es-*

tudios sobre la cultura actual del Perú, 221–272. Lima: Universidad de San Marcos.

Avila, Francisco de (see Taylor 1987).

Betanzos, Juan Diez de. [1550] 1987. *Suma y narración de los Incas.* Edited by María del Carmen Martín Rubio, with Horacio Villanueva Urteaga and Demetrio Ramos Pérez. Madrid: Atlas.

Burga, Manuel. 1988. *Nacimiento de una utopía: Muerte y resurrección de los Incas.* Lima: Instituto de Apoyo Agrario.

Cabello Balboa, Miguel. [1586] 1951. *Miscelánea Antártica.* Edited by Luis E. Valcárcel. Lima: Universidad de San Marcos.

Cantú, Francesca. 1979. Introduction to *Descubrimiento y conquista del Perú,* by Pedro de Cieza de León. Edited by F. Cantú. Rome.

———. [1553] 1984. *Crónica del Perú. Primera parte.* Introduction by Franklin Pease G. Y. Lima: Pontificia Universidad Católica del Perú y Academia Nacional de la Historia.

———. 1985. Introduction to *Crónica del Perú. Segunda parte,* by Pedro de Cieza de León. Lima: Pontificia Universidad Católica del Perú y Academia Nacional de la Historia.

———. 1987. Introduction to *Crónica del Perú. Tercera parte,* by Pedro de Cieza de León. Lima: Pontificia Universidad Católica del Perú y Academia Nacional de la Historia.

Cieza de León, Pedro de. [1554] 1979. *Descubrimiento y conquista del Perú.* Edited by Francesca Cantú. Rome.

Covarrubias, Sebastián de. [1611] 1987. *Tesoro de la lengua castellana o española.* Edited by Martín de Riquer. Barcelona: Alta Fulla.

Estete, Miguel de (see Larrea 1918).

Esquivel y Navia, Diego de. 1980. *Noticias cronológicas de la gran ciudad del Cuzco.* Edited by Félix Denegri Luna, with Horacio Villanueva U. and César Gutiérrez M. Lima: Fundación Augusto N. Wiese.

Fioravanti, Antoinette Molinié. 1987. "El regreso de Viracocha." *Boletín del Instituto Francés de Estudios Andinos* nos. 3–4:71–83.

Flores Ochoa, Jorge. 1973. "Inkarrí y Qollarí en una comunidad del altiplano." In *Ideología mesiánica del mundo andino,* edited by Juan M. Ossio, 153–213. Lima.

Guaman Poma de Ayala, Felipe. [1615] 1980. *Nueva corónica y buen gobierno.* Edited by Franklin Pease G. Y. Caracas: Biblioteca Ayacucho.

Jiménez de la Espada, Marcos. 1879. *Tres relaciones de antigüedades peruanas.* Madrid: Imprenta de M. Tello.

Lara, Jesús. 1957. *La "Tragedia del fin de Atawallpa."* Cochabamba: Imprenta Universitaria.

Larrea, Carlos M. 1918. *El descubrimiento y la conquista del Perú. Relación inédita de Miguel de Estete.* Reprinted from *Boletín de la Sociedad Ecuatoriana de Estudios Históricos Americanos* 1, no. 3.

Lechner, J., ed. 1988. *Essays on Cultural Identity in Latin America: Problems and Repercussions.* Leiden: Rijksuniversitait.

MacCormack, Sabine. 1988. "Pachacuti: Miracles, Punishments and Last Judgement: Visionary Past and Prophetic Future in Early Colonial Peru." *American Historical Review* 93, no. 4:960–1,006.

Maticorena Estrada, Miguel. 1955. "Cieza de León en Sevilla y su muerte en 1554. Documentos." In *Anuario de Estudios Americanos,* vol. 12, 518–674.

Meneses, Teodoro L., ed. 1983. *Teatro quechua colonial. Antología.* Lima: Edubanco.

Molina, Cristóbal de. [1575] 1943. *Fábulas y ritos de los incas.* Edición los Pequeños Grandes Libros de Historia Americana, serie 1, vol. 4. Lima.

Noticia del Perú (see Larrea 1918).

Ossio, Juan M., ed. 1973. *Ideología mesiánica del mundo andino.* Lima: Ignacio Prado Pestor.

Oviedo y Valdés, Gonzalo Fernández de. *Historia general y natural de las Indias.* 5 vols. 1959. Madrid: Biblioteca de Autores Españoles.

Pease G. Y., Franklin. 1973. *El dios creador andino.* Lima: Mosca Azul.

———. 1982a. *Pensamiento mítico. Antología.* Lima: Mosca Azul.

———. 1982b. "Mesianismo andino e identidad étnica: Continuidades y problemas." *Cultura* 6, no. 13:57–71.

———. 1984a. Introduction to *Crónica del Perú. Primera parte,* by Pedro de Cieza de León. Lima: Pontificia Universidad Católica del Perú y Academia Nacional de la Historia.

———. 1984b. "Cieza de León y la tercera parte de la *Crónica del Perú.*" *Revista Interamericana de Bibliografía* 34, nos. 3–4:103–118.

Porras Barrenechea, Raúl. 1937. *Las relaciones primitivas de la conquista del Perú.* Paris: Les Presses Modernes.

———. [1962] 1986. *Los cronistas del Perú y otros ensayos.* Edited by Franklin Pease G. Y. Lima: Banco de Crédito del Perú.

Ravines, Rogger. 1985. *Dramas coloniales en el Perú actual.* VI Congreso Peruano del Hombre y la Cultura Andina. Lima: Universidad "Inca Garcilaso de la Vega."

Rivarola, José Luis. 1985. *Lengua, comunicación e historia del Perú.* Lima: Lumen.

Rowe, John Howland. 1985. "Probanza de los incas nietos de conquistadores." *Histórica* 9, no. 2:153–215.

Sáenz de Santa María, Carmelo. 1976. "Los manuscritos de Pedro de Cieza de León." *Revista de Indias* 36:145–146.

Sancho de Hoz, Pedro. [1534] 1962. *Relación de la conquista del Perú.* Madrid: Porrúa Turanzas.

Sarmiento de Gamboa, Pedro. [1572] 1947. *Segunda parte de la historia general llamada Indica.* Edited by Angel Rosenblat. Buenos Aires: Emece.

Solano, Francisco de. 1975. "El intérprete: Uno de los ejes de la aculturación." In

Estudios sobre política indigenista espanola en América 1, 265–278. Seminario de Historia de America. Valladolid, Spain: Universidad de Valladolid.

Taylor, Gerald. 1980. "Supay." *Amerindia* 5. Paris.

————. 1987. *Ritos y tradiciones de Huarochirí del siglo* XVII. Lima: Instituto de Estudios Peruanos.

Titu Cusi Yupanqui. [1570] 1985. *Ynstruçión del Ynga Don Diego de Castro Titu Cusi Yupanqi. . . .* Introduction by Luis Millones. Lima: El Virrey.

Todorov, Tzvetan. 1982. *The Conquest of America: The Question of the Other.* Translated by Richard Howard. New York: Harper & Row.

Xerez, Francisco de. 1534. *Verdadera relación de la conquista del Perú.* Seville: Bartolomé Pérez.

Zárate, Augustín de. [1555] 1944. *Historia del descubrimiento y conquista del Perú.* Edited by Jan M. Kermenic. Prologue by Raúl Porras Barrenechea. Lima: Librería e imprenta D. Miranda.

Allegory
and
Ethnography
in
Cabeza de Vaca's
Naufragios
and
Comentarios

José Rabasa

Alvar Núñez Cabeza de Vaca's *Naufragios* is among the chronicles of the Indies that literary critics have traditionally singled out for their literary value. Insufficient attention, however, has been paid to the ideological implication of reading colonial texts for their artistic worth. Why privilege the *Naufragios* over the *Comentarios*, an account of his tribulations as governor of the Río de la Plata written by his amanuensis Pero Hernández, which after all presents itself as an exemplary history with moral and political lessons? What cultural forms and reading patterns inform literary appraisals of colonial texts, in particular the *Naufragios*, to the point of ignoring their colonialist impulse and their reduction of Native Americans to either servile or hostile characters in the Spanish imperial plot in the Americas? What deeply embedded historiographical prejudices keep these readings today from making allowances for indigenous resistance? Obviously historians and anthropologists also tend to partake of these ethnocentric constructs in their use of colonial documents. If I highlight literary criticism it is because this discipline purports to do the kind of textual and discursive analyses that ought to make manifest the rhetorical strategies that authorize representations of colonial encounters. I shall begin by quoting from a letter by Joseph Conrad to R. B. Cunninghame Graham, dated December 26, 1903, congratulating him on the publication of a book on Hernando de Soto, conqueror and explorer of Florida and the southeastern United States. The tone of the praise and the general colonial context in which it is inscribed exemplify the ubiquitous recurrence of what I have defined in this paper as the "culture of conquest."

. . . H. de Soto is most exquisitely excellent: your very mark and spirit upon a subject that only you can do justice to—with your wonderful English and your sympathetic insight into the souls of the Conquistadores. The glamour, the pathos and the romance of that time and of those men are only adequately, truthfully, conveyed to us by your pen; the sadness, the glory and the romance of the endeavour together with the vanity of vanities of the monstrous achievement are reflected in your unique style as though you had been writing of men with whom you had slept by the camp fire after tethering your horses on the threshold of the unknown. (Watts 1969:148)

Alvar Núñez Cabeza de Vaca (or simply Cabeza de Vaca, as he preferred to be called) is without a doubt along with Soto one of the most romantic of the conquistadors. His writings inaugurate some of the most vivid and familiar *topoi* in representations of colonial encounters (by *topoi* I mean those discursive spaces and places of memory—barbarism, cannibalism, superstition, evolutionary stages, as well as shipwreck and its travails, saintliness, going native— that written accounts reelaborate in the construction of a Western self and a colonial subject as its Other).[1] If there is in Cabeza de Vaca's narratives a self-conscious hesitation to spell out symbolic meanings, autobiographical gestures and novelesque episodes interrupt the straightforward chronicle of events and thus call our attention to an expected tropological reading—one attentive to the vehicles that carry the imagination from the concrete to the abstract, from the particular to the universal (see Tyler 1986:132; White 1978:1–25). For a sixteenth-century European audience avid for adventure stories in exotic places, the wanderings through oceans, rivers, deserts, and jungles were not just traces on the face of the earth, to be reproduced in maps and written accounts, but historical figures, events with a transcendental significance. Indeed explorers and conquerors wrote and designed their narratives anticipating that allegorical meanings would be drawn from the events. The conquistadors knew that their feats would be read as if they were in themselves inscriptions in golden letters on the pages of history. Therein lies the power and seduction of their self-consciously elaborate narratives and their contribution to the culture of conquest with colonial myths and anthropological categories that still haunt much of Western ethnography, literary criticism, and fiction.

Recent studies of the literary character of the so-called *crónicas* (a generic term that encompasses texts ranging from letters to multivolume histories) and in particular Cabeza de Vaca's *Naufragios* have broadened our understanding and appreciation of their rhetorical and aesthetic sophistication (e.g., Carreño 1987; Pupo-Walker 1987; Invernizzi 1987; Molloy 1987; Dowling 1984; Pastor 1983; Lewis 1982; Lagmanovich 1978; Hart 1974). It is my belief, however, that we ought to step back and consider wherein lies the literary quality and charm of conquest narratives before defining a literary canon that would tend to perpetuate a whole array of ethnocentric terms—for example, the uncritical use of evolutionary categories, the reduction of the corpus of Spanish-American literature to texts written in Spanish, and the definition of literary value exclusively according to Western conventions.[2] Furthermore, we should note that Cabeza de Vaca is a benevolent colonial official who nonetheless reproduces on a symbolic level the colonial myths that structure and articulate the same violence he condemns. His denunciations, for instance, retain and reiterate the belief in the natural subordination of Native Americans to Spanish rule, the definition of cannibalism as a culinary aberration that warrants the destruction of a culture, and the reduction of native knowledge to sham and superstition inspired by the devil.

Conrad's letter to Cunninghame Graham, also known as Don Roberto, calls attention to the notion that we always write from a specific time and place and that ultimately we should be responsible for our participation within the colonial legacy that determines our discourse. In an essay on *Nostromo,* Conrad's novel of exploitation and revolution in South America, Said has pointed out that to the extent that we can see Conrad both "criticizing and reproducing the imperial ideology of his time," we have today the alternative between "the projection, or the refusal, of the wish to dominate, the capacity to damn or the energy to comprehend and engage other societies, traditions, histories" (Said 1988:72). Indeed, we can further define the culture of conquest, what Said calls our "Gringo eyes," with Conrad's letter. Conrad's praise of Don Roberto's book on Hernando de Soto for its splendid, realistic capturing of the spirit of the conquistadors is followed by an indictment of the Belgian enterprise in the Congo and its recruits from "the souteneurs, sous-offs, maquereaux, fruits-sec of all sorts on the pavements of Brussels and Antwerp" (Watts 1969:149). Don Roberto's book, adds Conrad, "gives me a furious desire to learn Spanish and bury myself in the pages of the incomparable Garcilaso—if only to forget all about our modern Conquistadores" (Watts 1969:148). There is a nostalgia for the conquistadors, even an escapist yearning for the delightful prose of El Inca Garcilaso de la Vega.

And yet in Conrad's letter the Belgian enterprise in the Congo still retains an aura of romance and adventure in the figure of Roger Casement, who has, as Conrad puts it, "a touch of the Conquistador in him too." Conrad explains: "For I've seen him start off into an incomparable wilderness swinging a crookhandled stick for all weapons, with two bull dogs: Paddy (white) and Biddy (brindle) at his heels and a Loanda boy carrying a bundle for all company"; he adds that "some particle of Las Casas's soul had found refuge in his indefatigable body" (Watts 1969:149). This image of Casement emerging from the wilderness "a little leaner, a little browner, with his stick, dogs, and Loanda boy" reiterates the commonplace in colonial literature of intrepid adventurers enduring the wilderness, but it also underlies much of the nostalgia in contemporary films—*Passage to India, Out of Africa, The Mission*—for the colonial period in the face of the absolutely unromantic Third World of the postcolonial world order (see Rosaldo 1989).

Those familiar with Taussig's (1987) study in terror and healing, as he subtitles his *Shamanism, Colonialism and the Wild Man,* will recall his discussion of Conrad's letter to Don Roberto, the allusion to "a man called Casement," the importance of the latter's critical report in the early 1910s of the atrocities committed by the Peruvian Amazon Company during the rubber boom along the Putumayo River, and more important for the purposes of this essay the *topoi* of nostalgia and its recurrence in the culture of conquest (Taussig 1987:11–15). Even the rubber boom has its myths and picturesque characters. Rivera's *La vorágine,* as Taussig reminds us, inspired more than one person to migrate "to the Putumayo on account of the mysterious excitement it conveyed about the jungle (1987:111); as critical as *La vorágine* might be of the rubber industry, "it is always the colonial view of the jungle that provides the means of representing and trying to make sense of the colonial situation" (1987:77). This colonial view of the jungle recurs in anecdotes about such historical characters, savvy in native ways, as Don Crisóstomo, who "would spend nights orating with Indian men around the tobacco pot, seducing them into doing his bidding with the power of *his* story telling" (Taussig 1987:108). According to Joaquín

Rocha, who traveled the region at the turn of the century, Don Crisóstomo became "not only for the Indians the seductive orator and the invincible man of arms but also by these means something greater—because for the Huitotos he was their king and God" (Taussig 1987:108). And we all know that stories of men who would be kings and gods abound in the European repertoire of colonial myths. But let me round off the question of nostalgia with one more quotation drawn by Taussig from the epigraph to París Lozano's *Guerrilleros de Tolima,* a study of the War of One Thousand Days (1899–1901), that implicitly comments on the picturesqueness of Don Crisóstomo: "Aquellos eran otros hombres, más hombres que los de los de tiempos presentes, más bravos en la acción y más sazonados en la palabra [Those were other men, more men than those of today, wilder in action and more seasoned in the word]" (Taussig 1987:109). The recent events in the Putumayo strike us as repetitions of legendary characters and atrocities already told in Cabeza de Vaca's accounts. Indeed many pages in Taussig's study illustrating terror, exploitation, and seduction could have been drawn from documents of Cabeza de Vaca's failed governorship in the Río de la Plata. Moreover, Casement, like Cabeza de Vaca, is a critic-ethnographer who reiterates on a symbolic level the mythology that structures and articulates the violence he denounces. We may accordingly define the culture of conquest as a set of beliefs, images, and categories that tends to determine the ideology not only of those who perpetrate atrocities but also of those who condemn them. With these preliminaries in mind, let us now examine Cabeza de Vaca's writings.

Born in Jerez de la Frontera sometime between 1490 and 1507 (little is known of his early life), Cabeza de Vaca participated as treasurer and *alguacil mayor* (provost marshal) in Pánfilo de Narváez's expedition to Florida. (This is the same Narváez who tried to topple Cortés at the beginning of the conquest of Mexico.) The expedition sailed from San Lúcar on June 17, 1527, stopped in Santo Domingo, and Santiago de Cuba, and tried to get from Trinidad to Havana when a wind blew them toward Florida, where they landed on April 12, 1528. Thus began a disastrous expedition in which "four hundred men and eighty horses in four ships and a brigantine" were reduced to four survivors who stumbled into Culiacán, Sinaloa, in March 1537 after crossing Texas, New Mexico, Arizona, and the Mexican states of Chihuahua and Sonora.[3] Those they encountered were left speechless and amazed:

Y otro dia de mañana alcance quatro christianos de cauallo que recibieron gran alteracion de verme tan extrañamente vestido y en compañia de indios. Estuuieronme mirando mucho espacio de tiempo, tan atonitos que ni me hablauan ni acertauan a preguntarme nada. (CLD: vol. 5, 126)[4]

The day after I overtook four of them on horseback, who were astonished at the sight of me, so strangely dressed as I was, and in the company of Indians. They stood staring at me a length of time, so confounded that they neither hailed me nor drew near to make an inquiry. (translated by Smith 1871:183–184)

Images of this kind convey the mythic stuff of Cabeza de Vaca's story and its attractiveness to both a sixteenth- and a late twentieth-century audience. The *Naufragios* exemplify, for instance, an evolved ethnographic view in Todorov's typology of attitudes towards Otherness in *The Conquest of America*:

. . . Cabeza de Vaca also reached a neutral point, not because he was indifferent to the two cultures but because he had experienced them both from within—thereby, he no longer had anything but "the others" around him; without becoming an Indian, Cabeza de Vaca was no longer quite a Spaniard. His experience symbolizes and heralds that of the modern exile. . . . (Todorov 1987:249)

Todorov's narrative of an evolving ethnographic consciousness manifests a Western need to believe in its privileged capacity to understand other cultures. It is far from obvious whether Cabeza de Vaca would recognize the value of not being the Other and yet not quite the same implicit in Todorov's characterization, but there is certainly in his accounts a self-representation of a benevolent, enlightened colonial official dutifully pursuing the interests of the Crown. Cabeza de Vaca sought the governorship of Florida, but by the time he returned to Spain, in 1538, it had already been assigned to Hernando de Soto. Nevertheless Cabeza de Vaca did gain the title of *adelantado* and governor of the province of Río de la Plata, where he sailed on November 2, 1540. Five years later Cabeza de Vaca returned to Spain in chains, accused of crimes ranging from such minor offenses as robbing the inhabitants of the Canary islands of three cows on his outward journey to murdering friendly Indians, confiscating the property of Spaniards, and, the ultimate crime of sedition, calling himself king of the land; he was first jailed and then held under house arrest in a Madrid inn for a total of eight years (see Bishop 1933:276–278; Graham 1968:157–160). The *Comentarios,* written by his secretary and amanuensis, Pero Hernández, tells about his political failures.

Although the *Naufragios* and the *Comentarios* are generally published together, at least in the original Spanish versions, the *Naufragios* has been singled out as one of the most accomplished narratives of the Conquest from a literary point of view. Literary critics generally agree in finding a tension between the historical account of events and novelesque episodes, between an exceptional objective capacity to relate simply what was seen and a notable autobiographical projection (e.g., Dowling 1984; Lewis 1982; Lagmanovich 1978). Scholars generally make this clear-cut separation and insist that the *Naufragios* can be studied as literature as well as chronicle. Dowling has defined the distinction between story and discourse as the terms that enable these literary claims (1984:94): Story (the chronicle of events) is presumed separate from discourse (the reflection on the events). Dowling then argues that such a distinction entails the priority of story to discourse, a concept that not only is suspect in fiction but also reintroduces a false opposition since "it is debatable whether a story exists at all apart from the discourse" (1984:97). The separation of story from discourse keeps us from seeing how both elements contribute to the formation and development of a plot in the *Naufragios*. The separation of story and discourse, then, does not make sense if we want to read the *Naufragios* as fiction. Only when we read the text as history is the distinction apt; then, as Dowling puts it, "the ferreting out of the true nature of the 'story' through historical investigation assumes real importance" (1984:97). This line of reasoning suggests that the opposition of story and discourse is not inherent in the text but a product of our reading. The tension between fiction and history would in the end be the tension between the *Naufragios*'s similarity with adventure stories and the text's classification as historical account.[5]

But it seems to me that displacing the tension to a historical reading creates, in turn, a false opposition since it is precisely the narrative form that draws the similarities between history and fiction and also makes each of them meaningful and truthful accounts (see White 1989a). The priority of story over discourse is false in fiction, but it is perhaps accurate to postulate the priority of meaning over facts—that is, of discourse over story in history (see Barthes 1981:16–17). The *Naufragios* is not simply an account of what happened because the significance of its facts depends on the instructions from the Crown, the required numerous readings of the *Requerimiento*, and in general an ideology of conquest that defines not only a legal framework but also general parameters of prudence and chivalry. The *Requerimiento* drew a short history of the world in which the Christian God established Saint Peter as head of the whole human race, an authority that was transferred to succeeding popes, one of whom had donated the islands and the mainland to the Spanish Crown; having been notified, the Indians were under the obligation to serve the Crown or else be subjected to war and slavery (Parry and Keith 1984: vol. 1, 288–290). Failure to mention the *Requerimiento* or insist on the several readings of it would hardly constitute an inconsequential factual detail, since the Spaniards had the obligation to read it aloud to the Indians before engaging in war against them. Dowling's reduction of history to "what really happened" presumes that events can be constituted independently of ideological constraints and legal frameworks. Furthermore Dowling's observation would imply that a *relación* could limit itself to just providing a truthful account. In fact, the opposition between fiction and history that literary critics have found in the *Naufragios* could be explained as a result of a coexistence of different modes of writing about the past that would correspond to the different degrees of narrativity in *relaciones,* chronicles, and histories in the proper sense of the term (White 1989b; see also Lewis 1982:686). There is indeed a self-conscious suspension of narrative resolution in the *Naufragios.*

Let us further observe how meaning and ideology define facts in some passages from the *Historia general y natural de las Indias,* by Gonzalo Fernández de Oviedo y Valdés, the official chronicler of the Indies. After giving a summary of the disaster according to a letter from Cabeza de Vaca, Alonso de Castillo, and Andrés Dorantes, the three surviving Spaniards (note that the fourth is a black man named Esteban, who has no last name, never counts as a full member of the expedition, and is mentioned only incidentally), Oviedo provides a parenthetical comment on the folly of Narváez and the Spaniards who followed him: "Querría yo que me dijesen qué les predicaron esos frailes a Pánfilo de Narváez a aquellos españoles que tan ciegos se fueron, dejando sus patrias tras falsas palabras [I wanted them to tell me what those friars and Pánfilo de Narváez preached to those Spaniards that led them to venture so blindly, leaving their fatherland behind]" (Oviedo 1959: vol. 4, 290). It is beside the point that Oviedo implicitly accepts Cabeza de Vaca's account of how he required Narváez not to continue the inland exploration without placing the ships in a safe haven. And, indeed, to suggest a ferreting out of the true story of who said what and when would ultimately be a minor detail if not an irrelevant point from a sixteenth-century understanding of history (cf. Dowling 1984:95–97). What matters is that the disaster holds a moral lesson for future explorations: "Es cosa que aunque no tiene remedio ni enmienda, tiene alguna parte aviso, o le causará esta relación . . . [Although this does not have a remedy nor correction, it does hold some kind of lesson that this account will draw . . .]" (Oviedo 1959: vol. 4, 291). There is a lesson in the disaster, and Oviedo adds that it will be brought forth by his own version of the events. History is allegorical beyond the intent of the participants; it is precisely the task of the historian to draw moral meanings and practical lessons from the events. Narváez and the friars were not only mistaken but also deceived the others into proceeding without a description of the territories by previous explorers:

> En este tractado hallarán de qué temer e de qué se deban recelar los que nuevas empresas de aquestas toman, pues cada día veo que las procuran e traen hombres al carnero, sin saber dónde los llevan, ni ellos adónde se van ni a quién siguen. (Oviedo 1959: vol. 4, 291)

> Those who are about to embark in this kind of new enterprise will find in this treatise what to watch out for and avoid, since every day I see how some begin new ones and lead men like sheep, without knowing where they are taking them, nor the others where they are going nor who they are following.

There is a moral lesson to be derived from the events, which to be meaningful must be informed by rules of procedure such as reading the *Requerimiento* several times, retaining a balance of power between the clergy, the officials of the Crown, and the governor, and keeping a written account of the exploration and the nature and peoples of the land. This dependence of relevant facts on instructions and the possibility of transforming the chronicle of the events into a moral history suggests not just that facts are the product of interpretation but that ideology or discourse, if that term is preferred, itself also underlies actions. Oviedo spells out a moral reading that Cabeza de Vaca suggests but never brings to closure.

Several drafts anticipated the version of the *Naufragios* as we know it today, and these reflect the transformation of what would have been one more account of events by one more functionary of the Indies into a self-consciously labored text with literary pretensions. Two early versions, in collaboration with the other survivors, were submitted to the viceregal authorities of New Spain and the Crown upon the author's arrival; there is a fragment with the title "Relación de Cabeza de Vaca, tesorero que fué en la conquista," which also includes the instructions to Cabeza de Vaca as a factor of the expedition (*CDI*: vol. 14, 265–279)[6]; we also have Oviedo's summary and commentaries to the letter by Cabeza de Vaca, Castillo, and Dorantes quoted earlier. The *Naufragios* was first published in 1542 (as *La relación que dio Alvar nu- / ñez Cabeça de vaca de lo acaescido en las Indias / en la armada donde yua por gouernador Pᵃ. philo de narbaez / Desde el año de veinte / y siete hasta el año d' treinta y seis / que bolvio a Sevilla con tres / de su compania*) and with further revisions with the *Comentarios* in 1555 (as *La relación y comentarios del gouerna / dor Aluar nuñez cabeça, de lo acaescido en las / dos jornadas que hizo a las Indias*); although the term *Naufragios* appears in the contents of the 1555 edition, the title *Naufragios* first appeared (and has been used since then) in 1749 as *Naufragios de Alvar Núñez Cabeza de Vaca, y Relación de la jornada, que hizo a la Florida con el adelantado Pánfilo de Narváez.*[7]

If this ongoing rewriting of a *relación* is particularly obsessive in Cabeza de Vaca, its impulse to draw a universal message does have, however, illustrious antecedents among the narratives of successful enterprises—for example, Columbus's *Diario* of the first voyage and Cortés's *Letters to Charles V* relate their particular feats as unique events with an implied universal significance that would affect the meaning of world history. Thus Columbus wrote his daily entries in the *Diario* as if every detail were an inscription bespeaking the coming of a new age, and Cortés insistently highlighted the Otherness of New Spain so that he could legitimize mutiny and claim political authority. Both Columbus and Cortés knew that their enterprises would be read as key parts of an emerging historical plot. Passages in their accounts underscore the uniqueness of their enterprises, but for the most part narrative is subordinated to an inconclusive chronological account. Cabeza de Vaca faced another task in the *Naufragios*; while retaining a truthful, open-ended account characteristic of the *relación,* he projects into the sequence of events the plot structure of romance. Emplotment, the constitution and organization of facts by means of a narrative structure, endows otherwise univocal statements with symbolism; nakedness, hunger, shipwreck, and healing become something more as they are given political, religious, and moral interpretations (see Pastor 1983:294–337, 1989:136–146). Narrative thus transforms the facts of a *relación* into an allegory. So that the straightforward account does not get filed away as one more report of a failed expedition, Cabeza de Vaca must underscore the uniqueness of his story with a narrative. By retaining the *relación*-like, inconclusive representation of events in time as well as the narration's apparent autonomy, Cabeza de Vaca allows several readings. His ethnographic register names and geographically situates the peoples he encounters but also invests them with symbols and characters significant within a narrative of evangelization and conquest whose meanings, in turn, exceed the adventures of Cabeza de Vaca and the other survivors.

From the point of view of reception, the adoption of the title *Naufragios* over the plain *La relación* illustrates the symbolic field in the text. We may wonder why the editor of the 1749 edition chose *Naufragios* and not *Milagros, Peregrinajes,* or even *Las aventuras de Cabeza de Vaca,* which is perhaps the closest to the title of the premier example of the novelesque genre— Daniel Defoe's *The Life and Strange Surprising Adventures of Robinson Crusoe* (1719), already published when the title *Naufragios* first appeared in a Spanish edition. Although the so-called *milagros* have been subject to polemic and speculation about their nature and Cabeza de Vaca's capacity to effect them, the symbolism of the shipwreck is the strongest motif; it dates to antiquity and recurs in the works of such prominent figures as Homer, Dante, and Defoe. Indeed, shipwrecks have a long tradition as vehicles for conveying the spiritual travails of saints and their miracles. Because Cabeza de Vaca undergoes a shipwreck, his account immediately lends itself to a religious reading, among others.[8]

The motif of the shipwreck calls to mind the notion of an unexpected mishap and its interpretation as a fall into chaos. The tendency among critics has been to read chaos as original or primitive, not simply as a complete loss of material culture. Primitive chaos is but one step from the characterization of Cabeza de Vaca's journey into North America as "un alucinante itinerario que lo llevó de la cultura renacentista a la barbarie indócil del paleolítico americano [a hallucinating itinerary that took him from the culture of the Renaissance to the hostile barbarism of the American Paleolithic Age]" (Pupo-Walker 1987:539) or "un viaje en el tiempo, de la civilización europea del siglo XVI a la edad de piedra [a journey in time, from European civilization of the XVI century to the stone age]" (Lagmanovich 1978:32), as Pupo-Walker and Lagmanovich have respectively defined what they perceived as a historico-temporal voyage in the *Naufragios*.[9]

If there is a lack of refinement in Cabeza de Vaca's narrative, it is among the Spaniards; for instance, when they are faced with the task of building ships, not one of them had the knowledge or the skills, "nosotros no lo sabiamos hacer" (*CLD*: vol. 5, 32) ["we knew not how to construct"] (Smith 1871: 46). Moreover, if the Indians are hostile one need not wonder why; the Spaniards raid villages for food, procuring "hasta cuatrocientas hanegas de maíz, aunque no sin contiendas y pendencias con los indios" (*CLD*: vol. 5, 33) ["as many as four hundred fanegas of maize; but these were not got without quarrels and contentions with the Indians"] (Smith 1871: 47). Cabeza de Vaca does not mention any form of peaceful request or even the numerous legalistic readings of the *Requerimiento* that the instructions to Pánfilo de Narváez demanded. And to the scandal of the Indians the Spaniards resort to cannibalism out of hunger:

> . . . se comieron los vnos a los otros hasta que quedo uno solo, que por ser solo no huuo quien lo comiesse. . . . Deste caso se alteraron tanto los indios y ouo entre ellos tan gran escandalo, que sin dubda si al principio ellos lo vieran, los mataran y todos nos vieramos en grande trabajo. . . . (*CLD*: vol. 5, 52)

> They ate one another until there was only one left, and since he was alone there was no one to eat him. . . . This produced great commotion among the Indians, giving rise to so much censure that had they seen it at the beginning, doubtless they would have destroyed any survivor, and we should have found ourselves in the utmost perplexity. (Smith 1871:74)

There is a certain irony in his insistence on the fact that there was no one left to eat the last Spaniard, considering that cannibalism among Native Americans is a recurring motif in European representations of the New World since the early publications of Amerigo Vespucci's accounts (c. 1503). In their abhorrence of Spanish cannibalism, the Indians embody European values, for Cabeza de Vaca imagines them inflicting death as a punishment. On closer inspection the Indians' character is one more component of the plot that in the final analysis depends on the Spaniards' attitude. If the peoples of Florida are hostile, it is because of Pánfilo de Narváez's excesses. It is true that Cabeza de Vaca eventually comes in contact with nomadic peoples, but there is no justification, even if the term "Stone Age" were applicable, for the qualifier "indocile barbarism" (Pupo-Walker 1987:539). Clearly one can make reference to indocility only from an imperialist perspective. Indocility would read as resistance in a nonethnocentric reading of Indian responses to Spanish invasion of their lands. If it is understandable that resistance is not documented in the *Naufragios*, whose primary concern is narrating the travails of the four survivors, or the *Comentarios*, which highlights the author's political struggles in Paraguay, as literary critics we should not contribute to the culture of conquest by turning the rights to resist into hostile barbarism.

In late twentieth-century studies of colonial texts we can do without such touches of color as the time-travels from European civilization to a Stone Age proposed by Pupo-Walker and Lagmanovich. On the other hand, it is interesting to note that immediately after making his time-travel metaphor Lagmanovich asserts that the *Naufragios* is the account of "una progresiva identificación del autor con el mundo que había partido para sojuzgar [a progressive identification with the indigenous world that he had come to conquer]" (1978:32). So in this sense the *Naufragios* suggests a transition and conversion to an overarching critique of the Spanish conquest of the New World. Following these indications by Lagmanovich, Pastor has precisely elaborated a detailed close reading of the *Naufragios* as an inversion of the Spanish imperial project (1983:294–337; 1989:136–146). Before discussing the question of an ideological and political conversion, let us examine some other inversions of the code of conquest.

Cultural inversions define Cabeza de Vaca's style and need to endow his *relación* with a narrative. Thus in his preface he anticipates the reception of his account, which has nothing to offer but a chronicle of disaster and survival:

Mas como ni mi consejo, ni diligencia, aprovecharon para que aquello a que eramos ydos fuesse ganado conforme al servicio de Vuestra Magestad, y por nuestros peccados permitiesse Dios que de quantas armadas a aquellas tierras han ydo ninguna se viesse en tan grandes peligros, ni tuuiesse tan miserable y desastrado fin, no me quedo lugar para hazer mas servicio deste, que es traer a vuestra Magestad relacion de lo que en diez años que por muchas y muy extrañas tierras que anduve en cueros, pudiesse saber y ver, ansi en el sitio de las tierras y provincias y distancias dellas como en los mantenimientos y animales que en ellas se crian y las diuersas costumbres de muchas y muy barbaras naciones con quien converse y vivi. . . . (*CLD*: vol. 5, 4)

Neither my counsel nor diligence were of any avail for what we set out to gain in the service of Your majesty, and for our sins God permitted that of all the armadas that have ever gone to those lands no one has found itself in straits as great as ours or come to such a miserable and disastrous end. To me, only one duty remains, to present an account of what was seen and heard in the ten years I wandered naked through many and very strange lands. My account provides information not only about the position of territories and provinces and distances between them, but also about the animals and vegetation, and the diverse customs of the many and very barbarous people with whom I talked and dwelt. . . . (Smith 1871: 11–12)

In one breath Cabeza de Vaca first insists on his loyalty and how his prudence and advice were to no avail in preventing the catastrophe that kept the armada from winning the lands and then highlights collective guilt ("por nuestros pecados [for our sins]") and the uniqueness of the failure ("ninguna se viesse en tantos peligros [no one has found itself in straits as great as ours]"). Having exculpated himself, he can move on to single out the event and the mysterious designs of God. All he has to offer is the account of ten years spent in strange lands among barbarous nations, specifying that he was "en cueros" (naked). Cabeza de Vaca insists again on nakedness in the concluding lines of the preface when he states that the only service he can account for is the knowledge contained in the relation, "pues este solo es el que un hombre que salio desnudo pudo sacar consigo" (*CLD*: vol. 5, 5)—"since it is the most that one could bring who returned thence naked" (Smith 1871:12). It contains information, certainly of value, for those who "fueren a conquistar aquellas tierras y juntamente traerlos a conoscimiento de la verdadera fee y verdadero señor y servicio de vuestra majestad" (*CLD*: vol. 5, 5)—"in your name go to subdue those countries and bring them to a knowledge of the true faith and the true Lord, and to the service of your Majesty" (Smith 1871:12). His account thus contributes to the stock of knowledge about the Indies, but his insistence on his nakedness in the closing remark places the emphasis on autobiography and "cosas muy nuevas y para algunos muy dificiles de creer" (*CLD*: vol. 5, 5)—"things very novel and for some persons difficult to believe" (Smith 1871:12). Ultimately all credibility depends on his claim to be truthful: "pueden sin duda creerlas . . . y bastará para esto auerlo yo ofrecido a Vuestra Magestad por tal" (*CLD*: vol. 5, 5)—"they may without hesitation credit this is the truth . . . and it is sufficient to say the relation is offered to your Majesty as such" (Smith 1871:12). Nudity assumes a symbolic dimension; all Cabeza de Vaca has to offer is his naked truth.

Thus the preface calls our attention to the allegorical nature of his text and ensures a reading in which Cabeza de Vaca emerges as an exceptional subject of Charles V. Knowledge of the territories as well as the specifics of the disaster and survival are subordinated to the production of a subject, the first person who surfaces in the narrative. It is not, however, an individual self but an ideal law-abiding, faithful servant. Cabeza de Vaca's narrative produces a subject that embodies in the exemplariness of his travails an allegory of the Spanish enterprise in the Indies—that is, of what it ought to be.

Cabeza de Vaca's narrative inverts the prototypical chronicle of conquest: Whereas the successful conquistadors justify violence, his personification of the ideals of conquest replaces material gains as a leading topic. In fact, Cabeza de Vaca embodies the possibility of peaceful conquest and evangelization. But these ideals not only literally follow the Crown's instruction but also morally absolve the emperor's conscience. We cannot ascertain from such inversions whether the *Naufragios* represents a conversion from an initial conquistador to a critic of conquest. What we can point out is that Cabeza de Vaca's position is not extraneous to the discourse of the Crown. In Pánfilo de Narváez's instructions (*CDI*: vol. 16, 80ff) we find next to the *Requerimiento* a condemnation of violence that Bishop describes as follows in his biography of Cabeza de Vaca: "The voice is that of Charles V, but the words are those of Bartolomé de las Casas" (1933:24). Cabeza de Vaca's instructions, likewise, specifically obligate him to report any form of injustice toward the Indians (*CDI*: vol. 14, 265–279). And so toward the end of the *Naufragios*, precisely in the chapter before Cabeza de Vaca encounters the Spaniards in Culiacán and denounces their cruelties and abuses, he elaborates a statement on colonial policy that echoes the title of a book Las Casas was writing in 1537:

> . . . claramente se vee que estas gentes todas para ser atraydos a ser christianos y a obediencia de la Imperial Magestad han de ser lleuados con buen tratamiento, y que este es camino muy cierto, y otro no. (*CLD*: vol. 5, 124)

> . . . clearly it can be seen that to attract all these peoples to Christianity and to the obedience of the Imperial Majesty, they must be won by kindness, which is a sure way, and no other is. (Smith 1871:175)

The full title in Latin of Las Casas's book is *De cura Regibus Hispaniarum habenda circa orbem indiarum et de unico vocationis modo omnium gentium ad veram religionem,* better known in Spanish with the shorter title *Del único modo de atraer a todos los pueblos a la verdadera religión* [*Of the Only Way to Attract All People to the True Religion*]. As is well known, the policies of this book inspired an experiment in peaceful evangelization in Vera Paz, Guatemala, from 1537 to 1550, but it is beyond the scope of this paper to examine in any detail the results. It suffices to note that in 1540 there was a surge of official support of Las Casas's position in a series of decrees destined to encourage peaceful conversions; on October 17 alone, just before Cabeza de Vaca's departure for the Río de la Plata on November 2, there were twelve such decrees (see Hanke 1942:50). The passage from the *Naufragios* quoted earlier corresponds to Las Casas's ideas in *Del único modo,* though in the narrative's temporal framework Cabeza de Vaca had not been in contact with Spaniards for ten years. Cabeza de Vaca's seemingly independent advancement of Las Casas's policies would certainly have been well received in the ideological climate of the late 1530s and very likely contributed to his gaining the governorship of the Río de la Plata.

We have seen that in the instructions of Narváez the ideal of peaceful colonization and evangelization was expressed in terms reminiscent of Las Casas.

In practice, however, the ideal of peace was prefaced with multiple readings of the *Requerimiento,* "una é dos é mas veces, cuantas pareciese á los dichos religiosos é clerigos que conviniere é fueren necesarias, para que lo entiendan . . . [one, and two and more times, as many as would seem to the said clerics and friars necessary for comprehension]" (*CDI*: vol. 16, 80). Only after a full comprehension of the Crown's right to demand obedience and submission could war be legitimate. *Del único modo* does not explicitly denounce the *Requerimiento* nor its ends—the submission of all Native Americans to the Crown. But it certainly restricts the means and condemns all abuse. Needless to say, *Del único modo* was not well received by colonizers and *encomenderos* (grantees of villages and even city-states who benefited from tribute products and labor). And yet we should not assume that Cabeza de Vaca was merely substituting some sort of evangelical success for his material failures, for Las Casas was bitterly opposed by members of other religious orders such as the Franciscan Motolinía, just to mention the most prominent figure.[10] The *Requerimiento* of course could be manipulated despite the controls of power exercised by the supervision of the clergy; nothing guaranteed the honesty of ecclesiastics. And this is precisely the ideological context of Cabeza de Vaca's political catastrophe in the Río de la Plata, where the virtuous governor encountered lascivious friars, murderous captains, and in general a colonial outpost ruled by terror. Cabeza de Vaca's actions appear to follow to the letter the *Requerimiento* and other instructions on fairness and peaceful colonization. And there is no reason to question his sincerity. He is in all respects a benign colonizer, especially when we compare him with his enemies Domingo de Irala and his followers, including the two Franciscan friars who traveled with a party of up to fifty Indian women.

Besides the *Comentarios* there are two other main accounts of Cabeza de Vaca's political shortcomings in the Río de la Plata; one, the *Relación general,* by Cabeza de Vaca, contains a shorter chronological account of the events, and the other, *Relación de las cosas sucedidas en el Río de la Plata* (1545), by Pero Hernández, the amanuensis of the *Comentarios,* provides detailed descriptions of cruelty to and sexual abuse of Guaraní women. Serrano y Sanz (*CLD*) has compared it to the lifting of roofs in the picaresque novel *El diablo cojuelo.* The following examples suggests Hernández's affinity for gory details and a voyeuristic sense of history:

Una Yndia les avia hurtado cierto bastimento e les dixo [Domingo de Yrala]: *pues tomá esa yndia y cavalgalda tantas veces hasta que seays pagados* [an Indian woman had stolen some supplies and (Domingo de Yrala) told them: *so take that Indian woman and ride her until you feel compensated*]

. . . el dicho Domingo de Yrala por celos que tuvo de Diego Portugues lo colgó de su natura, de lo cual quedó muy malo e lastimado [the aforementioned Domingo de Yrala out of jealousy he felt for Diego Portugal had him hung from his genitals, which resulted in great injury]

un Francisco Palomyno rronpio a muchacha que tenia en su casa, de edad de seys o siete años, hija de su manceba . . . e la madre la truxo al pueblo corriendo sangre e llorando . . . [a Francisco Palomyno deflowered a girl six or seven years old, the daughter of his mistress . . . and the mother brought her to town bleeding and crying. . . .] (*CLD*: vol. 6, 318)

From Hernández we also learn of the accusation "quel governador avia dicho que era rrey . . . [that the governor had said he was the king . . .]" (*CLD*: vol. 6, 347). Beyond the immediate conflict with Cabeza de Vaca, other letters confirm Irala's tactics, such as using "friendly" Indians to terrorize the land:

. . . echando sus axcas y corredores por la tierra, robando y destruyendo los indios, tomandoles sus mugeres paridas y preñadas, y quitando a las paridas las criaturas de los pechos . . . [sending his axcas and runners through the land, stealing and destroying the Indians, taking their wives who had recently given birth or were pregnant, and removing the infants from the breast of those who had recently given birth. . . .] (letter from Juan Muñoz de Carvajal to the emperor, Asunción, June 15, 1556, *Cartas de Indias*, 598)

Another letter tells us that "a sucedido vender Yndias libres naturales desta tierra por caballos, perros y otras cosas, y ansi se usa dellas, como en eso reynos la moneda [it has happened that they sell free Indian women native from this land for horses, dogs and other things, and so they use them, as money is used in those kingdoms]" (letter from Martín González, cleric, to the emperor, Asunción, June 25, 1556, *Cartas de Indias*, 609). These passages are comparable to atrocities detailed in Las Casas's *Brevíssima relación de la destrucción de las Indias* and more recently to events during the rubber boom on the Putumayo River and the ongoing practice of torture and terror in Latin America and elsewhere.

Though the *Comentarios* avoids descriptions of specific instances of abuse, it does denounce the general climate of terror and the exchange of women. However, what interests us about the *Comentarios* is not the specific atrocities Cabeza de Vaca condemns but that through Hernández he represents himself as an exemplary *adelantado*. In the preface to the *Comentarios*, dedicated to the young Prince Don Carlos, Cabeza de Vaca implies—and all but states outright—that his account contains lessons, "preceptos de christiandad, caualleria y philosophia [Christian, chivalric and philosophical precepts]," for the education of the young prince (*CLD*: vol. 5, 154). Thus the *Comentarios* takes special care to underscore how he abided by the law in his proceedings with the Indians. Every time Cabeza de Vaca obtains food from the Indians, for instance, he insists that it was the result of a fair exchange with such repetitive assurances as:

. . . y demas de pagarles el precio que valian, a los indios principales de los pueblos les dio graciosamente e hizo mercedes de muchas camisas [and besides paying them the fair price, he graciously and freely gave them many shirts] (*CLD*: vol. 5, 170);

. . . demas de pagarles los mantenimientos . . . les hazia muchas mercedes . . . en tal manera que corria la fama por la tierra . . . y todos los naturales perdian el temor y venian a ver y a traer todo lo que tenian y se lo pagauan [besides paying them for their provisions . . . he would give them many gifts . . . and so his fame extended throughout the land . . . and all the natives lost their fear and came to see them and brought all they had and we paid for it] (*CLD*: vol. 5, 171–72);

. . . los salieron a rescebir, mostrando grande plazer con la venida del gouernador y gente, y les truxeron al camino muchos bastimentos, los quales se los pagaron segun lo acostumbrauan [they came out to receive them, showing great pleasure at the arrival of the governor and his people, and brought out many provisions to the path, which they paid for them, as it was the custom] (*CLD*: vol. 5, 174);

. . . los salieron a rescebir como hombres que tenian noticia de su venida y del buen tratamiento que les hazian, y le truxeron muchos bastimentos, porque los tienen [they came out to receive them as men who had news of their arrival and the fair treatment they gave them, and they brought many provisions, because they have them] (*CLD*: vol. 5, 182).

And again one sentence later, "En toda esta tierra los indios les seruian porque siempre el gouernador les hazia buen tratamiento [throughout the land the Indians would serve them because the governor treated them well]," which closes his triumphant march from the coast to the falls of Iguazu. Cabeza de Vaca makes the gesture of a humble but seasoned explorer by removing his shoes and leading the march barefoot at the start of the expedition; as he explains in the colorful language of his *Relación general*, "yo camyné sienpre a pie y descalço por animar la gente que no desmayase [I always walked barefooted to encourage the people so they would not lose heart]" (*CLD*: vol. 6, 15). And likewise, he emphasizes how peaceful the penetration was: "Por . . . tienpo de cinco meses syn que diese alteración, ni rompimiento con los Yndios [for . . . approximately five months without causing disturbance nor quarrel with the Indians]" (*CLD*: vol. 6, 15). In both the *Relación general* and the *Comentarios* the falls of Iguazu mark the first natural obstacle and the first conflict with the Indians.

Conflict with the Indians increases and becomes commonplace after Cabeza de Vaca's meeting with Irala in Asunción; conflicts obviously are implicitly blamed on Irala's policies. The dancing and celebrating of his triumphant entrances to villages on his way from the coast now give place to the equally reductive and emblematic war cries, to "grande grita y toque de tambores . . . tan grande la bozeria y alaridos . . . que parescia que se juntaua el cielo con la tierra [great shouting and beating of drums . . . that it seemed as if the sky and the earth were coming together]" (*CLD*: vol. 5, 194), and to the formulaic and repetitive insistence on reading the *Requerimiento* as a preface and justification of war:

. . . mando juntar todos los indios naturales vassallos de Su Magestad, y assi juntos delante y en presencia de los religiosos y clerigos les hizo su parlamento diziendoles como . . . avian de venir en conocimiento de Dios . . . debaxo de la obediencia de Su Magestad y fuessen sus vassallos, y que desta manera serian mejor tratados y fauorescidos que hasta alli auian sido. (*CLD*: vol. 5, 198)

. . . he asked all the Indians natural vassals of Your Majesty to gather, and so together in front of the friars and clerics he addressed them telling them how . . . they had to come to the knowledge of God . . . and under the jurisdiction of Your Majesty and be your vassals, and that thus they would be better treated and favored than they had been up to then. . . .

But Cabeza de Vaca does not insist merely on the repetition of the *Requerimiento* and how he solicited the opinion of the friars and clergy but also over and over again on how he took care to "hazer los apercebimientos vna e dos e tres vezes con toda templança [make the warnings soberly, one, two and three times]" (*CLD*: vol. 5, 207). These repetitive readings of the *Requerimiento* throughout the text—"vna y dos y tres vezes y quantas mas deuiessen [one and two and three, and as many times as needed]" (*CLD*: vol. 5, 254)—are expressed in the same words and thus emphasize the legality of his procedures.

We should note that in the *Comentarios* the *Requerimiento* is first read after the initial conflict with the Indians on Cabeza de Vaca's arrival in Asunción and is followed by a long description of cannibalism among the Guaraní. Although it is most likely that Cabeza de Vaca did not observe the ritual, the *Comentarios* provides an elaborate description of the captive's preparation: ". . . lo ponen a engordar y le dan todo quanto quiere a comer, y a sus mugeres e hijas para que aya con ellas sus plazeres [. . . they fatten him and they give him all he wants to eat, and his wives and daughters to have pleasure with them]" (*CLD*: vol. 5, 198). From the start of his march Cabeza de Vaca had mentioned cannibalism as one more cultural trait alongside the enumeration of foodstuffs, houses, dances, and so on. All along, he had also taken care to write how he had taken possession of the territories and to comment on the Guaranís' natural inclination to Christianity. His long statement on cannibalism precisely when conflict arises clearly suggests that cannibalism is a sufficient reason to declare war and enslave those who refuse to abandon its practice. Moreover, to overlook and tolerate cannibalism is the most unacceptable breach of the Conquest's rationale. Such passages justify Cabeza de Vaca's recourse to violence and war and substantiate a distinction between friendly and enemy Indians. These passages obviously condemn all military action against friendly Indians but also emphasize the gravity of Cabeza de Vaca's ultimate accusation against Irala:

Para valerse los oficiales y Domingo de Yrala con los indios naturales de la tierra les dieron licencia que matassen y comiessen a los indios enemigos dellos, y a nuchos destos a quien dieron licencia eran christianos nueuamente conuertidos . . . cosa tan contra el seruicio de Dios y de Su Magestad. . . . (*CLD*: vol. 5, 357)

In order to be favored by the native Indians of the land the officers and Domingo de Yrala gave them permission to kill and eat their Indian enemies, and many of those to whom they gave license to eat human flesh were recently converted Christians . . . a thing so against the service of God and Your Majesty. . . .

This permission to practice cannibalism, condemnable especially among those who had been Christianized, closes a long list of accusations of Irala's unjust treatment of the Indians and the rebellion against Cabeza de Vaca's rule in the Río de la Plata.

We should recall here that in the *Naufragios,* after the collapse of authority, it is the Spaniards who eat each other and scandalize the Indians. In the *Apologética historia sumaria,* Las Casas cites these passages from Cabeza de Vaca's *Naufragios* to counter all usages of cannibalism as reason to justify conquest (Las Casas 1967:2, 354). Indeed Las Casas derives a certain satisfaction in recounting these examples of cannibalism among Christians, especially since the Indians who condemn the Spaniards are, according to Cabeza de Vaca, so poor and hungry "que si en aquella tierra ouiesse piedras, las comerian [that if there were stones in that land, they would eat them]" (*CLD*: vol. 5, 70). Such passages in the *Naufragios* cause Las Casas to argue in favor of ritualistic anthropophagy and dismiss all notions of cannibalism as a nutrition substitute. Cabeza de Vaca, however, never draws this corollary since these passages in the *Naufragios* are ultimately self-serving: He does not eat meat from the horses, much less human flesh. We must note, however, that in the same chapter Cabeza de Vaca includes a funerary practice of burning the remains of shamans, whose ashes are diluted in water and consumed a year later by the immediate members of the family: "a los parientes dan esos polvos a beber, de los huesos, en agua" (*CDI*: vol. 5, 54). Thus Cabeza de Vaca suggests that if anthropophagy does occur among Native Americans, it assumes a highly symbolic form. One does not need to emphasize the irony implied in this description of ritual anthropophagy right after the anomie that led Spaniards to kill and devour each other.

If at the end of the *Naufragios* Cabeza de Vaca echoes Las Casas's *Del único modo,* he never explicitly denounces the absurdity of the *Requerimiento* or the illegality of all wars of conquest in the New World. Even when in the *Naufragios* he alludes to peaceful measures as the only acceptable form of evangelization and subjection to the Crown, he follows the terms of the *Requerimiento*. Thus, in the *Naufragios* he threatens the Indians after offering good will if they submit: ". . . mas que si esto no quisiessen hazer, los christianos les tratarian muy mal y se los llevarian por esclavos á otras tierras [. . . and if they were not willing to do this, the Christians would greatly mistreat them and would take them as slaves to other lands]" (*CLD*: vol. 5, 134). This dutiful compliance with the *Requerimiento* is ultimately what differentiates Cabeza de Vaca's position from the slave raiders in Culiacán and Pánfilo de Narváez who apparently never bothered reading the document after landfall in Florida. Cabeza de Vaca could never have assumed the position Las Casas takes in the 1550s (a unique one indeed) of total condemnation of the Spanish enterprise in the New World (see Rabasa 1989). Cabeza de Vaca certainly strikes us as a conscientious and law-abiding servant of the Crown. We should not, however, project an anti-imperialist position or be seduced by his heroic, colorful narratives of colonial adventures and especially not by his similarly vivid and colorful ethnographic sketches of servile or hostile Indians. Because of the self-serving nature of his narratives, resistance has no place in his representation and interpretation of the Indians.

Through the *Naufragios* Cabeza de Vaca first sought to gain the governorship of Florida; as a compensation he was eventually granted governorship of the Río de la Plata. He emerges in the *Comentarios* and other documents as an exemplary *adelantado,* with worthy lessons for the young Don Carlos. Irala is appointed to the governorship in 1555, which perhaps explains the absence of all claims to the Río de la Plata in the preface to the *Comentarios,* and his settling for fame as a writer:

Que cierto no hay cosa que mas deleyte a los lectores que las variedades de las cosas y tiempos y las bueltas de la fortuna, las quales, aunque al tiempo que se experimentan no son gustosas, quando las traemos a la memoria y leemos, son agradables. (*CLD*: vol. 5, 148)

There is certainly nothing that delights readers more than the variety of things and times and turns of fortune, which although they are not delightful when experienced, are pleasurable when we recall them and read them.

We do not know the exact date of Cabeza de Vaca's death, but most likely he did not learn of Irala's in 1557, probably from "peritonitis following on appendicitis" (Bishop 1933:289). Nonetheless Cabeza de Vaca knows the lessons to be derived from the whims of fortune and, perhaps, how the *relaciones* of his misfortunes would in the end redeem him.

Whether his accusations of Irala and his followers are reliable representations of the events need not concern us, and perhaps the Paraguayan historian Gandía is justified when he defines the two parties as follows:

. . . los españoles del Paraguay, sin frenos capaces de liberarlos de las tentaciones de las bellas Guaraní, se condenaban el alma con aquellas infieles de las cuales cada uno poseía treinta, cuarenta y aún más, según las indignadas relaciones de los contados puritanos de aquel entonces, que sólo disfrutaban de media docena de indias. (Gandía 1932: 119)

. . . the Spaniards from Paraguay, without the restraints that could free them from the temptations of the beautiful Guaranís, would condemn their souls by living with those infidels of which each possessed thirty, forty and even more, according to the outraged relations of the few puritans of those times, who only enjoyed having half a dozen Indian women.

We may question, nevertheless, Gandía's ironic detachment that allows him to blame not "los sentimientos de los españoles, que se pervertían al llegar a estas tierras, sino al medio ambiente en que ellos vivían y que, hasta un cierto punto los hacía irresponsables de sus actos [the feelings of the Spaniards, that were perverted upon arrival, but the natural milieu in which they lived and that, up to a point, exempted them from responsibility for their acts]" (1932:127). In support of this statement Gandía quotes Francisco de Andrada, a cleric, who asks how the Spaniards could avoid taking Indian women when they had the "maldita costumbre [damned custom]" of being responsible for sowing and reaping. Gandía further substantiates the natural milieu with "las delicias de aquellas tierras paradisíacas, como la dulzura del clima, la facilidad de la vida y, sobre todo, la extraordinaria abundancia de mujeres [the delights of those paradisaical lands, the sweetness of the climate, the ease of life and, above all, the extraordinary abundance of women]" (1932:127). This "inimaginable Paraíso de Mahoma," as Gandía defines it, which leads Spaniards to abuse and exploit Guaraní women, could easily be replaced by another explanatory commonplace in the colonial representation of the tropics—the infernal jungle, which also leads Europeans to commit the worst of atrocities. With these closing remarks on Gandía we come full circle to Conrad, Cunninghame Graham, and Casement. They provide one more example of what I have attempted to define as the culture of conquest in which we historians, literary critics, and anthropologists are still implicated today.

In treating the discursive violence that the culture of conquest perpetuates in reading and interpreting colonial texts, this essay has reiterated the lack of attention given by literary readings to indigenous resistance. The vulnerability of the four survivors in the *Naufragios* does not lend itself to a documentation of resistance, nor does the almost exclusive concern with the political conflicts with Irala in the *Comentarios*. But forms of resistance can be reconstructed from descriptions of military encounters in the so-called *entradas* (raids) without recurring to that all too imperialistic *topoi* of the hostile Indian. We should also resist the impulse to identify Cabeza de Vaca's function as a shaman in the *Naufragios* with the *topoi* of the Western hero whose perspicacity enables him to play the role of a quack doctor and manipulate the *hijo del sol* [son of the sun] attribute (see, for example, Pastor 1989:141–142; see also Molloy 1987:439–449).

It is precisely because the *topoi* of the ignorant and warlike Indian have played an integral function in colonialist literature that they lend artistic and literary value to the *Naufragios*. But in following Cabeza de Vaca's conception of Indians literary critics not only perpetuate the culture of conquest but also lose track of the rhetorical devices that enabled him to convey knowledge of Native

American cultures and personal experiences that questioned European taboos. The faithful and benevolent colonial official that I have traced in this essay may also have an exceptional story to tell. It seems to me that only after we make room for this paradoxical coexistence of an imperial and an empathetic perspective will we be able to trace voices of resistance in Cabeza de Vaca. Those passages that critics tend to read at face value may turn out to be allegorical—saying one thing but meaning another.

Notes

1. See Fabian (1983:109–113 and *passim*) on *topoi* of discourse and their function in anthropology.
2. Mignolo (1986) has drawn an extensive critique of the reduction among literary critics of the multicultural reality of the Americas to Spanish and Western cultural norms.
3. This rough itinerary does not pretend to give the reader the actual trajectory but a feeling for the distances. Cabeza de Vaca's exact route is a highly debated issue involving all sorts of nationalistic feelings; for example, Robert E. Hill, a distinguished geologist working at the University of Texas in the 1930s, felt that to favor a trans-Mexico route would take away Cabeza de Vaca's citizenship. I draw these observations from Chipman's (1987) review of the historiography of Cabeza de Vaca's route across Texas.
4. For the *Naufragios* and the *Comentarios* as well as other documents pertaining to Cabeza de Vaca's governorship of the Río de la Plata, I am using *Colección de libros y documentos referentes a la historia de América* (1906), ed. Serrano y Sanz, vols. 5 and 6. Hereafter citations will be *CLD*, volume, and page number. For the English version of the *Naufragios* I am following, with some emendations where I have felt necessary, the 1871 translation by Buckingham Smith. I have given page numbers from this edition after the English versions. Unless otherwise indicated, all other translations are mine.
5. As William Taylor has pointed out to me in a personal communication, this opposition by literary critics presupposes an understanding of "'history' . . . as an ideal type—as what objectively happened. Few historians would say that this is what they are able to produce."
6. *Colección de documentos inéditos, relativos al descubrimiento, conquista y organización de las antiguas posesiones en América y Oceanía* (1864–84), eds. Pacheco, Cárdenas, Torres Mendoza. Hereafter citations from this collection will be *CDI*, volume, and page number.
7. For bibliographical information on both the *Naufragios* and the *Comentarios*, see Cardozo (1959: vol. 1, 133–144), Hart (1974: xi–xix), and Lastra (1984:150–151).
8. Lafaye (1984) has studied the reception and the different values the *milagros*

have assumed since the first comments in the sixteenth and seventeenth centuries; see also Pupo-Walker (1987).

9. These time-travel metaphors by Lagmanovich and Pupo-Walker exemplify a tendency in Western anthropology to deny the coevalness of the people it studies—that is, to place them in another time, obviously anterior to the observer. For a definition of this denial of coevalness as the allochronism of anthropology, see Fabian (1983:32 and *passim*). Ferrando, in his edition of the *Naufragios y Comentarios* (1984:17–20), uncritically reproduces allochronic metaphors as primitives and insists on placing the different groups within an evolutionary cultural schema ranging in his case from the Mesolithic to the Neolithic ages. In the face of such prehistorical cultures Ferrando feels the need to imitate evidence that physical anthropology uses in the study of human evolution by reproducing information on cranial forms, facial shapes, and other physical data as height. He obviously did not feel the need to provide measurements for Cabeza de Vaca's cranium.

10. See, for instance, Motolinía's bitter critique of Las Casas in his letter of January 2, 1555, to Charles V (documentary appendix to Motolinía 1971).

References

Barthes, R. 1981. "The Discourse of History." In *Rhetoric and History: Comparative Criticism Yearbook*, edited by Elinor Shaffer, 7–20. Cambridge: Cambridge University Press.

Bishop, Morris. 1933. *The Odyssey of Cabeza de Vaca*. New York and London: The Century.

Cardozo, Efraín. 1959. *Historiografía paraguaya*. 2 vols. Mexico City: Instituto Panamericano de Geografía e Historia, Comisión de Historia, 83.

Carreño, A. 1987. "Naufragios, de Alvar Núñez Cabeza de Vaca: Una retórica de la crónica colonial." *Revista Iberoamericana* 53: 499–516.

Cartas de Indias. 1887. Ministerio de Fomento. Madrid: Imprenta Manuel G. Hernández.

Chipman, D. E. 1987. "In Search of Cabeza de Vaca's Route across Texas: An Historical Survey." *Southwestern Historical Quarterly* 91:127–148.

Colección de documentos inéditos, relativos al descubrimiento, conquista y organización de las antiguas posesiones en América y Oceania (CDI). 1864–84. Edited by J. F. Pacheco, F. de Cárdenas, and L. Torres Mendoza. 42 vols. Madrid: Imprenta de José María Pérez.

Colección de libros y documentos referentes a la historia de América (CLD). Edited by M. Serrano y Sanz. Vols. 5–6. Madrid: Librería General de Victoriano Suárez.

Dowling, Lee. 1984. "Story vs. Discourse in the Chronicle of Indies: Alvar Núñez Cabeza de Vaca's Relation." *Hispanic Journal* 5:89–99.

Fabian, J. 1983. *Time and Its Other: How Anthropology Makes Its Object*. New York: Columbia University Press.

Gandía, Enrique de. 1932. *Indios y conquistadores en el Paraguay*. Buenos Aires: Librería de A. García Santos.

Graham, R. B. Cunninghame. 1968 [1924]. *The Conquest of the River Plate*. New York: Greenwood Press.

Hart, B. T. 1974. "A Critical Edition with a Study of the Style of 'La Relación' by Alvar Núñez Cabeza de Vaca." Ph.D. diss. University of Southern California.

Hanke, L. 1942. Introduction to *Del único modo de atraer a todos los pueblos a la verdadera religión*, by Bartolomé de las Casas. Mexico City: Fondo de Cultura Económica.

Jara, R., and Spadaccini, N., eds. 1989. "1492–1992: Re/Discovering Colonial Writing." *Hispanic Issues* 4:261–289.

Invernizzi, L. 1987. "Naufragios e infortunios: discurso que transforma fracasos en triunfos." *Revista Chilena de Literatura* 29:7–22.

Lafaye, Jacques. 1984. "Los milagros de Alvar Núñez Cabeza de Vaca (1527–1536)." In *Mesías, cruzadas, utopías: El judeo-cristianismo en las sociedades ibéricas*, 65–84. Mexico City: Fondo de Cultura Económica.

Lagmanovich, David. 1978. "Los Naufragios de Alva Núñez como construcción narrativa." *Kentucky Romance Quarterly* 25:23–37.

Las Casas, Bartolomé de. 1967. *Apologética historia sumaria*. 2 vols. Mexico City: Universidad Nacional Autónoma de México.

———. 1942. *Del único modo de atraer a todos los pueblos a la verdadera religión*. Mexico City: Fondo de Cultura Económica.

Lastra, P. 1984. "Espacios de Alvar Núñez: Las transformaciones de una escritura." *Cuadernos Americanos* 3:150–164.

Lewis, R. E. 1982. "Los Naufragios de Alvar Núñez: Historia y ficción." *Revista Iberoamericana* 48:681–694.

Mignolo, W. 1986. "La lengua, la letra, el territorio (o la crisis de los estudios literarios coloniales)." *Dispositio* 11:137–160.

Molloy, S. 1987. "Alteridad y reconocimiento en los Naufragios de Alvar Núñez Cabeza de Vaca." *Nueva Revista de Filología Hispánica* 35:425–449.

Motolinía, T. de Benavente. 1971. *Memoriales o libro de las cosas de la Nueva España y de los naturales de ella*. Mexico City: Universidad Nacional Autónoma de México.

Núñez Cabeza de Vaca, Alvar. [1871] 1966. *Relation of Alvar Núñez Cabeça de Vaca*. Translated by Buckingham Smith. Ann Arbor, Mich.: University Microfilms.

———. 1984. *Naufragios y Comentarios*. Edited by Roberto Ferrando. Madrid: Historia 16. Oviedo y Valdés, G. Fernández de. 1959. *Historia natural y general de las Indias*. 5 vols. Madrid: Biblioteca de Autores Españoles.

París Lozano, Gonzalo. *Guerrilleros de Tolima*. Bogotá: El Ancora, 1984.

Parry, J. H., and R. G. Keith, eds. 1984. *New Iberian World: A Documentary History of the Discovery and Settlement of Latin America*. Vol. 1. New York: Times Books.

Pastor, Beatriz. 1983. "Del fracaso a la desmitificación." In *Discurso narrativo de la conquista de América*, 237–337. Havana: Casa de las Américas.

———. 1989. "Silence and Writing: The History of the Conquest." In *1492–1992:*

Re/Discovering Colonial Writing, edited by R. Jara and N. Spadaccini. *Hispanic Issues* 4:121–163.

Pupo-Walker, Enrique. 1987. "Pesquisas para una nueva lectura de los Naufragios de Alvar Núñez Cabeza de Vaca." *Revista Iberoamericana* 53:517–539.

Rabasa, José. 1989. "Utopian Ethnology in Las Casas's Apologética." In *1492–1992: Re/Discovering Colonial Writing*, edited by R. Jara and N. Spadaccini. *Hispanic Issues* 4:261–289.

Rivera, José Eustacio. 1974. *La vorágine*. Bogotá: Editorial Pax.

Rosaldo, R. 1989. "Imperialist Nostalgia." *Representations* 26:107–122.

Said, Edward. 1988. "Through Gringo Eyes: With Conrad in Latin America." *Harper's Magazine* 278 (April): 70–72.

Taussig, Michael. 1987. *Shamanism, Colonialism, and the Wild Man: A Study in Terror and Healing*. Chicago and London: University of Chicago Press.

Todorov, Tzvetan. 1987. *The Conquest of America: The Question of the Other*. New York: Harper Torchbooks.

Tyler, S. A. 1986. "Post-Modern Ethnography: From Document of the Ocult to Ocult Document." *In Writing Culture: The Poetics and Politics of Ethnography*, edited by J. Clifford and G. E. Marcus, 122–140. Berkeley and Los Angeles: University of California Press.

Watts, C. T., ed. 1969. *Joseph Conrad's Letters to Cunninghame Graham*. Cambridge: Cambridge University Press.

White, H. 1978. *Tropics of Discourse: Essays in Cultural Criticism*. Baltimore and London: Johns Hopkins University Press.

———. 1989a. "The Question of Narrative in Contemporary Historical Theory." In *The Content of Form: Narrative Discourse and Historical Representation*, 26–57. Baltimore and London: Johns Hopkins University Press.

———. 1989b. "The Value of Narrativity in the Representation of Reality." In *The Content of Form: Narrative Discourse and Historical Representation*, 1–25. Baltimore and London: Johns Hopkins University Press.

The Art
of
Survival
in
Early
Colonial
Peru

Rolena Adorno

It gave me much toil to fulfill my desire of presenting to your Majesty this said book . . . written and drawn by my own hand and talent, so that the variety of the pictures and the invention and artistic creation to which your Majesty is inclined, might make less heavy the burden and bother of reading a work lacking genius and that ornament and polished style that is found in great and talented writers.[1]

With this statement a native Andean, Don Felipe Guaman Poma de Ayala, dedicated to King Philip III of Spain about 1615 the book that he had written in Spanish and Quechua and illustrated with four hundred pictures. The title-page drawing (fig. 1) encapsulates the features of a self-portrait that the author presented some five times in the course of his work. Although he is dressed in a European courtier's costume and assumes a position of Christian piety, nevertheless his European hat covers an Andean haircut, and under his Spanish cape and over his European knee breeches he wears a traditional Andean tunic (*uncu*).

Figure 1. Title page of the *Nueva corónica y buen gobierno* showing Guaman Poma (lower right-hand corner), the king of Spain next to him, and the Roman Catholic pope presiding over all. All illustrations are reproduced from the 1987 edition of the *Nueva corónica y buen gobierno,* with the permission of the publisher, Historia-16, Madrid.

In this ideal representation he is subordinated to the Spanish king but, like him, is a sovereign prince. On Guaman Poma's European-style coat of arms are displayed the symbols of his totemic names *guaman* (falcon) and *poma* (lion).[2] Both the Spanish king and the Andean prince submit to the higher authority of the Roman Catholic pope. As solicitous of the king's good will as Guaman Poma's introductory remarks and drawing may seem to be, they preface a profound criticism of colonialism. As part of an act of resistance, Guaman Poma's words highlight the problem I wish to explore—namely, the use of writing as resistance and an art of survival.

Born shortly after the Spanish conquest of Peru, Guaman Poma was raised in contact with Spanish colonial society and was employed by the institutions of the Spanish colonial administration as an interpreter.[3] Like other Andeans versed in the language and customs of the Spaniards, he was identified by Europeans as an *indio ladino*. The social and political reality of the native Andeans who came to be called *indios ladino*s is too complex and varied to take up here (Solano 1975; Adorno 1991). However, on a spectrum in which the extremes are *indio ladino* accommodation to European ways and messianic *indio ladino* resistance to all that was not Andean, the experience of Guaman Poma stands somewhere in the middle.[4] As such, his case can illuminate the complexities and contradictions of accommodation and resistance to colonialism. Although Guaman Poma's testimony offers only a single instance and not a comprehensive pattern of Andean colonial experience, it provides a richness of detail and nuance that a single source's sustained reflection can provide.

I have called the topic of this essay the art of survival within a specific scholarly context. More than thirty years ago Garibay (1953–54) and most prominently León-Portilla (1959) brought to international attention the sixteenth-century Nahua oral traditions on the Spanish conquest of Mexico. The themes of defeat in the texts recovered led logically to the consideration of that testimony as "the vision of the vanquished" (León-Portilla 1959). Inspired by that initial body of work, a second, more recent phase in the study of the process of post-Conquest reflections and memorializing has placed the emphasis on resistance. Work on individual native and mestizo writers of the early colonial period, such as the Andean Don Juan de Santacruz Pachacuti Yamqui Salcamayhua, exemplify this trend (see Harrison 1982 and Salomon 1982). The theme of writing as resistance of this second phase complements the first insofar as it attempts to refine the issues and elaborate the paradigms of action and response. The topic of this essay is resistance *and* survival, and their simultaneous consideration is significant. Guaman Poma's work allows us to describe some forms of resistance—mediated and accommodating though they may be—that suggest that the keys to cultural survival may also have been mediated and accommodating.

Writing—that is, the phonetic writing of European culture—was already in the world into which Guaman Poma de Ayala was born.[5] Although Andeans under colonial rule had learned to use literacy in their own interest to initiate lawsuits and litigation, Guaman Poma typically portrayed his compatriots as victims of the administrative and juridical workings of written culture, while occasionally acknowledging the effectiveness of native legal petitioning. His own commentary on written culture has two manifestations: (1) what he had to say about its uses and abuses in colonial society and (2) the uses to which he put it in his own literary and pictographic production.[6] Pursuing each of these lines of inquiry, we find that they ultimately converge in his consideration of writing in relation to the exercise of political influence and power.

To set the stage for this discussion, I would like to begin (and later conclude) with Guaman Poma's version of the initial encounter between the Inca Atahualpa and Francisco Pizarro's expedition during the first phase of the Spanish invasion of Peru. Guaman Poma tells how, in that fateful meeting in Cajamarca in November 1532, Atahualpa was defeated by the book containing the silent Word of God—which did not speak (Adorno 1985a:2–3; see also MacCormack 1988a).

Drawing a picture of that encounter to accompany his narrative description, Guaman Poma freezes the moment of initial confrontation when the Inca Atahualpa, sitting on his *usno* (ceremonial seat), stares straight ahead as before and beneath him Fray Vicente de Valverde holds a book—a Bible or breviary— in his left hand and a cross in his right and the Indian interpreter Felipillo gesticulates with his left hand (fig. 2) (1987:386). The scene would quickly and disastrously change, but it is this moment of the European-Andean confrontation that the artist immortalizes in a picture. In Guaman Poma's account, Fray Vicente tells the Inca that Atahualpa should be his friend, adore the cross, and believe only in the Christian Gospel. Atahualpa asks who has told him all this, and the friar answers that the book has told him. Atahualpa demands the object so that "it may say the same to me." Handling the book, hearing nothing, Atahualpa throws it to the ground declaring, "It does not speak to me!" With that, according to Guaman Poma (1987:387–388), Fray Vicente called for the attack. The Spanish soldiers killed the assembled Andeans "like ants" and captured Atahualpa without a struggle.

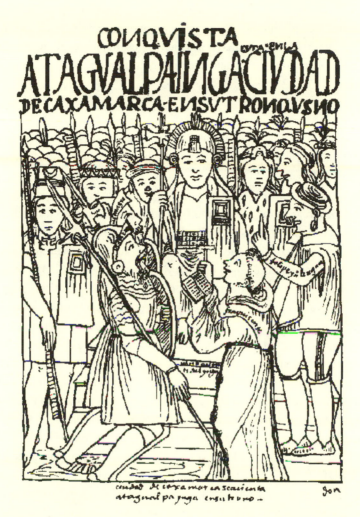

Figure 2. Atahualpa Inca, Fray Vicente de Valverde, and the sacred book (1987:386).

It is as if, in Guaman Poma's and many other similar interpretations of that event, the Inca and all Andeans were punished for failing to recognize the ultimate emblem of religious and political power that the sacred book represented. Clearly, Atahualpa had failed the "ritual test of literacy."[7] The ritual dimension of Atahualpa's response—the Inca's apparent disregard and scorn for the silent sacred book, not his inability to read it—sealed his fate. To be able to read the book, to believe in the power of the written word, and to subscribe only to the values that it represented—these were the challenges presented and rejected in that historic confrontation. Picking up the gauntlet some sixty or seventy years later, Guaman Poma evaluated those challenges, funneling all his energies into dominating the written word and attempting to appropriate the power that it represented.

"The good lord must be examined in the language and letters of Spanish." Briefly, the linguistic politics of Spain in the Peruvian viceroyalty during the early colonial period can be summed up as "the simultaneous efforts to restrict the inroads of [Spanish-Quechua] bilingualism in the legal and political domain and to encourage bilingualism among local headmen so as to facilitate indirect rule" (Mannheim 1984:291). Bilingual mestizos were allowed only restricted participation in the clergy and were prohibited outright from exercising "the juridically important occupation of notary" (Mannheim 1984:294).[8] At the same time bilingualism was encouraged among the noble elites, and the clergy in particular cultivated literacy among youths, such as Guaman Poma, who were taught not only to speak but also to read and write Spanish.[9] At the local level both the ecclesiastical and civil establishments depended on native interpreters in the negotiations between Europeans and *criollos* on the one hand and the native Andean population on the other. As mentioned earlier, Guaman Poma spent a considerable amount of time working for the colonial administration.

Guaman Poma's views on European written culture and its relation to Andean cultural survival can be set forth best by reference to his drawings. Guaman Poma (1987:685, 686) prescribed a program for Andean literacy not unlike the efforts of a few outspoken members of the ecclesiastical establishment, which may be summarized as follows: Andean children and adolescents of both sexes should be taught to read and write "in order to become Christian"; being literate, they would lose their superstitious practices and idolatries. He therefore recommended the establishment of schools in every settlement "for the service of God and His Majesty and good government and Christianity"; special schools should be set up for the sons of ethnic lords (1987:686). In his program for colonial reform, which included the governance of Andeans by Andeans under the nominal leadership of the Spanish monarch, Guaman Poma recommended as a qualification for all Andean leaders literacy in Castilian and, at the highest levels, in Latin (1987:756, 758, 760, 762, 764, 766, 768, and 770).

Guaman Poma's vision of the future is materialized in a picture of an Andean *curaca* (ethnic lord) sitting at his desk, listening and writing, as one of the

Andeans living under his jurisdiction gesticulates and enumerates on the fingers of his right hand the charges he wishes to be presented in his petition (fig. 3) (1987:784). The picture is entitled "The good lord must be examined in the language and letters of Spanish." Thus envisioned, writing was to become the force that would integrate the traditional and colonial structuration of the polity and represent the citizen's prerogatives within it.

Figure 3. Now a colonial intermediary, the ethnic lord writes formal petitions on behalf of his people (1987:784).

Opposing Guaman Poma's advocacy of Andean literacy is his portrayal of colonial efforts to control its spread. He complained often that colonial functionaries mistrusted literate Andeans and that the former attempted to block the development of literacy: "They all want us to be ignorant, asses, so that they can take away all we have, our wives and daughters" (1987:604; see also 609, 637, 799, and 920). At the same time he acknowledged—significantly and perhaps unwittingly—that native Andean literacy was not an uncommon phenomenon. A priest, newly arrived to the parish to which he has been assigned, requests that all writing materials in the settlement be rounded up (fig. 4) (1987:636). His Andean assistant brings him a great number of such items and promises to deliver a great many more. Upon discovering that so many of the inhabitants of this Andean settlement know how to read and write Castilian, the priest understands that any and all native grievances against him are likely to be translated into written complaints. "My son," declares the priest, "I do not seek a town that has so many notaries! Tomorrow I'll be on my way!" (Guaman Poma 1987:637).

Understanding through his own experience how potentially dangerous the colonizers considered the Andeans' literacy in Castilian, Guaman Poma set his own agenda to promote the cause of literacy among his people. His political activism consisted of presenting petitions and suits against the colonial overlord, and he claims to have had many Andean students (*decípulos*) to whom he taught reading and writing. Literacy—not as a simple set of skills but as the command of an entire cultural repertoire—was the way the colonized could become part of the Spanish colonial legal system. It was, potentially at least, the most effective means for combating disenfranchisement or dispossession.

Despite Guaman Poma's belief in literacy as an antidote to the excesses of virulent colonialism, we find evidence that his confidence came to be seriously eroded. His disillusionment is hinted at in the repetitiveness that characterizes and mars his prose text. Guaman Poma's remark that "to write is never to be finished" belies an anxiety about the ability to communicate through the written medium and his fear that the silence imposed by the conclusion of his polemical project might create a vacuum to be filled by other, antagonistic voices. In addition, his extraordinary use of pictorial signification reveals that he took care not only to entertain his princely reader but also to assure himself of a more direct mode of communication.[10] Before anticipating our conclusion, let us look first at Guaman Poma's own uses of written culture.

Figure 4. The priest tells his native assistant that he does not want to serve a parish in which so many native Andeans are literate (1987:636).

"The author personally presents the chronicle to His Majesty."

That Guaman Poma considered writing one of the indispensable arts of survival is most compellingly demonstrated by the composition of his own book. One of the most remarkable of Guaman Poma's pictures is his self-portrait and interview with the Spanish king, Philip III (fig. 5) (1987:975). Splendidly costumed, as in the title-page drawing, he kneels at the foot of the king's throne

Figure 5. In an imagined audience with the Spanish king, Guaman Poma presents his book (1987:975).

and gesticulates with his right hand while holding the book in his left. I shall return to this scene later, but for the moment let us concentrate on the presence of the book. The book—Guaman Poma's own book—makes possible the very idea of such a dreamed-of interview. The book effects the interview through its representative powers of bringing the vassal before the king. It magically materializes the ideas and sentiments of the absent author to the present reader. It is an instrument of power worthy of occupying the site of maximum authority—the monarch's domain. In this drawing the book is the fulcrum of the power relations between superordinate and subordinate.

Given the looming Christian image of the book as sacred object and conveyer of divine knowledge, it is not surprising that Guaman Poma should take for his immediate model the didactic works of religious instruction published for the proselytization of the native populations: "I spent much time and many years," he states in his prologue "to the Christian reader," "remembering that my work should be useful to faithful Christians for correcting their sins and evil ways and errors and for confessing the said Indians and for the said priests to learn to confess the said Indians (1987:11)." [11] This idea of the book as didactic and prescriptive replicates the program for proper conduct that had been prescribed by his literary models. The *New Chronicle and Good Government*, for example, outlined for the European and *criollo* readership the codes of conduct Guaman Poma considered appropriate and just in the management of secular colonial affairs, just as the catechisms and sermon texts with which he was so familiar had set forth codes of religious and moral conduct for the Andeans.

Looking backward in time as well as forward, Guaman Poma used the book to enter the debate on the philosophical and legal status of the native Andean peoples under colonialism. [12] Understanding full well the ways in which such innocent titles as Francisco de Jerez's *True Account of the Conquest of Peru (Verdadera relación de la conquista del Perú)* embraced and masked the arguments of the juridical treatises, the polemics on colonization, and the prejudices against the colonized, Guaman Poma crafted his own *New Chronicle* to reinterpret the conquest and deny the rights of the colonizers to the lands and labors of the peoples of Peru. Because writing tended to reduce the past and render its record fixed, Guaman Poma entered the fray with an account he described as the first of the "new" chronicles. [13] He did not present his contestatory views by argument but rather by narration (Adorno 1986:6) [14]—so familiar to him as an explanatory discourse through the oral traditions, so comfortable to him in light of his own recent experience reading the European chronicles of the Peruvian conquest. What is most remarkable about Guaman Poma is the degree to which he apprehended the ultimately political subtexts of European writings and the "texts" of European culture in general. Here, he denies Inca resistance to the invading Spaniards in order to deny the rights of the Spanish *encomenderos* as the natives' new overlords (fig. 6) (1987:377, 404, and 406).

In light of European historiography on the Indies, Guaman Poma's own polemical literary agenda was easily set. One priority was to salvage autochthonous culture from its interpretation by the foreign. Another was to recover the fullness of the native cultural traditions, which implied that being "written down" caused distortion and transformation. A third was the reconciliation of the tra-

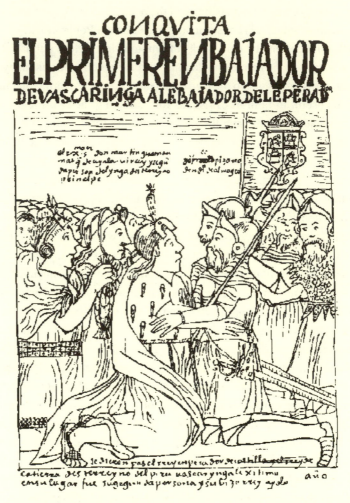

Figure 6. Guaman Poma denies the military conquest of Peru by showing the diplomatic submission of the Inca's emissaries to Pizarro (1987:377).

ditional with the foreign culture, not in the sense of acculturation but rather as the adaptation or the grafting of two disparate traditions.[15] In this context I would like to address three points that reflect Guaman Poma's literary engagement with the political agendas of written culture and illuminate his own art of survival.[16]

The first may be considered under the rubric of the devil and the dispossessed, for it concerns the fact that the European colonizers always seemed to find Satan palpably present among the colonized; Guaman Poma attempted to erase that image. The second concerns the use of writing as an attempt to reconcile opposing cultural systems—that is, as an instrument of analysis and interpretation to reconcile the irreconcilable.[17] Finally, there are the political implications of oral culture as these are represented in the visual text, by the *indio ladino* looking back.

The Devil and the Dispossessed

The most fundamental project of the writings of the colonized was to radically alter the European discourse of Satanic intervention. In the earliest printed European accounts of Andean culture, such as those of Pedro de Cieza de León and Juan de Betanzos, the Andeans' inspiration by Satan was a prominent theme not only in prose but also pictorially (see Adorno 1990:110). In rescuing Andean culture from such European interpretations, the colonized literary subject engaged in a procedure of admitting within a limited and highly qualified context the presence of practices considered demonic by Europeans and identified by them as sacrifice, idolatry, witchcraft, and superstition (fig. 7) (Guaman Poma 1987:279). Writings such as Guaman Poma's attempted to erase the discourses in which evil forces were consistently read into the traditions and practices of newly colonized peoples. As a profoundly political act involving the transaction of exchange in the currency of the colonizers, Guaman Poma replaced the horned demon set on the non-European landscape by Europeans with the dove of the Christian Holy Spirit (fig. 8) (1987:837). He framed his attack against the injustice of the Spanish conquest of Tawantinsuyu (and therefore against the rights of all foreigners to rule Andean lands and peoples) on the claim that the Andeans were already Christian in 1532—in spirit if not in fact—when the invaders arrived (1987:89, 91). What this apparently naive statement reveals to us is the colonized's full understanding of the political content of the foreign religious message. Guaman Poma responded to it using the same idiom but with an economy of expression that synthesized European juridical arguments and native Andean lore.

Writing and Cultural Synthesis

In addition to his efforts to salvage the dignity of the autochthonous tradition by translating its values into those a European reader would appreciate, Guaman Poma attempted to integrate the systems of thought of both cultures—that is, he sought to coordinate his understandings of the Andean tradition with those of colonial Spanish culture. For this purpose writing became a tool of complex

Figure 7. Guaman Poma restricts demonic intervention in the
Andes to the Inca's religious specialists (1987:279).

cultural and historical interpretation and analysis.[18] The act of understanding
colonialism came through the interpretation of history. For the colonized subject no matter was more pressing than the need to explain the present—that is,
to understand how conquest and colonization from abroad could have taken
place. The recovery of history, as González-Echevarría (1976:21) has observed,
is an act of decolonization. Guaman Poma attempted to achieve this goal by
synchronizing and harmonizing the oral traditions of the myths of origins of

Figure 8. The Holy Spirit (the dove) blesses an Andean woman
engaged in her devotions (1987:837).

civilization in the Andes with the written traditions of biblical chronologies (see
Ossio 1973). But writing itself could not provide the hoped-for synthesis of very
different ways of understanding and interpreting historical experience or of rec-
onciling different concepts of history. Such irreconcilable concepts as, for example, the *pachacuti* (the destruction and renovation of the universe) of the Andean tradition and the Christian concept of divine punishment did not lend
themselves to a systematic integration of cosmic and personal causalities (see
Adorno 1985b; MacCormack 1988b).

Guaman Poma confronted the European claim that the subjugation of Peru was an act of divine justice and that the destruction of the Andean empire was its ultimate form. Attempting to refute that interpretation, he framed his own treatise on the fall of Tawantinsuyu in terms of good and evil, sin and virtue. Yet as he worked through Christian theological language, he was also led to return to classic formulas of the Andean system of thought. For Guaman Poma the traditional explanations no longer existed in their pristine, pre-contact forms. In attempting to equate the Andean concept of *pachacuti* with the biblical notion of divine punishment (*castigos de Dios*), he discovered that these concepts, either separately or together, could not explain or justify the disastrous effects of European colonization in the Andes (Adorno 1985b). Guaman Poma in effect ended his book where he began, reformulating the ancient Quechua prayer *"Pachacamac, maypim canqui?"* ("Creator of the universe, where are you?") into a contemporary lament.

I believe that we can reconstruct Guaman Poma's thought in this regard by the following trajectory. First, an ancient Andean, representing the second age of Guaman Poma's pre-Incaic history of the Andean world, looks heavenward and asks, "Creator of the World, where are you?" (fig. 9) (1987:53). Next, in Inca times the traitor in the imperial cave prison, surrounded by predators, implores: "Where are you, Creator of the wrongdoer?" (fig. 10) (1987:304). Finally, in a pose reminiscent of those ancient ancestors, the Andean of colonial times is surrounded by the predators who exploit him (fig. 11) (1987:708). This Andean's beseeching attitude is the same one we saw in the supplication of the ancient Andeans of the second pre-Incaic age that Guaman Poma called *Vari Runa*. Yet the words that issue from this colonized Andean's mouth are not a prayer but a desperate plea: "Don't despoil me, for the love of God! I will give you more!" (1987:708). It is to this contemporary catastrophe that Guaman Poma provided his final commentary. Near the end of his book he asks, "Where are you, God of Heaven?" (1987:1,114, 1,122).

Guaman Poma concludes his speculation on matters cosmic and imperial by asking: "How is it that the true lieutenant of God, the Holy Pope, is far away? Where are you, our lord, king Philip?" (1987:1,122). His final answer is: "There is no God and no king. They are in Rome and in Castile" (1987:1,136). Neither the cultural systems of the victor nor those of the vanquished were adequate to deal with the problems of interpreting historical Andean experience.

At the same time the struggle to interpret that experience was no doubt an act of survival that helped keep such individuals as Guaman Poma from the swirling

Figure 9. An Andean of ancient times asks his maker, "Creator of the universe, where are you?" (1987:53).

madness of the open contests between the old gods and the new. These very real struggles were remembered in the early colonial oral traditions and are found recorded in the only compendium of Andean lore and history that we know from the early colonial period. The Quechua manuscript *Runa yndio ñiscap machoncuna*, collected by Francisco de Avila sometime after the turn of the seventeenth century (Acosta 1987:596), records the frightening and maddening appearance of the Andean deity Llocllay Huancupa to the newly con-

Figure 10. A man condemned to the imperial cave prison of Inca
times is devoured by predators (1987:304).

verted Don Cristóbal Choque Casa (Salomon and Urioste 1991:103–110). Two
chapters are devoted to Don Cristóbal's struggle against the old gods, both when
he is awake and when he dreams. Salomon has analyzed these episodes as the
experience of the convert as the enemy of the ancient and colossal deities who
still dominated the Andean landscape and its societies.[19]

For Guaman Poma and other writers of his generation, writing imposed the
illusion of rationality on the zone of madness where spiritual combat took place.[20]
Just as Don Cristóbal Choque Casa was haunted by the old gods he dared to

Figure 11. In an allegory of colonial times, the Andean victim is tormented by his overlords (1987:708).

abandon, Guaman Poma was haunted by his failure to assimilate European modes of thought and expression with the deeper passions with which they were unable to contend. Eighty years after the Spanish conquest he could not salvage for himself the traditional system of thought in its integrity, yet it was impossible to discover any rationale in the new that would make sense of the course of recent history or explain the domination of Andeans by foreigners. Written discourse was unable to resolve the disparities. Writing, the apparent gesture of affirmation, revealed itself as the source of doubt and interrogation. Although we have examined writing as an art of survival, we begin to wonder whether we are witnessing the proof of survival or merely the testimony of the struggle to do so.

The Visual Representation of Oral Tradition

We return now to the scene in which Guaman Poma addresses the king. Perhaps no comments of the newly literate are more intriguing than those concerning the practice of political and social life under oral and scribal cultural regimes. Guaman Poma himself was aware of the uncontrollability of the written medium, and he complained that he needed to write to the king simply to contradict all the false accounts that he knew the monarch would be receiving. The keepers and communicators of information were no longer the "very, very Christian" *quipu camayoc* (keeper of the *khipu*, knotted cord mnemonic records) (Guaman Poma 1987:360) and *quilca camayoc* (keeper of graphic or pictorial information) of Inca times, whose special status and inherited vocation assured the veracity of their administrative and historical accounts.[21] Guaman Poma's precise concern was that any scoundrel could write or have something written. Yet he himself was caught because, unlike some other ethnic lords who actually traveled to Spain to petition the Council of the Indies, he was unable to make the trip. For him the face-to-face encounter with the highest authorities was impossible. Against the written and printed chronicle accounts about the Andeans that portrayed them as communities of devil worshipers mired in a mental chaos of superstition and pagan beliefs, the colonized subject, Guaman Poma, poised his own pen, painfully aware that traditional avenues of recourse were gone.

It is thus as an unsolicited but worthy advisor to the king that this colonial subject presented himself. In the dialogue he created between himself and King Philip (fig. 5), the king asks the questions, and the "author and prince" provides fully all the answers and advice he can give. Holding his book in his left hand, the author gesticulates with his right; the king patiently listens, his right hand at rest, his left holding the scepter. The caption reads: "The author personally presents the chronicle to His Majesty." In the accompanying narration Guaman Poma explains that writing has become the surrogate for the face-to-face meeting:

I would like to serve Your Majesty as a grandson of the king of Peru,[22] to see you face to face and talk, communicate at present about the said topics, but I cannot, because of being eighty years old and sick, go so great a distance. . . . Thus, through that which is written and by means of this letter we shall see each other. And thus Your Majesty should go about asking me, and I shall go along responding, in the following manner. (1987:976)

This scene recreates the model of the traditional oral culture in which the Inca solicited advice and counsel from his royal ministers and listened to their accounts.[23] Guaman Poma had represented this face-to-face communication of the oral cultural setting in another drawing in which the Inca listened to his gesticulating subjects (fig. 12) (1987:366). In still another Guaman Poma pictured himself surrounded by Andean compatriots to whose oral accounts, verified or denied by other witnesses, he listened (fig. 13) (1987:368). In the first of these two depictions the traditional royal council of Tawantinsuyu is assembled; the Inca has gathered together the lords of Cuzco and those of the subdivisions of the empire to settle matters of state. The Inca is gesticulating, but so too are two or three of the lords gathered round him. On the following page Guaman Poma appears. Dressed in the costume in which we have seen him twice previously, he stands now where the Inca stood, and he, like the Inca before him, is surrounded by Andean lords. He and they are gesticulating, hands raised, all under the title "The author asks." Commenting on this tableau, Guaman Poma explained how these lords from all parts of the kingdom deciphered for him the contents of the *quipu* records of ancient times "so that he [Guaman Poma] may write and register it in the said book so that order and justice may prevail" (1987:369).

With these drawings Guaman Poma visualized the characteristics of the oral culture, and he reproduced them subsequently in the picture of his audience with the king. Through these pictorial reiterations he grafted the virtues of the old system onto the new: As the Inca sought the counsel of his ministers, so too Guaman Poma gathered reports from his compatriots. In turn, Guaman Poma would become the counselor and minister of the Spanish monarch who reproduced, in Guaman Poma's imagination, the traditional solicitation of information and guidance institutionalized by the Inca. To the new colonial society, in which oral testimony was without value unless authorized and legalized in writing, Guaman Poma posed the superiority of the traditional oral culture revivified in modern times.

The local circumstance, the autochthonous local courts, and the imperial court of last resort had been replaced by a foreign system for the administration of justice. Writing, which colonialism had brought, was the only means of participating in the new system and transcending the local setting. In Gua-

Figure 12. The Inca seeks the counsel of the lords of the realm
(1987:366).

man Poma's case going abroad to see the king was out of the question. The
Andean author's encomium of the honorable comportment of the officials of
the Inca state betrayed his concern that what had been gained with the introduction of written culture was mitigated by what was lost in the traditional
forms of political and social organization and administration. The art of writing was to be a defense, perhaps the only viable one, against the ruthless exercise of colonial power. This message is conveyed in the drawing of the Inca's
quilca camayoc, now turned notary of the town council (*cabildo*) (fig. 14)

Figure 13. Guaman Poma seeks information and advice from the lords of the Andes (1987:368).

(1987:828). The notary's earnestness communicates the notion that writing and written culture represented a loss at least as much as a gain; writing was only one aspect of a complex network of relations out of which power was created and exercised.

The book at the center of the picture of Guaman Poma's interview with the king thus has at least two meanings. First, it brings full circle the story that began with Atahualpa. As the Inca had gazed past the book and ultimately rejected it, the Spanish king is absorbed in discourse with Guaman Poma, gazing at him and listening to the opinions that he presents. With this drawing the Inca who

Figure 14. The *quilca camayoc* of Inca times becomes in colonial
times the municipal notary "appointed by His Majesty"
(1987:828).

rejected the book (Atahualpa) is succeeded by the colonial Andean who reveres
it (Guaman Poma). But Guaman Poma's idealism is betrayed by the representation itself. Given his acknowledged age, infirmity, and poverty, it is significant
that Guaman Poma did not portray the only possible version of his book's reception by the king—namely, a tableau in which the king would sit alone and
read it. Instead, Guaman Poma presents both himself *and* his book to the monarch.

The insertion of the author's own person into the scene and the representation of himself reading aloud from his own open book reveal his unease in relying exclusively on the one-way communication made possible by the written word. As a surrogate for the interview of lord and subject, the book could not guarantee its desired outcome; the silent book could not talk back to its reader.

Guaman Poma considered the personal interview far preferable to the written report. The ideal communication would take place in a dialogic setting in which one could read not only the written word but also the face of the interlocutor. If every cross-cultural encounter between Europeans and Andeans was to be ruled by the written word, Guaman Poma made clear that it would be considered a necessary but not sufficient constituent in the creation of relationships between peoples and polities.

Guaman Poma's testimony shows us, from the inside, the second emblematic moment (the first being Atahualpa's rejection of the book) in the history of European colonialism in the Andes. He and many other optimistic members of his generation had picked up the book that the Inca Atahualpa had thrown to the ground. Convinced of its potency, persuaded of its ability to speak to them and of themselves to speak through it, they learned, much more agonizingly than did Atahualpa, that in itself the book was not a reliable instrument of power. Its efficacy was available only through processes and procedures in which the colonial subject participated with uneven success. In Guaman Poma's final assessment of writing and power, Atahualpa's "reading" of the book—"It does not speak to me!"—was the most accurate and surely the most prophetic of all.

Notes

1. This statement is from Felipe Guaman Poma de Ayala's *Nueva corónica y buen gobierno* (1987:10). All citations to the *Nueva corónica y buen gobierno* are from the 1987 edition and refer to the corrected version of Guaman Poma's original pagination used there. The translation from Castilian to English in this and all following instances is my own.

2. He associated these names with his patrilineal descent from the Yarovilca dynasty of Huánuco, which predated the Incas and was later colonized by them (Varallanos 1959). Guaman Poma is one of a handful of ethnic Andeans whom we know to have written works in Castilian in the seventeenth century. Unlike Juan de Santacruz Pachacuti Yamqui Salcamayhua (fl. 1613) and El Inca Garcilaso de la Vega (1539–1616), Guaman Poma discussed extensively the problems of native life under European colonialism.

3. Guaman Poma assisted in colonial campaigns against native religion and in veri-

fying the land titles of Andean and colonial owners; see Guillén Guillén (1969), Duviols (1967), Adorno (1978), and Stern (1978).

4. *Indios ladinos* were often leaders in the messianic and prophetic movements of native resistance to colonialism in Peru during the sixteenth century. In general, they called for the return of Andean gods and the rejection of European customs and beliefs. See Pease (1977, 1981), Cock and Doyle (1979), and MacCormack (1988b).

5. Although Guaman Poma (1987:1,104) claimed to be about eighty years old around 1615, there is cause for wide speculation on the date of his birth, which could have taken place from the late 1530s to the 1550s. It is fair to say that he had not been born "in the time of the Incas" but that he thought of himself as "very old" after about 1610. The detail of his drawings and writings reveals that he had a lifelong familiarity with the institutions and customs of Spanish colonial culture.

6. My readings of the works of Jack Goody, Brian Stock, Benedict Anderson, Roberto González-Echevarría, and Irene Silverblatt have been most helpful in suggesting directions for this discussion.

7. The term was coined by Geoffrey Hartman in his analysis of the fundamental dimensions of literacy (cognitive and functional on the one hand, ritual on the other) at the symposium "Literacy, Reading, and Power," Whitney Humanities Center, Yale University, November 14, 1987.

8. Unlike Mexico, where extensive colonial notarial records in Nahuatl are known to exist into the eighteenth century, the picture for the Andes is less clear. In addition to Mannheim's (1984:305) discovery of a notebook of fragments of a Quechua notarial register, George Urioste has discovered some late seventeenth-century Quechua documents from central Peru that Lockhart (1988:24) describes as "closely comparable to Nahuatl materials; they imply that Quechua was routinely written by native speakers in at least some parts of the Andean region and arouse the hope that larger caches will yet surface." Recent studies on Quechua-Castilian contact in the written Spanish of Guaman Poma and other colonial sources (Carranza Romero [forthcoming]; Godenzzi [forthcoming]) make further work in this area promising.

9. Guaman Poma (1987:15) said that his older half-brother, a mestizo priest, taught him reading and writing, ostensibly for the purpose of religious indoctrination.

10. That Guaman Poma found in the pictorial medium a most trustworthy vehicle of communication cannot be disputed, given his acknowledgment of European predilections (1987:10) and Andean antecedents (in particular, the *quilca camayoc*, secretaries to the Inca and keepers of graphic information) (1987:361). As yet undetermined is the possible influence of the Andean iconographic tradition on Guaman Poma's art, although his use of Andean spatial symbolism in pictorial composition has been much discussed; see Wachtel (1973), Adorno (1979), and López-Baralt (1979).

11. This statement directly paraphrases a doctrinal text, the Franciscan Luis Jerón-

imo de Oré's *Symbolo Catholico Indiano*, which was published in Lima in 1598. Guaman Poma's exaggerated use of "the said" and "the afore-mentioned" probably results from the convergence of a Quechua language trait (Urioste 1980:xxx; Carranza Romero (forthcoming]) with the legalistic phraseology of juridical documentation in the Spanish tradition with which he was familiar.

12. Guaman Poma read not only catechisms and sermons written for the evangelization of the native Andean populations and the devotional works of Fray Luis de Granada but also histories of the Spanish conquest of Peru and juridical treatises on the just war. All these readings are apparent in his own paraphrasings and reproductions of these texts; see Guaman Poma (1987: vol. 3, 1,317–1,359). Most striking is his reading of Fray Bartolomé de las Casas; Guaman Poma rewrote the history of the conquest of Peru to conform to the arguments presented by Las Casas in his *Tratado de las doce dudas* (1564) and to deny the legitimacy of the conquest altogether (see Adorno 1986:13–35).

13. It is difficult to interpret what Guaman Poma meant by the title "new chronicle," of which he was obviously proud. Did he mean his chronicle was new with respect to the European chronicles of the conquests, which told only the Spanish side of the story? Or did he consider it new with respect to the historical record-keeping of his own oral cultural tradition?

14. I have also benefitted from the analysis by Jerome Bruner (1986:11–43) of this fundamental distinction.

15. I have in mind here the theorizing of George Foster (1960) and Fernando Ortiz (1978), who have studied the processes of cultural transformation under colonialism as a series of overlapping and complex interactions between "donor" and "recipient" cultures.

16. The following section reiterates arguments I made at the symposium "Literacy, Reading, and Power," Yale University, Whitney Humanities Center, November 14, 1987 (see Adorno 1988:222–225).

17. See Stock (1983); on this problem among indigenous American writers of Guaman Poma's generation, see Salomon (1982).

18. Brian Stock's (1983) discussion of the transformation of the basic skills of reading and writing into instruments of analysis and interpretation has been particularly helpful in this regard.

19. Frank Salomon, lecturing on the manuscript of Huarochirí, N.E.H. Summer Institute on Transatlantic Encounters, The Newberry Library, Chicago, June 29, 1987 (see also Salomon and Urioste 1991:26–28).

20. Stock (1983:31ff) has identified and explored the injurious notion, which developed with medieval literacy, that literacy itself was identical with rationality.

21. Guaman Poma (1987:361) described these keepers of the *quipu*, as well as those of the pictoriographic tradition and astronomy and calendrics, as those who "recorded without lying and without being bribed whatsoever." For this reason he called them, metaphorically, "very, very Christian." The remark carried with it not only nostalgia for traditional systems of signification of limited access but

also a criticism of the colonial European notaries who used their access to information to serve their own interests.

22. On this occasion and in corrections to his completed text Guaman Poma emphasized his claim to maternal descent from the Tupa Inca Yupanqui (Adorno 1989:78–82).

23. Goody's (1986:108–110) discussion of political functioning in oral cultures, emphasizing the indispensableness of face-to-face meetings and oral consultation between the principal ruler and his lords for decision making, underscored for me the significance of Guaman Poma's pictures on the subject.

References

Acosta, Antonio. 1987. *Francisco de Avila: Cusco 1573(?)–Lima 1647.* In *Ritos y tradiciones de Huarochirí del siglo XVII*, translated and edited by Gerald Taylor, 551–616. Lima: Instituto de Estudios Peruanos and Instituto Francés de Estudios Andinos.

Adorno, Rolena. 1978. "Felipe Guaman Poma de Ayala: An Andean View of the Peruvian Viceroyalty, 1565–1615." *Journal de la Société des Américanistes* 65:121–143.

————. 1979. "Paradigms Lost: A Peruvian Indian Surveys Spanish Colonial Society." *Studies in the Anthropology of Visual Communication* 5, no. 2:78–96.

————. 1985a. "The Inca Prince and the Dominican Friar." In *JCB: An Occasional Newsletter of the John Carter Brown Library* 4:2–3.

————. 1985b. "The Rhetoric of Resistance: The 'Talking Book' of Felipe Guaman Poma." *History of European Ideas* 6, no. 4:447–464.

————. 1986. *Guaman Poma: Writing and Resistance in Colonial Peru.* Austin: University of Texas Press.

————. 1988. "Selections from the Symposium 'Literacy, Reading, and Power,' Whitney Humanities Center." *Yale Journal of Criticism* 2, no. 1:222–225.

————. 1989. *Cronista y príncipe: La obra de don Felipe Guaman Poma de Ayala.* Lima: Pontificia Universidad Católica del Perú.

————. 1990. "The Depiction of Self and Other in Colonial Peru." *Art Journal* 49, no. 2:110–118.

————. 1991. "The Image of the *Indio ladino* in Early Colonial Peru." In *Transatlantic Encounters: Europeans and Andeans in the Sixteenth Century*, edited by Kenneth J. Andrien and Rolena Adorno, 232–270. Berkeley: University of California Press.

Anderson, Benedict. 1983. *Imagined Communities: Reflections on the Origin and Spread of Nationalism.* London: Verso Editions.

Betanzos, Juan de. [1551] 1987. *Suma y narración de los Incas*, edited by María del Carmen Martín Rubio. Madrid: Atlas.

Bruner, Jerome. 1986. *Actual Minds, Possible Worlds.* Cambridge, Mass.: Harvard University Press.

Carranza Romero, Francisco. Forthcoming. "Resultados lingüísticos del contacto quechua y español en 'El primer nueva corónica.' " In *XXVIII Congreso: Letras coloniales: Interacción y vigencia*. Pittsburgh: Instituto Internacional de Literatura Iberoamericana.

Casas, Bartolomé de las. [1564] 1958. "Tratado de las doce dudas." In *Obras escogidas de fray Bartolomé de las Casas V*, edited by Juan Pérez de Tudela Bueso. Biblioteca de Autores Españoles 110. Madrid: Atlas.

Cieza de León, Pedro de. 1553. *Parte primera de la crónica del Perú*. Seville: Martín de Montesdoca.

Cock, Guillermo, and Mary Eileen Doyle. 1979. "Del culto solar a la clandestinidad de Inti y Punchao." *Historia y cultura* 12:51–73.

Duviols, Pierre. 1967. "Un inédit de Cristóbal de Albornoz: La instrucción para descubrir todas las guacas del Pirú y sus camayos y haziendas." *Journal de la Société des Américanistes* 56:7–39.

Foster, George M. 1960. *Culture and Conquest: America's Spanish Heritage*. Viking Fund Publications in Anthropology, no. 27. New York: Wenner-Gren Foundation for Anthropological Research.

Garcilaso de la Vega, El Inca. [1609] 1966. *Royal Commentaries of the Incas and General History of Peru, Part One*. Translated by Harold V. Livermore. Foreword by Arnold J. Toynbee. Austin: University of Texas Press.

Garibay, Angel K. 1953–54. *Historia de la literatura nahuatl*. Mexico City: Porrúa.

Godenzzi, Juan Carlos. Forthcoming. "Discordancias de ayer y de hoy: El castellano de escribientes quechuas y aimaras." In *XXVIII Congreso: Letras coloniales: Interacción y vigencia*. Pittsburgh: Internacional de Literatura Iberoamericana.

González-Echevarría, Roberto. 1976. *Relecturas: Estudios de literatura cubana*. Caracas: Monte Avila.

Goody, Jack. 1986. *The Logic of Writing and the Organization of Society*. Cambridge: Cambridge University Press.

Guaman Poma de Ayala, Felipe. [1615] 1980. *El primer nueva corónica y buen gobierno*. Edited by John V. Murra and Rolena Adorno. Quechua translations by Jorge L. Urioste. Mexico City: Siglo Veintiuno.

———. 1987. *Nueva corónica y buen gobierno*. Edited by John V. Murra, Rolena Adorno, and Jorge L. Urioste. Madrid: Historia 16.

Guillén Guillén, Edmundo. 1969. "El cronista don Felipe Guaman Poma y los manuscritos hallados en el pueblo de Chiara." *Amaru, Revista de Artes y Ciencias* 10:89–92.

Harrison, Regina. 1982. "Modes of Discourse: The 'Relación de antigüedades deste reyno del Pirú' by Joan de Santacruz Pachacuti Yamqui Salcamaygua." In *From Oral to Written Expression: Native Andean Chronicles of the Early Colonial Period*, edited by Rolena Adorno, 65–99. Syracuse, N.Y.: Maxwell School of Citizenship and Public Affairs, Syracuse University.

León-Portilla, Miguel. 1959. *Visión de los vencidos*. Mexico City: Universidad Nacional Autónoma de México.

Lockhart, James. 1988. "Charles Gibson and the Ethnography of Postconquest Central Mexico." La Trobe University Institute of Latin American Studies Occasional Papers 9:3–27.

López-Baralt, Mercedes. 1979. "La persistencia de las estructuras simbólicas andinas en los dibujos de Guaman Poma de Ayala." *Journal of Latin American Lore* 5, no. 1:83–116.

Mannheim, Bruce. 1984. " 'Una nación acorralada': Southern Peruvian Quechua Language Planning and Politics in Historical Perspective." *Language and Society* 13: 291–309. Cambridge: Cambridge University Press.

MacCormack, Sabine. 1988a. "Atahualpa y el libro." *Revista de Indias* 48, no. 184:693–714.

———. 1988b. "*Pachacuti*: Miracles, Punishments, and Last Judgment: Visionary Past and Prophetic Future in Early Colonial Peru." *American Historical Review* 93, no. 4:960–1,006.

Oré, Luis Jerónimo de. 1598. *Symbolo catholico indiano.* Lima: Antonio Ricardo.

Ortiz, Fernando. 1978. *Contrapunteo cubano del tabaco y el azúcar.* Caracas: Biblioteca Ayacucho.

Ossio, Juan M. 1973. "Guaman Poma: Nueva corónica o carta al rey: Un intento de aproximación a las categorías del mundo andino." In *Ideología mesiánica del mundo andino*, edited by Juan M. Ossio, 155–213. Lima: Biblioteca de Antropología, Ignacio Prado Pastor.

Pachacuti Yamqui Salcamayhua, Juan de Santacruz. [1613] 1879. "Relación de antigüedades deste reyno del Pirú." In *Tres relaciones de antigüedades peruanas*, edited by Marcos Jiménez de la Espada, 229–238. Madrid: Ministerio de Fomento.

Pease G. Y., Franklin. 1977. "Las versiones del mito de Inkarrí." *Revista de la Universidad Católica* 2:25–41.

———. 1981. "Felipe Guaman Poma de Ayala: Mitos andinos e historia occidental. *Caravelle* 37:19–36.

Salomon, Frank. 1982. "Chronicles of the Impossible: Notes on Three Peruvian Indigenous Historians." In *From Oral to Written Expression: Native Andean Chronicles of the Early Colonial Period*, edited by Rolena Adorno, 9–39. Syracuse, N.Y.: Maxwell School of Citizenship and Public Affairs, Syracuse University.

Silverblatt, Irene. 1982. *Moon, Sun, and Witches: Gender Ideologies and Class in Inca and Colonial Peru.* Princeton, N.J.: Princeton University Press.

Salomon, Frank, and George L. Urioste, eds. and trans. 1991. *The Huarochirí Manuscript: A Testament of Ancient and Colonial Andean Religion.* Austin: University of Texas Press.

Solano, Francisco. 1975. "El intérprete, uno de los ejes de la aculturación." In *Estudios sobre la política indigenista española en América. Terceras Jornadas Americanistas de la Universidad de Valladolid*, 265–278. Valladolid: University of Valladolid.

Stern, Steve J. 1978. "Algunas consideraciones sobre la personalidad histórica de Don Felipe Guaman Poma de Ayala." *Histórica* 2, no. 2:225–228.

Stock, Brian. 1983. *The Implications of Literacy: Written Language and Models of Interpretation in the Eleventh and Twelfth Centuries*. Princeton, N.J.: Princeton University Press.

Urioste, Jorge L. 1980. "Estudio analítico del Quechua en la *Nueva Corónica*." In *Guaman Poma de Ayala*, edited by John V. Murra and Rolena Adorno, xx–xxxi.

Urioste, Jorge L., ed. 1983. *Hijos de Pariya Qaqa: La tradición oral de Waru Chiri (Mitología, Ritual y Costumbres)*. 2 vols. Syracuse, N.Y.: Maxwell School of Citizenship and Public Affairs, Syracuse University.

Varallanos, José. 1959. *Historia de Huánuco*. Buenos Aires: Imprenta López.

Wachtel, Nathan. 1973. "Pensamiento salvaje y aculturación." In *Sociedad y ideología: Ensayos de historia y antropología andinas*, 165–228. Lima: Instituto de Estudios Andinos.

——. 1976. *Los vencidos: Los indios del Perú frente a la conquista española (1530–1570)*. Translated by Antonio Escohotado. Madrid: Alianza.

Part 2
Strategies
of
Resistance
and
Survival
in
Late
Colonial
Mexico

▲ ▲ ▲

Colonial Expansion and Indian Resistance in Sonora: The Seri Uprisings in 1748 and 1750

José Luis Mirafuentes Galván

Perhaps with the exception of the Apache Indians, no ethnic group in north-western Mexico has ever been the target of so many or such cruel epithets as the Seri Indians under Spanish rule. Because of their nomadic lifestyle and the hostile geographic environment in which they lived, the Seri were regarded as barbarian, savage, shiftless, useless, lazy, crude, and wild. However, it was their refusal to renounce their autonomy and traditional lifestyle that earned them their harshest characterizations: irrational, treacherous, ungrateful, tyrannical, depraved, and murderous. Other descriptions, just as cruel, included capricious, ungrateful, brutal, rebellious, provocative, arrogant, and contemptuous.

The Spaniards' attitude toward the Seri was an expression of Spanish violence toward the Indians, a violence born as much from the Spaniards' lack of understanding of the Seri culture as from the many difficulties—nearly always insurmountable—they faced in their efforts to conquer the Seri. This essay attempts to show that this violence, exacerbated by the belief that the Seri Indians stood in the way of Spanish expansion to the Colorado River and northern California, was at the root of the Seri Indian uprisings of 1748 and 1750.

The Seri and the Efforts to Convert Them

At the time of the first contact between the Indians and the Spaniards in north-western Mexico, the Seri were living along the coastal desert of western Sonora. This territory covered an area of 20,400 square kilometers, stretching approximately from the mouth of the Yaqui River, its southernmost point, north to the Concepción River. On the east, it extended to the banks of the San Miguel River, and on the west it extended to the coast, including Tiburón and San Esteban islands (Nolasco 1967:135). The Seri Indians belonged to the Hokana linguistic family. They were organized in autonomous groups or bands with subgroups consisting of nuclear and extended families. They lived as nomads, sustaining themselves as hunters, gatherers, and seafarers. During certain periods of the year they traded with neighboring Indians who farmed the land, exchanging salt and deer hides for maize (Pérez de Ribas 1944: vol. 2, 148). The Seri population numbered less than five thousand (Radding 1978:5) and was divided into six groups: the Seri (the name used by the Spaniards to refer to the entire group), the Tepoca, the Salinero, the Tiburón, the Guayma, and Upanguayma. The Seri were surrounded by sedentary tribal societies who belonged to the Uto-Aztec family: the Pima Alto, the Opata-Eudeve, and the Pima Bajo. The Pima Alto lived north of the Seri, the Opata-Eudeve to the east, and the Pima Bajo to the south. These groups were farmers as well as hunters and gatherers and lived in incipient villages established on the river meadows. They were much more numerous than the Seri: The Pima Alto numbered about thirty thousand; the Pima Bajo about twenty-five thousand; and the Opata-Eudeve about sixty thousand (Radding 1979:5). Together, these groups inhabited an area that covered more than three-fourths of Sonora. Their very dominance in the region was decisive in limiting initial relations between the Seri and the Spaniards.

When Jesuit missionaries began their formal colonization of Sonora in the early seventeenth century, they directed most of their efforts toward the sedentary groups. They even tended to view the Seri Indians with contempt. In his celebrated chronicle from the mid-1600s, Andrés Pérez de Ribas referred to the Seri as

exceedingly wild, without villages, houses, or fields. They have no rivers nor streams and drink from some small pools and puddles of water. They sustain themselves by hunting, although during the maize harvest season they go with deer hides and the salt they gather from the sea to trade with other nations. (Pérez de Ribas 1942: vol. 2, 148)

Some forty-five years later another missionary noted that the Seri lived "like cattle, without God, without law, without faith, without princes, and without houses" and explained that the missionaries were not interested in them because the Spaniards considered them "a wretched people from whom the fruits of evangelism could not be gathered" (Di Peso 1965:43).

The Jesuits thus began to establish their missions in the areas inhabited by sedentary groups—that is, along the Yaqui, Sonora, and San Miguel rivers—leaving the western plains and coast free of Spanish settlements. Their interest in the Seri did not begin until the end of the 1660s, after members of this group, perhaps suffering the devastating effects of the isolation that followed the successful missionization of their neighbors, began to maraud the San Miguel River mission settlements. These raids were isolated, most likely carried out by the bands who lived nearest to the missions. However, after the indiscriminate reprisals suffered by the majority of the Seri, the raids generalized and ultimately led to an uprising of such extensive proportions that the Spaniards were unable to subdue it until the end of the following decade (Navarro García 1967:65–67). In 1678, as a result of this pacification, missionaries converted an undetermined number of Seri in the lower portion of the San Miguel River. There, in a site abundant with water, grass, and farmland, they founded the first mission for the Seri, naming it Our Lady of the Pópulo of the Seri (AGN, H, 19, f. 343). Shortly afterward, the Jesuits apparently converted about three hundred Indians, aborigines who came primarily from the high part of the river, perhaps from the vicinity of the Cucurpe mission. We do not know the name given to this settlement, but we do know that it was short-lived. Shortly after the mission was founded, its inhabitants fell victim to an epidemic; those who did not succumb to disease returned to their deserts and beaches (AGN, H, 308, f. 393v). Our Lady of Pópulo met a similar fate, and by 1683 the mission was completely abandoned (Di Peso 1965:43).

The Seri continued to live peacefully, and the missionaries did not concern themselves with them again for another six years. At that point their interest in converting the Seri was most likely linked to Father Eusebio Francisco Kino's plans to convert the Pima Alto and extend the missions to the Colorado and Gila rivers. Perhaps the missionaries felt that the Seri, because of their proximity to the Pima, could well interfere with the plans if they were not incorporated into the missions. At Father Kino's initiative Father Adamo

Gilg was sent to reestablish the Pópulo mission in 1689 (Kino 1926:16). Father Gilg apparently did not encounter any great difficulty in renewing contact with the Seri. His problems began, however, when he tried once again to bring them into the mission. Possibly as a result of their initial experience in the missions the Seri forcibly resisted abandoning their territory and traditional practices. "The longer I struggled with these people," said the missionary, "the more offensively they opposed my undertaking" (Di Peso 1965:43). The few Indians whom he was able to convert not only resisted carrying out the activities he taught them but soon afterward returned to their old domains. It was difficult for Father Gilg to devote himself to a group who, as he said, "would neither work nor stay long in one place . . ." (Di Peso 1965:43). These problems became even more serious for Gilg when shortly after the Pópulo mission was reestablished the Pima Cocomacaquetz, a neighboring group of the Seri with whom they were continually warring, turned violently against the mission. As a result of the destruction and attacks by the Cocomacaquetz, most of the Seri left. The villages of San Tadeo and San Eustaquio, which Gilg had begun to build for the Tepoca Seri, also were abandoned and destroyed (Di Peso 1965:46).

Despite everything, however, Gilg did not abandon the mission. With the assistance of several soldiers who were able to achieve a peace agreement between the Seri and the Pima, Gilg began to realize the first fruits of his labor. By 1690 the Seri had begun to reassemble in Our Lady of Pópulo and the Tepoca in the Cucurpe mission. In addition, three hundred Seri and one hundred Tepoca had been baptized, although the Indians had still not been convinced to remain permanently in the towns (AHH, T, 279–22). By 1692, however, Gilg seemed to have overcome this problem, at least in the Pópulo mission. He said that here the Seri had learned to farm the land as skillfully as the sedentary groups, had begun to build a church and their own houses, were practicing Christianity, and were setting up a Spanish model of government (Di Peso 1965:47, 56). Gilg did not indicate how many Indians were part of this process of change, but he was so encouraged by the results that by 1692 he was proposing to establish new missions, particularly among the Tepoca Seri (Di Peso 1965:47). It was probably through his initiative that the town of Los Angeles and Santa Magdalena de Tepocas were founded. We do not know the precise date of the founding of Los Angeles; we only know that it was built four leagues southeast of the Pópulo mission as a *pueblo de visita*. Santa Magdalena de Tepocas was established in 1699 northeast of Pópulo, near the Cucurpe mission.

Subsequently, however, Gilg as well as the missionaries who followed him in Pópulo encountered many problems in their work with the Seri. A significant problem—one that gave rise to many others—was the lack of assistance provided by soldiers and residents to the mission. This problem cannot be adequately addressed in this essay; however, it is important that we at least mention the following facts:

During the seventeenth century the Jesuits in Sonora opened a territory about two hundred leagues wide for colonization (Navarro García 1965:312–313). The aboriginal population at the time of contact was about 125,000 (Radding 1979:6). Until 1692, however, the responsibility of providing military protection to Sonora fell to a single presidio—the Sinaloa presidio—whose seat was located in Sinaloa Province, more than fifty leagues south of Sonora. This military post had no more than fifty troops, which meant that in an emergency only about fifteen soldiers could be sent to Sonora. In 1692 the decision was made to establish a new presidio in Sonora. It was built in the far northeastern part of the province in Santa Rosa del Corodéguachi, also known as Fronteras. Its purpose was to handle the growing threat of Apache invasions in that part of the region (Viveros 1981:202). Like Sinaloa, Fronteras had no more than fifty armed troops; thus from the outset the situation was similar to that in Sinaloa—the military presence was insufficient to lend effective assistance to the regions in the province. The troops from Fronteras and Sinaloa were small, defensive, and somewhat isolated units without the resources to operate outside their region. Despite the fact that the Fronteras presidio proved completely unable to contain the Apache, the number of soldiers and presidios in Sonora was not increased until 1742. Thus during those fifty years the western region was left virtually unprotected.

As for other Spaniards living in the vicinity, the amount of assistance they required from the presidios and missions outweighed any assistance they could provide. Gerhard has estimated that the non-Indian population of Sonora was 1,400 in 1678 and about 3,000 in 1730 (Gerhard 1982:285). Among this population, certainly small with regard to the size of the territory opened to colonization by the missionaries, only a small proportion could use weapons. In 1684 only 186 of the inhabitants could do so (Navarro García 1967:69); in 1730, although the non-Indian population of Sonora had grown, the number of those able to use weapons actually dropped to 155 (AGN, CyP, 12, f. 150).

The Spanish population of Sonora was not only small but also extremely mobile. It was not concentrated in villages or towns but rather was widely dispersed throughout the province. In 1726 Pedro de Rivera, inspector for the internal presidios, wrote to the viceroy:

I recognize that this province and borderland [of Sonora] is an open field in which the inhabitants are as much as 80 leagues apart, some working in the mines and others raising cattle and farming. Among them, no larger or smaller population is concentrated in a town, royal or otherwise, that can be called a village or hamlet. They are 80, 60, 50, 40, and 30 leagues away from the presidio, and the closest ones, 18. (AGN, CyP, 12, f. 240)

It is clear that this situation further reduced the defensive capacity of these Spaniards and thus their ability to provide assistance of any significance to the missions.

The immediate problem the missionaries faced was stopping the Seri from leaving their towns during certain periods to search for their traditional plant and animal food. According to Gilg, the Seri continued to remain interested in those foods, although their food supply was guaranteed in the mission. It seems that the persistence of this problem gradually negated the progress made by Father Gilg. In 1718 Father Miguel Javier de Almanza, the missionary who succeeded Father Gilg, described the Seri this way:

Were it not for the assistance of the military, these Indians would not have food in their towns; these lazy people are happy with only the wild plants from the forest, such as *pitahaya, tuna, bledo, mezcal, mesquite*, and *saya* in addition to the deer they kill with their bows and arrows for food. Since they do not esteem the essential foods from the ground, it is very difficult for them to plant and grow them. (AGI, G, 109)

For Almanza this meant that the few converted Seri living in the mission were merely waiting for an extended absence by the soldiers so they could return to the deserts and beaches, where, as he said, they could once again practice "their old depraved customs" (AGI, G, 109).

But the missionaries faced a more serious problem: containing the ethnic conflicts that were again erupting in the region. Perhaps as a result of the new settlements organized by Father Gilg, the Pima Cocomacaquetz renewed their raids against the missions in Pópulo, destroying the agricultural installations and food supplies of the converted Indians. Troops arrived to contain the hostilities in 1700 and 1704 but did not return to the region again until 1716. Meanwhile, the Seri and Pima renewed the fighting between them (AGI, G, 109).

For the missionaries the continued fighting was disastrous—not only because of the death and destruction it wreaked on the missions but also because it caused the Indians who had already been Christianized to flee. In 1704, for example, after the attacks against the Pópulo mission, all the Indians from Los Angeles fled, making it known almost immediately that "they did not want to either live or be present in any way in that town" (BNM.AF, 12/200 bis, f. 104). The town of Santa Magdalena de Tepocas met a similar fate. In 1699 it had a population of about four hundred Indians; by 1710, however, the town was almost completely abandoned, the inhabitants having either been killed by disease or attacks by enemy tribes (AGN, H, 308, f. 393v). According to the missionary Miguel Javier de Almanza, when the soldiers returned to the region in 1716 "everyone converted before was lost, Christians had become apostates as a result of the renewed fighting among the inhabitants themselves after 1704" (AGI, G, 109). By 1718 the Seri and Pima were once again at war. Father Fernando Bayerca went to the military inspector of Sonora, Antonio Becerra, hoping that the soldiers could achieve a lasting peace between the tribes. He said that this was the only way to get "the countless apostates [to return] to their towns . . ." (AGI, G, 109).

In addition to driving off the missionized Indians in droves, the fighting also damaged efforts to concentrate into towns the Seri who had still not been converted and continued to live on their traditional lands. They refused to be baptized because they associated baptism with a commitment to living in the towns, where they felt their lives were endangered. In 1715, for example, when missionaries offered to baptize a Seri chief and his entire family, the Indian responded

that neither he nor his family had been baptized; that he knew Christianity was a very good religion but that they feared death, since becoming Christian would mean they would have to live in the town which was the same as guaranteeing their enemies, the Pima, the opportunity to kill them with little or no effort. (AGI, G, 109)

The exodus of converted Indians and the refusal of unconverted Indians to live in towns were matters of grave concern for the missionaries because these phenomena were accompanied by another no less serious and recurrent one: banditry. Perhaps as a result of the destruction and hardship of war, the Indians who fled the missions did not always return to a hunting-and-gathering lifestyle; many turned to theft as a means of subsistence. And these were clearly not actions by isolated Indians. Because the Indians fled in families and groups of families, they were able to form bands to carry out their raids and thefts more effectively. They were also welcomed in the deserts and beaches by Seri who had not converted. This situation not only provided the raiders with allies but also gave them a wider territorial base for cover from possible persecutors (AGI, G, 109).

Thus sheltered on inhospitable land, the Seri regularly raided their enemies' missions. However, the targets of the forays soon expanded to include the Spaniards' haciendas and mining camps as well. "Entire bands even came to steal cattle from these estates," noted Father Almanza, referring to these raids. By 1718 they were already occurring in a large part of the south and west of Sonora (AGI, G, 109).

The raids by the Seri, despite their extent, did not seem to reflect a particularly anti-Spanish attitude. As far as we know, they did not attack people, houses, or other buildings belonging to the Spaniards. However, given the confrontations that inevitably occurred between the groups, it was not long before these tactics changed. We know that after these confrontations, several Seri bands joined forces to defend themselves against the Spaniards and that these activities crystallized in a successful armed revolt in 1725. As a result of this revolt, authorities in Sonora granted local autonomy to two bands of Indians who had fled the missions. In exchange, these bands promised to end their raids (AGN, CyP, 12, exp. 2).

But the clashes between the Seri Indians and Spaniards were far from over. As a result of the successful uprising of 1725, the Seri were considered a threat to the Spanish presence in the region. Thus, controlling and concentrating the Seri into towns was no longer the exclusive interest of the missionaries. In 1729 the captain of the Sinaloa presidio, Manuel Bernal de Huidobro, attempted to convert the Seri by force (AHH, T, 17–34, 17–35). However, he succeeded only in inciting a new uprising that involved the majority of the tribe (AGN, HJ, 16, exp. 2). The Spaniards were unable to crush this revolt until 1735 and then only after making certain new concessions to the Seri. Huidobro, who was by then governor of Sonora y Sinaloa, was prepared to grant autonomy to nearly the entire group in their old territory. According to the missionary Nicolás Perera, he told the Seri that "since they were to live together and not cause any harm, they could live wherever they wanted" (AGN, J, 1–12, exp. 2). The majority of the Seri chose to remain outside the mission. In exchange, Huidobro would not take any new action against them. At the end of 1735 he had to journey to California to crush an indigenous uprising there and did not return to the provinces until mid-1738. At that time his sole objective was to deal with the fighting that had broken out between the missionaries and the Yaqui Indians, fighting that led to a general revolt by the Yaqui in 1740 (Navarro García 1967:24, 38).

It was not until 1741, when the pacification of the Yaqui was complete, that the Spaniards undertook any new efforts to convert the Seri. That year Huido-bro was replaced as governor of Sonora y Sinaloa by Agustín de Vildósola, a long-time wealthy resident of Sonora (Mirafuentes 1986:71). When he took office, Vildósola implemented several measures aimed at guaranteeing peace in Sonora and the defense of its borders. His first step was to move the seat of government from its old location in Sinaloa to a site facing Seri territory known as Pitic, twenty leagues southeast of the Pópulo mission. The following year he established two new presidios in Sonora: the Terrenate presidio was established along the northern border to strengthen the defense against Apache attacks and another was built in Pitic, the new seat of government. With this presidio Vildósola committed himself to defeating the Seri once and for all. He believed that they had already become an obstacle to colonial expansion in the region (and that, for example, fear of the Seri was keeping the Spaniards from working the many salt mines in the coastal plains. "And out of fear of these savages," he added, although it is the best and wealthiest in the Province of Sonora, it has been and still is the most underpopulated" (AGN, H, 17, exp. 1; AGN, M, 27).

Vildósola, however, ultimately used the resources of the Pitic presidio to promote his own interests. On land intended for fortification he had built a hacienda that he used for refining metals extracted from the mines in the area as well as for agricultural production, cattle raising, and the manufacture of liquor and textiles, using soldiers for nearly all the work involved (AGN, I, 1,282). In addition to promoting his own business interests, Vildósola also concentrated all decision-making power at the regional level in his own person. Here, however, he clashed with the captains in the border presidios, who wielded strong political power. This caused a split among the governing groups in Sonora and raised the possibility of his being replaced as governor.

Given these circumstances, it was clearly not in Vildósola's interest to provoke a new conflict with the Seri. Thus, rather than trying to convert the Seri by force, he attempted to keep the peace. He was quite tolerant of their autonomy and succeeded in establishing friendly relations with them. We know that he had trade agreements with the Seri Indians from Tiburón Island and that he personally took responsibility for supplying the converted Indians with food. He also allowed the latter to continue their hunting-gathering activities while they learned how to farm (AGN, M, 27). The inspector from Sonora y Sinaloa,

José Rafael Rodríguez Gallardo, stated that Vildósola allowed the converted Seri to continue living as hunters and gatherers.

Everything indicates that this policy won Vildósola not only the friendship of the Seri but also many converts to Christianity beginning in the early years of his administration. By 1743 some six hundred Indians had moved into Pópulo and Los Angeles (AGN, M, 27, f. 322; AGN, J, 1–11, f., 30). This number certainly continued to increase until shortly before the 1748 uprising; by mid-1749, when many converted Seri had already joined the revolt, one missionary stated that eighty families still remained in Pópulo (AHH, T, 278–18).

Vildósola was still far short of his goal of converting the entire Seri nation. In 1745 the total Seri population was estimated to be approximately three thousand (AGN, M, 27). Furthermore, not only missionized Seri lived in the mission. Many who continued hunting and gathering spent certain periods of time on their traditional lands, where they could more closely adhere to their old lifestyles. Even the missionized Indians retained a good deal of autonomy. It could almost be said that for them the Pópulo mission served as a source of supplemental resources, resources that probably only a small number of Indians helped produce. In 1749 Pópulo missionary Tomás Miranda noted that the Seri were "extremely lazy" and that they subsisted by "hunting deer with bows and arrows" (AGN, J, 1–12, 2).

Vildósola was unable to do much to change the situation. The conflicts that faced the border presidio commanders ultimately forced the Mexican authorities to intervene directly in Sonora. At the end of 1747 they decided to send an inspector to the province with instructions to definitively settle these conflicts and handle the problems Vildósola had left unresolved. In early 1748 José Rafael Rodríguez Gallardo arrived from Mexico to do just that (Rodríguez Gallardo 1975:xiii–xiv).

José Rafael Rodríguez Gallardo's Visit

Once in Sonora Rodríguez Gallardo immediately implemented his first set of instructions: to remove Agustín de Vildósola as governor. In his report he explained the reasons for this measure:

The charge against Mr. Vildósola was not specifically that he was living in Pitic, but rather that he was living in Pitic without doing anything, without resolving the issue of the Seri, without securing the presidio by distributing land; and that he was living in Pitic, which was his hacienda, not the capital (Rodríguez Gallardo 1975:60).

With regard to his second set of instructions, Rodríguez Gallardo had two objectives. First, he was to visit the Seri mission and, after confirming the advisability of moving the Pitic presidio to that mission, choose the most appropriate site for the presidio (AGI, G, 301). This was the first step in the complete subjugation of the Seri. Second, he was to build one or more Spanish settlements in well-placed locations using allocated land, preferably in the northern part of the province. This was a first attempt to establish stable population centers, which did not yet exist in Sonora. The purpose of these centers was to concentrate the Spanish population and strengthen political-administrative control of the province. In addition, the Spaniards hoped that these population centers would help counter the Apache raids in the border region (AHH, T, 278–28).

Before continuing the account of Rodríguez Gallardo's experience, it is important to discuss in somewhat greater detail the reasons that led Mexican authorities to move the Pitic presidio to Seri mission territory. This will help us better understand both the importance of the move and the means used by Rodríguez Gallardo to accomplish it.

In 1744 Cristóbal de Escobar, the provincial head Jesuit of Mexico, received a royal edict to convert to Christianity all the inhabitants of the California peninsula. To accomplish this he was advised to simultaneously move the missions on the peninsula and of the Pima Alto in Sonora northward as far as the mouth of the Colorado River. This was where some of the missions would merge and where it was hoped the Sonora missions would serve as a source of support for the expansion of the California missions (Ortega 1944:363).

This order was based on the observations made to the king, Philip V, by the then–Council on Indian Affairs. The council recommended that the king carry out the "complete discovery, conversion, and pacification" of the peninsula so that Spain could take advantage of the wealth contained there and prevent another foreign nation from "getting a foothold" along its coasts (AGI, G, 137, exp. 1, f. 299–299v).

In his response de Escobar stressed the inadvisability of expanding the missions northward without first strengthening the Seri, Pima Alto, and Pápago (Tohono O'odham) missions that had already been established in Sonora. He pointed out that many of these Indians had not yet been converted and that this situation would interfere with the success of any new conquests. He described the Seri Indians as living "far from any doctrine, in their unlimited freedom and natural barbarianism." He added that because they had already rebelled in the past, the inhabitants and missions in his territory were continually suspect. He therefore felt that if the situation remained unchanged, the Seri would inevitably carry out new attacks and raids and perhaps even another uprising if they were attacked by the Spaniards during any of their forays.

De Escobar proposed establishing another mission for the Seri in addition to the one in Pópulo. It could be built on Tiburón Island to reach the Indians on the coast. He suggested allowing the Seri who had already been converted to return to the Pópulo mission. To guarantee a better fate for these missions, de Escobar made two recommendations. First, he suggested assigning about ten armed men from the Pitic or Sinaloa presidios to the missions for the first three or four years so they could force the Seri to farm the land and thwart any attempt by them to return to the deserts or beaches. Second, he suggested giving the Seri a year's worth of clothing and supplies so that they would not have to abandon their towns in search of food while awaiting the fruits of their first harvest, as occurred in the Pópulo mission. De Escobar also suggested that the Pitic presidio not be moved to the Colorado and Gila rivers, as was planned, but rather remain in its current location, where he felt its services were key to the successful missionization of the Seri Indians (AGN, M, 27). Thus the Pitic presidio was placed twenty leagues southeast of the Pópulo mission.

On December 4, 1747, the First Count Viceroy of Revilla Gigedo received a direct order from the king "to make a very serious effort to finish converting the Seri nation inhabiting the province of Sonora, the Pima Alto nation, and the Pápago nation" (AGI, G, 137). This date perhaps marked the decision to move the Pitic presidio to the Seri mission as a first step to guaranteeing the expansion of the missions toward the Colorado River and northern California.

Shortly after his arrival, Rodríguez Gallardo was briefed on the Seri:

The Seri nation, with the exception of a few families residing in the towns of Los Angeles, Pópulo, and Nacameri, continued almost within view living in rancherías and mud flats in all their wildness, regularly traversing the area around the Pitic presidio, carrying weapons as dangerous and offensive as arrow tips poisoned with preparations of herbs and deadly insects, making it impossible to cure even the most minor wound, [which] makes them live more proudly and not content to simply continue stealing (AGN, I, 1,282, exp. 10, f. 371).

Rodríguez Gallardo immediately made the Seri Indian issue a matter of concern. He ordered a group of soldiers to meet with some of the Indians who lived outside the towns, instructing them to carefully observe the Indians' stance toward them. They should then inform the Indians why Rodríguez Gallardo had been brought to Sonora and of his interest in meeting with them when he arrived at the Pitic presidio (AGN, I, 1,282, exp. 10., f. 371–371v). When they returned, the soldiers informed the inspector that the Seri Indians were not only living peacefully but also were prepared to demonstrate their obedience to him; they asked to be given advance notice of his arrival in Pitic "so that they could send messages to other *rancherías* located faraway" (AGN, I, 1,282, exp. 10, f. 370–370v).

However, Rodríguez Gallardo was not satisfied with the report. Perhaps, in accordance with his instructions, he felt that the sole fact that the Seri had not been converted "to social and political life" was reason enough to mistrust them (AGN, I, 1,282, exp. 10, f. 371).

At the end of August he moved to the Pópulo mission. From there he would go to the town of Mátape, where he had agreed to meet with the leaders of Sonora and work with them to choose the site for the future Spanish settlement. Once in Pópulo he was able to see firsthand the progress of missionization among the Seri. On the basis of his observations he wrote a report—of which only a small portion has survived—in which he discussed the Seri:

As I examined Pópulo, I was astonished to see close up the poverty, the miserable conditions of the Seri nation. There were only a few families in Los Angeles, just as in the Pópulo mission. Some of them did no work or farming of the lands, were completely idle, relying on their arrows for food, and as a result, open to thievery and treachery. [The Seri also showed themselves to be] arrogant and imperious, with the privilege or permission to carry weapons, the most poisonous imaginable, and this, in full view of the Pima Bajo, Yaqui, and Mayo Indians, who do not have weapons and are prohibited from having them because they do not have (as neither do the Seri) any enemy at their border. (AGI, G, 301)

This seemed to be reason enough for Rodríguez Gallardo to approve moving the presidio to the Seri mission, although he made the decision only after verifying that the site was indeed suitable for the move: "I have been assured that the splendid, fertile bottomland by the river offers an appropriate location as a foothold for defense and a good size settlement without causing any harm to the Indians, even if all the Seri Indian families went to live in Pópulo" (AGI, G, 301).

Once the decision was made, Rodríguez Gallardo carefully examined the towns that made up the Pópulo mission at that time—Our Lady of Pópulo, Los Angeles, and Santa Rosa de Nacameria—and the *ranchería* of San Miguel. He quickly decided on San Miguel, where he felt the presidio troops would predominate and be closer "to the mission, where those who have lived until now in the mud flats and beaches in depravity, incivility, and savagery must be converted" (AGI, G, 301). San Miguel did, in fact, offer the best conditions for monitoring the missionization of the Seri since it was located closest to the two main mission settlements, Pópulo and Los Angeles. It was a league and a half from Pópulo and two leagues from Los Angeles (AGI, G, 137). Nacameri, on the other hand, was seven leagues north of the headwaters. San Miguel also had the advantage of size: It covered an area of four leagues, estimated to be large enough to hold fifteen towns, according to land regulations from New Spain (AGI, G, 301). And finally, San Miguel was a *ranchería* rather than a town, which meant that the presidio would not affect the land belonging to the mission towns (AGI, G, 301).

Having resolved this final point and after ordering the Seri living in San Miguel to assemble in Pópulo, Rodríguez Gallardo went to the town of Mátape. He met with the town's inhabitants, who proposed that the Spanish settlement be established in Cumpas. Rodríguez Gallardo, however, did not particularly favor that proposal (AHH, T, 278–20) and after discussing it with a missionary rejected it. He had learned that Cumpas was the *pueblo de visita* for the Oposura mission and therefore could be eliminated only if he compensated residents with equivalent nearby lands, lands that in this case were nonexistent. Furthermore, Cumpas was the only town for that mission; thus its destruction would violate royal directives stating that each mission must have its own *pueblo de visita* (AHH, T, 278–20).

Under these circumstances and lacking a better site, Rodríguez Gallardo decided to establish the Spanish settlement in San Miguel. He had already considered this possibility when he first contemplated San Miguel's fertile land and size; at that time he had pointed out that the area could accommodate the presidio as well as "a good size settlement." However, it is important to examine all the reasons that may have led to his decision.

First, San Miguel had an abundant water supply. Besides the Pópulo and San Miguel rivers, there were several springs that, according to Rodríguez Gallardo, "divine providence had reserved for the inhabitants" (AGI, G, 137).

Second, San Miguel had enough land to divide among soldiers and inhabitants, a situation difficult to find in any other region in Sonora since most of the area's arable land was in the hands of the missions through the Indian towns. Furthermore, Rodríguez Gallardo would also be able to reallocate land from Los Angeles in the event that there was not enough land in San Miguel. That mission still had two towns where, according to his calculations, there was more than enough land to distribute among the Seri of Los Angeles (AGI, G, 301).

Third, the Seri would have the example of the Spaniards' lifestyle nearby, which Rodríguez Gallardo felt would invite swift civilization of the entire group. The viceroy supported this point in particular:

The Indians are so literal they only can conceive what they see in front of them; this is verified by the many years of experience in New Spain. It is only in proximity to the Spanish settlements that they submit to socialization; to work the land; to recognize their priests and colonial judges; and to trade, commerce, and use of their goods. Without substantial Spanish settlements, Indian settlements would never become permanent and secure. (AGI, G, 301)

Fourth, the settlement would benefit from the protection of the presidio, which would also guarantee the establishment and development of the first Spanish community in Sonora.

Finally, establishing the Spanish settlement in San Miguel would enable Rodríguez Gallardo to resolve simultaneously the problem of the Spanish settlement and that of the Seri resistance. This would in turn allow him to turn his attention to other matters before being called from Mexico to present a report on his tenure.

Once his plan was initiated, Rodríguez Gallardo named the site of the first Spanish *villa* in Sonora San Miguel de Horcasitas in honor of the viceroy.

The Uprisings

Before the move of the Pitic presidio to San Miguel Rodríguez Gallardo did not encounter any kind of opposition by the Pópulo Seri Indians. The problems started when he allocated the first mission lands.

In mid-1748 José de Meza, at that time the only person in Sonora involved in mining in the Seri territory (AGI, G, 301), offered to lend Rodríguez Gallardo one thousand pesos to help build the presidio. Rodríguez Gallardo, who at the time had only five hundred pesos for the project, accepted the offer and entered into a contract with de Meza (Viveros 1981:211). In exchange for his help de Meza was given the concession to build the presidio as well as two *caballerías* (about 210 acres) of arable land and a house. The house was located on one side of the presidio—that is, in San Miguel (AGN, I, 1,282, exp. 8)— while the land was located in the town of Los Angeles (AHH, T, 278–18). When the contract was drawn up, Rodríguez Gallardo and de Meza agreed to relocate the Seri families in Los Angeles to the town of Nacameri. For the relocation they asked the district governor of Sonora to determine the amount of arable land in Nacameri. However, just as de Meza began the relocation process, several Seri initiated an armed revolt. The revolt involved only nine persons headed by an Indian named Manuel (AGN, J, 1–12, exp. 2), whom the Seri called "el Queretano," most likely in reference to the numerous years he spent at work camps in Querétaro. Manuel was probably one of the Seri Indians deported to Querétaro by Manuel Bernal de Huidobro, then commander of the Sinaloa presidio. He had escaped and recently returned to Sonora. Rodríguez Gallardo said that he had returned to the area only "to get his degree in provocation" (Rodríguez Gallardo 1975:103). In fact, Manuel had more than sufficient reason to rebel and even more to lead the rebellion. The resentment he most certainly harbored for the years he had spent in prison could very well have caused him to revolt at de Meza's actions, particularly because de Meza supposedly stripped him of a "plot of land" (AHH, T, 278–18). Furthermore, Manuel's firsthand knowledge of Spanish colonialism, gained through his experience in Querétaro, and the standing this earned him among his compatriots were perhaps factors that placed him at the forefront of the Seri and channeled his discontent toward armed rebellion.

The first actions by Manuel and his group were to steal horses from the town of Opodepe, where they also killed an undetermined number of cattle (AGN, J, 1–12, exp. 2). When Rodríguez Gallardo learned what had happened, he charged de Meza, because of his knowledge of the Seri and Seri territory, with the pacification of the rebellious Indians. De Meza proceeded cautiously. He attempted to defeat Manuel peacefully rather than militarily, offering him a general pardon and inviting him to return to Los Angeles. Manuel seemed amenable to those terms but also took certain precautions himself. He sent a message to de Meza through two Indian followers that he would shortly accept the offer. As a guarantee he sent de Meza a "*replicario.*" De Meza, however, ordered Manuel's messengers disarmed and then, angry at Manuel's delay, sent the messengers back to search for him. In response, Manuel and his followers limited their negotiations to the return of the confiscated weapons. According to Father Nicolás Perera:

They asked for their arms for a third time. They were not returned and so, angered, instead of heeding de Meza, they went to his settlement in Chupi-Sonora and, after killing eleven people and burning the houses, took . . . his herd of horses in order to satisfy the hate they already felt for him. (AGN, J, 1–12, exp. 2)

De Meza then organized a posse of troops to find Manuel, but it was unsuccessful. Meanwhile Manuel and his group raided the Alameda settlement, killing one Spaniard (AGN, J, 1–12, exp. 2). Struck by these actions, one Spanish inhabitant commented, ". . . it seems that a very large uprising is forming, larger than those in the past . . ." (AGI, G, 188, exp. 25).

Up until this point, however, Manuel and his followers seemed to be seeking reparation only for the wrongs they had suffered at de Meza's hands. As one missionary observed:

In order to hurt him or his things, they hurt other inhabitants. With every attack by the Seri, you hear: they burned de Meza's house, they killed his relatives; and the Seri have said that they will not be happy until they can make a drum out of his stomach. (AHH, T, 278–18)

Toward the end of 1748 Rodríguez Gallardo personally took charge of the conflict. Not limiting his efforts to Manuel, he took aim against the entire group. In an attempt to contain the uprising before it spread among the rest of the Seri, particularly those living near the mission, he ordered the death penalty for any Indian who carried weapons, lived on the *rancherías*, or refused to live in the towns (AGI, G, 301). He also made the decree effective inside the Pópulo mission itself, sentencing to death one Indian carrying his bow and arrow who was perhaps only preparing to go out hunting. After being beaten and whipped, the Indian was ordered shot without, as several witnesses stated, being allowed to explain his actions: "Why are you killing me?" the Indian cried out desperately. "My wounds are real. Haven't you already cut me? I've already paid for my crime. If you were going to kill me, why did you whip me?" (AGI, G, 188).

The results were diametric to what Rodríguez Gallardo had hoped to achieve because the decree failed to recognize existing peace treaties between the Seri and regional authorities. Those treaties allowed the Seri to remain on their traditional lands, granting them a certain degree of local autonomy; the Seri who lived in the towns were permitted to continue hunting and gathering for a substantial part of their food supply. Furthermore, Rodríguez Gallardo frustrated possible expectations of the Seri that had developed as a result of their relationship with Vildósola—to live in peace with the Spaniards without unconditionally relinquishing their autonomy and traditions.

Complications ensued because Manuel quickly linked the intentions of the new government with the problems of the Seri. According to Father Cristóbal de Lauria, when Manuel and his followers were "ordered by the magistrate [the *visitador*] to submit and surrender, they responded that they would submit only to Agustín de Vildósola, who was their legitimate governor, and that they would accept only him as their ruler (AGI, G, 135, exp. 25). Thus Manuel broadened the goals of his movement. He was no longer merely seeking reparations for the injustices committed by de Meza; he was now challenging the legitimacy of Rodríguez Gallardo's authority and demanding that Vildósola be reinstated as governor.

The Seri who had remained on their traditional lands, who were perhaps already in close contact or alliance with Manuel, took a similar stance. In early 1749, when the Seri who lived on Tiburón Island received a message from Rodríguez Gallardo urging them to convert and granting a pardon to Manuel, they responded

> that they did not want any such pardon because they were lies and the Spaniards were doing this only to deceive them . . . that they lived there without causing harm to anyone, that if the Spaniards came after them and entered their lands, they would fight and finish off [the Spaniards]. That if Governor Agustín Vildósola were to call them, they would all go, including Manuel *El Queretaro*, and would live wherever he sent them because [Vildósola] did not deceive them; he loved them and they loved his lordship, and that was why they never hurt his property. That when this governor came and called them, every member of the nation would go. (AGI, G, 188)

Rodríguez Gallardo also faced the problem of feeding the missionized Seri. As he himself noted, he had to provide them with food so they would not go hungry and have reason to rebel. His plan was to feed the Indians while they, obligated to farm the land, waited for the fruits of their first harvests. Very quickly, however, he changed his mind. Perhaps as a result of the Seri resistance to giving up their hunting and gathering practices, he decided that everyone would participate in the construction of the presidio (AGI, G, 301). His reasoning perhaps was that the troops from San Miguel could keep an eye on the Indians and the presidio could be completed more quickly. Everything indicates that this decision sparked new resistance among the missionized Seri; one missionary affirmed that the Spaniards brought the Indians against their will to the presidio, "whipping and beating them" as if they were rebel Indians (AHH, T, 278–18). The Seri began to flee, joining the movement led by Manuel. Thus, by mid-1749 the missionary Carlos de Rojas reported that very few of the missionized Indians remained in the Pópulo mission: "All the others . . . have joined the uprising. Our weapons have been useless against them. They have caused significant damage, burning many settlements and killing many horses and cattle" (AHH, T, 278–18).

As a result of the events at Pópulo and the violence unleashed by Rodríguez Gallardo, Manuel further radicalized his stance. Following the execution of several of his followers, he rejected a new peace offer, advising the Spaniards "that he did not want God nor justice nor the missionaries, but rather to die while killing" (AHH, T, 278–18). In what appears to be another version of this response the rebel Indians reputedly told the peace messengers sent by Rodríguez Gallardo "that the Spaniards asked for peace out of fear and wanted to capture them by using deception; that they did not believe in the missionary nor in justice nor in anything; that they all lie; that they only love the devil and want to die wild" (AGI, G, 188).

Manuel's and his followers' responses were reflected in their actions. Their sole objective seemed to be to destroy everything in the region that represented Spanish dominion. In early June one Spaniard wrote:

The incendiary Seri [are] more contemptuous than other times because they operate during the day and steal everything in their path so that the people as far as Cedros de los Encinas have fled their homes, some taking refuge in the mining camps and others in the missions. (AGI, G, 188)

At the end of June the rebel Seri threatened to destroy the town of Nacameri, which at that time was home to the missionary from Pópulo (AHH, T, 278–18). Over the next few months they burned down settlements and mining camps in the west and south (AHH, T, 278–18). One example of the momentum of these actions as well as of the radical anti-Spanish sentiment behind them was reflected in the Seri attack on the Real de Aguaje in early September. The attackers killed forty-three people, pillaged the town, burned down the houses, and, as one missionary said, "desecrated the Church, spattered holy oil, and, with an infernal rage, thrust spears nine times into a painting of the Our Lady of Guadalupe. They took sacred ornaments, which, after using them to eat on, they burned" (AGN, J, 1–12, exp. 2).

The Spaniards did not remain idle. After a failed attempt to invade Tiburón Island (AHH, T, 278–18), they mounted a large-scale ground operation, using resources no less violent and fraught with symbolism than those of the rebellious Seri. After two battles near Pitic, for example, the Spaniards decapitated the dead Indians and mounted the heads in the corners of the towns closest to the plains where some of the missionized Seri still lived (AGN, J, 1–12, exp. 2). The Spaniards ultimately concentrated their efforts in the west, taking advantage of the fact that the rebel Indians had limited their actions in that area. They forced the Indians to retreat and gradually prevailed. In addition to those successful operations, Spanish troops dealt several successive blows against the Seri during January 1750. They destroyed three camps almost simultaneously, killing more than one hundred people and taking an undetermined number of prisoners. Manuel was apparently among those killed, for his name was never again mentioned by Seri leaders. Following those defeats, the rebel Indians took refuge on Tiburón Island (AGN, PI, 176, exp. 4).

The victory over the Seri Indians marked the conclusion of Rodríguez Gallardo's commission in Sonora. Before returning to Mexico he held a war council with the new governor of Sonora y Sinaloa, Diego Ortiz Parrilla. During that meeting Rodríguez Gallardo indicated to the new governor that the war with the Seri was the most pressing problem he faced and offered two suggestions. First, he suggested deporting the entire Seri nation to work camps in Mexico. By way of justification he pointed out that all peaceful means of solving the Seri problem were impractical because the Seri were declared enemies of the Spaniards (Rodríguez Gallardo 1975:127). Second, he suggested invading Tiburón Island with the objective of eliminating the island as a refuge for the Seri and thus facilitating their capture (Rodríguez Gallardo 1975:103).

On March 17, 1750, Rodríguez Gallardo was called to Mexico. Later that month Governor Ortiz Parrilla received a letter from the viceroy in which he ordered the deportation of the Seri to Mexican work camps. He indicated, however, that this measure was to be taken only with the agreement of the missionaries (AGN, J, 1–12, exp. 2). The missionaries, who had already met with the governor, supported the viceroy's order. They believed that deportation of the Seri "was not only necessary, but imperative and urgent" and proposed that they be sent preferably to "foreign islands" to prevent their return to Sonora (AGN, J, 1–12, exp. 2). At that point, according to the governor, the missionaries believed that every possibility for converting the Seri Indians had been exhausted, and they perhaps feared that any resistance by the Seri would halt expansion of the missions toward the Colorado River and northern California.

Thus, with the missionaries' blessing Ortiz Parrilla put a plan into action to capture the Seri. He would entice the inhabitants of Los Angeles, Pópulo, Cucurpe, and Nacameri with new peace offerings and promises to return their lands and then arrest them along with those who had already converted. He would then invade Tiburón Island to flush out those who had taken refuge there and finally deport them.

This plan was implemented in May 1750. The 252 Seri who responded to the peace offerings and arrived at the mission were apprehended by the soldiers and immediately deported. After separating the men, women, and children Ortiz Parrilla ordered that the women be sent throughout Sinaloa, Culiacán, and Copala "in the most secure houses so that they cannot communicate among themselves nor return to this territory." The children were sent to the border towns of Cuquiárachi, Cuchuta, and Teuricachi, which had been destroyed in Apache raids, so that they could help repopulate these towns. Ortiz Parrilla also recommended that the missionaries marry the Seri with Opata Indians so that "they can forget they were ever Seri." The men were concentrated in the San Miguel presidio while the governor attempted to capture the Indians who had taken refuge on Tiburón Island and prepared to send some to Mexican work camps (AGN, PI, exp. 4).

In early June Ortiz Parrilla began to prepare his invasion of the island; by August he had assembled an expeditionary force of 565 men, including soldiers, inhabitants, and Indians. The force landed on September 19 of that year (AGN, J, 11, exp. 5). However, before the actual landing Ortiz Parrilla tried to defeat the islanders by employing the same trickery he had used to capture the mainland Indians. He sent three Seri, who had just been captured and imprisoned in the San Miguel presidio, with a peace offering. These Indians were dressed "in [clothing] that was in keeping with the customs of the country and which had been presented as gifts so that, obligated by this hospitable treatment, they would persuade their compatriots to enter into this benevolent and benign agreement."

Only one of the three messengers returned from the mission. The other two sent back with the third the cross that Ortiz Parrilla had given them as a peace token and the message

that they were staying to help their fellow Seri, who were unyielding in their refusal to surrender and had resolved to attack the camp, kill him that night [and] fight until the death. That they felt this resolve was necessary for their own safety and their own protection before they allowed themselves to resist or yield to the suggestions of the Spaniards, who have already shown their promises to be false, untrue, and the product of cowardice rather than the graciousness they always express in their embassies and petitions. (AGN, PI, 176, exp. 4)

The governor then ordered the pursuit and capture of the Seri. The fighting continued until October 3. During the course of the campaign, despite the magnitude of the attack force, Ortiz Parrilla seized only one *ranchería*, resulting in about thirty persons dead and twenty taken prisoners, mainly women and children (AGN, J, 11, exp. 5). Nevertheless, on his return Ortiz Parrilla declared that the Seri had been annihilated. He even informed the viceroy that, taking into account the number of Indians killed and about to be deported to Mexico City, the Seri Indians had been completely wiped out in Sonora (AGN, PI, 176, exp. 3).

But the expeditionary force had hardly been dissolved when the Seri launched a series of attacks on the towns and missions nearest the desert. Their desire for revenge increased when most of the Indians who had been deported returned to Sonora. They had managed to escape through Sinaloa and, as the missionaries recounted, returned "to their beaches with their spirit more poisoned and resolved for greater vengeance" (Burrus 1963:31).

The next phase of the Seri movement extended well beyond the local area. It spread throughout nearly the entire province of Sonora, reaching the southern part of what is today the state of Arizona. The Spaniards were unable to contain the Seri until 1770. One of the most significant effects of the uprising was that it interrupted Spanish expansion to the Colorado River and northern California for more than twenty years.

Abbreviations

Archives

AGI	Archivo General de Indias, Sevilla
AGN	Archivo General de la Nación, México, D. F.
AHH	Archivo Histórico de Hacienda, México, D. F.
BNM. AF	Biblioteca Nacional de México, Archivo Franciscano, México, D. F.

Sections in Archives

C y P	Cárceles y Presidios
G	Guadalajara
H	Historia
HJ	Hospital de Jesús
I	Inquisición
J	Jesuitas
M	Misiones
PI	Provincias Internas
T	Temporalidades

References

Burrus, Ernest J. 1963. *Misiones norteñas mexicanas de la Compañía de Jesús 1751–1757*. Mexico City: Antigua Libería Robredo de José Porrúa e Hijos.

Di Peso, Charles, and Daniel S. Matson. 1965. "The Seri Indians in 1692 as Described by Adam Gilg, S.J." *Arizona and the West* 17: 33–56.

Gerhard, Peter. 1982. *The North Frontier of New Spain*. Princeton, N.J.: Princeton University Press.

Kino, Eusebio Francisco. 1926. *Las misiones de Sonora y Arizona*. Paleographic version and index by Francisco Fernández del Castillo, with bibliographic notes by Father Kino and his explorations and foundations by Dr. Emilio Bose. Mexico City: National Archives.

Mirafuentes Galván, José Luis. 1986. "Elite y defensa en Sonora, siglo XVIII." *Historias*, January–March: 67–69.

Navarro García, Luis. 1967. *Sonora y Sinaloa en el siglo XVII*. Seville: Escuela de Estudios Hispano-Americanos.

———. 1966. *La sublevación Yaqui de 1740*. Seville: Escuela de Estudios Hispano-Americanos.

Nolasco, Margarita. 1967. "Los seris, desierto y mar." *Anales del Instituto Nacional de Antropología e Historia* 18 (n.s.):125–194.

Ortega, José. 1944. *Maravillosa reducción y conquista de la provincia de San Joseph del Gran Nayar y descubrimiento de los pp. Kino y Sedelmayer en la Pimería Alta*. Mexico City: Layac.

Pérez de Ribas, Andrés. 1944. *Páginas para la historia de Sinaloa y Sonora. Triúnfos de nuestra santa fé entre gentes las más bárbaras y fieras del nuevo orbe*. 3 vols. Mexico City: Layac.

Radding, Cynthia. 1979. "Las estructuras socio-económicas de la misiones de la Pimería Alta, 1768–1850." *Noroeste de México* 3:1–124.

Rodrígucz Gallardo, José Rafael. [1750] 1975. *Informe sobre Sinaloa y Sonora*. Edition, introduction, notes, appendices, and indices by Germán Viveros. Mexico City: National Archives, Archivo Histórico de Hacienda.

Viveros, Germán. 1981. "Origen y evolución del presidio de San Miguel de Horcasitas, Sonora." *Estudios de Historia Novohispana* 7:199–270.

Cultural Creativity and Raiding Bands in Eighteenth-Century Northern New Spain

William L. Merrill

The Indians of northern New Spain adopted two major forms of violent resistance to challenge the expansion of the Spanish colonial empire. The first was large-scale revolts, which erupted irregularly during the colonial period in disparate areas of northern New Spain. The most famous of these revolts were those of the Tepehuanes in Durango between 1616 and 1618, the Tarahumaras of Chihuahua in the mid- and late seventeenth century, the New Mexico Pueblos in 1680 and 1696, and the Yaquis of Sonora in the 1740s (for brief overviews of these revolts, see Spicer 1962). Organized for the most part by sedentary agriculturalists, all these revolts were short-lived and rarely disrupted the Spanish conquest for more than a decade or two. In contrast, small-scale raiding of Spanish settlements by nomadic Indian groups—the second form of violent resistance—was continuous across the northern frontier for most of the colonial period, preventing colonization of many areas of the north and seriously disrupting the development of the regional economy.

By the second half of the eighteenth century, frustrated by its inability to contain these raiding bands, the Spanish royal government reorganized northern New Spain into a vast military zone known as the General Command of the Interior Provinces (Navarro García 1964; Moorhead 1968). In the center of this zone lay the province of Nueva Vizcaya (fig. l). Established in the mid-sixteenth century, Nueva Vizcaya extended a thousand kilometers southward from its border with Texas and New Mexico to encompass all of what is now the Mexican state of Durango along with most of the state of Chihuahua and a portion of Coahuila (Gerhard 1982:161). During the sixteenth and seventeenth centuries

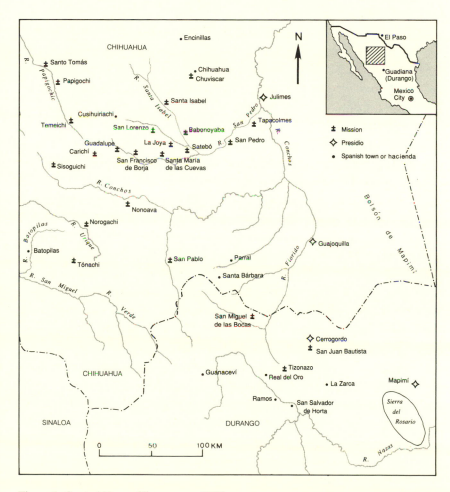

Figure 1. Central Nueva Vizcaya, ca. 1773.

the various Indian groups that raided the Spanish in Nueva Vizcaya were native to the province, but by the early decades of the eighteenth century most of these groups had been eliminated through deportation and wars of extermination (Griffen 1969). Almost immediately, various Apache groups from the north replaced them, attacking Spanish and later Mexican settlements in the region until the late nineteenth century (Griffen 1988b). In the nineteenth century other groups from north of the Rio Grande, such as the Comanches and Kiowas, also raided in the area (Fehrenbach 1974; Mooney 1898).

Such raiding was conducted primarily but not exclusively by nomadic Indian groups. South of Nueva Vizcaya, bands of escaped African slaves, Indians, and people of other ethnic backgrounds began raiding in the second half of the sixteenth century (Davidson 1966; Powell 1952:173–174). In Nueva Vizcaya itself such multiethnic bands were attacking Spanish settlements as early as 1617, during the Tepehuan Revolt (Porras Muñoz 1980:151–162), and by the second half of the eighteenth century a number of such bands operated in the province.[1] These bands drew their membership from all the various ethnic groups on the northern frontier: Apaches and other nomadic Indians; sedentary Indians affiliated with Catholic missions; individuals of mixed Indian, European, and African descent known as *castas* or *gente de razón*; and, in a few cases, Europeans or Creoles. Before joining these raiding bands, most of these people—Indians and non-Indians alike—had participated extensively in colonial economic enterprises, typically as peons or laborers in haciendas or, less frequently, in mining camps. The Europeans in these bands often were military deserters or for other reasons fugitives from justice. Spanish administrators and settlers considered these bands especially dangerous because their members could infiltrate the frontier settlements with ease and were also intimately familiar with the colonial defense system.

The emergence of such multiethnic bands presumably was a widespread frontier phenomenon, yet no detailed study of these bands has been completed. To begin to fill this gap, I consider here the available documentation regarding what appears to have been the largest multiethnic band operating in Nueva Vizcaya in the eighteenth century. After evaluating the sources of information on this band, I present a sketch of its organization, economy, and raiding practices. I then explore the factors that promoted cultural creativity within the band, considering in particular how the band's violent opposition to the Spanish colonial system affected the culture that its members created.

Most studies of colonial resistance movements tend to ignore their cultural dimensions, focusing instead on the political, military, or sociological (e.g., Crummey 1986; Katz 1988). The creation of new cultural forms is widely recognized as one of the most important features of the interaction that occurred during the colonial period between peoples of the Old and New Worlds. Yet, this interaction and the cultural creativity associated with it often are portrayed as taking place on the level of grand collectivities such as nations and producing consequences that on the whole can be characterized as positive. Such a view obviously distorts the reality of the so-called Encounter as the consequence of a European invasion of the New World. It also obscures the fact that the cultural creativity associated with this invasion was most exuberant among the oppressed classes of colonial society and more often than not was counterhegemonic in tone.

Examining the relationship between cultural processes and resistance in northern New Spain serves to correct this depoliticized and overgeneralized view while providing insights into the formation of the cultural foundations of colonial and postcolonial life. In Nueva Vizcaya, Indians, Africans, and Europeans from the lower strata of colonial society formed ethnically heterogeneous communities in mining camps, haciendas, ranches, and missions, creating a "mestizo" culture that eventually became dominant in the region. The members of the multiethnic bands that raided these Spanish economic centers also contributed to the emergence of this colonial culture. In contrast with the multiethnic communities established within Spanish colonial society, however, these bands brought people of diverse ethnic backgrounds together on the margins of colonial society where cultural creativity and life in general were much less constrained by the social and economic relations of the dominant colonial order.

Documentary Sources

The multiethnic band considered here was described in some detail in 1773 and then disappears from the historical record. All information on this band, which reportedly was under the leadership of an Indian named Calaxtrin, comes from official colonial records of two types: (1) summaries of depositions recorded during judicial proceedings against individuals accused of collaborating with Calaxtrin's band, and (2) reports of various Spanish officials to their superiors on these proceedings and related events.[2]

The principal description of the band's raiding activities and military strategy is found in the deposition of José Manuel Moreno de los Reyes. Reyes was arrested on June 7, 1773, for spying on the Hacienda de San Salvador de Horta. Two weeks later he was interrogated in the capital city of Durango by José Fayni, governor and commandant-general of Nueva Vizcaya. In the records of his interrogation, Reyes was characterized as a thirty-year-old *negro* or *mulato* shepherd, married but separated from his wife. Born and raised on the Hacienda of San Juan Bautista, located in the jurisdiction of the Presidio de Cerrogordo, Reyes testified that he had fled this hacienda three years earlier after stabbing the hacienda's head rancher to death in an argument. During his first two years as a fugitive, he lived a peripatetic existence, working in seven different haciendas in southern Chihuahua and northern Durango. Then in April 1772, he claimed, a party of "enemies" composed of five Tarahumara Indians and two non-Indians captured him near the Hacienda de la Zarca as they were returning to their base after having attacked another hacienda in the area. Threatened with death unless he joined them, Reyes accompanied the party to a rendezvous with members of allied raiding parties in a nearby sierra. He then returned with them to Calaxtrin's main camp in the Sierra del Rosario, a line of low, arid mountains located near the current junction of the states of Durango, Chihuahua, and Coahuila.

Reyes reported that during the following fourteen months he participated in two raids against Spanish haciendas, explaining that he remained with the band because they promised him a share of the spoils; by the time of his interrogation, however, he had received only one used shirt. In May 1773 Calaxtrin sent Reyes and another captive-turned-band-member named José del Río to spy on the Hacienda de San Salvador in preparation for an attack. To avoid suspicion, Reyes and del Río arrived separately at the hacienda and asked for work, Reyes staying with a sister who lived on the hacienda, del Río with another household. A few days later, on June 7, they were arrested by Alexandro de la Carrera, manager of the hacienda, after one of them inquired about the grazing schedule for the hacienda's mules, the principal target of Calaxtrin's planned attack.

For reasons not specified in the documents, Reyes confessed immediately to being a spy, but del Río admitted his guilt only after he had been given seven lashes. Both prisoners agreed that the raiding party with which they were affiliated was in the area, but they disagreed as to its size and location. Carrera organized a party of seventy-four men from the hacienda and, forcing del Río to serve as their guide, set out in search of the raiders. After the group traveled several hours without encountering any sign of the raiders, del Río admitted that he had lied about where the other members of his raiding party had been hiding. He said that they had been waiting near the hacienda for Carrera and his men to leave so they could attack the hacienda, kill the people there, steal the horses and mules, and then pursue Carrera and his men to finish them off. Enraged, the men from the hacienda demanded that Carrera turn del Río over to them so they could cut him to pieces. With difficulty Carrera prevented his men from killing del Río, but he could not dissuade them from flogging him. They rushed back to the hacienda to confront the raiders but found everything as they had left it.

On June 10 Carrera sent a letter to Governor Fayni, notifying him that he would deliver the prisoners to Durango shortly. On June 17 they arrived in Durango, where Reyes and del Río were immediately placed in the royal jail and assigned a lawyer. Two days later Carrera gave his sworn declaration, summarizing the information he had extracted from Reyes and del Río at the Hacienda de San Salvador. Between June 21 and June 23 Governor Fayni interrogated del Río and Reyes twice, first separately and then together to clarify contradictions in their individual accounts.

These contradictions were remarkably minor, the principal disagreement being whether del Río had participated in an attack on the Hacienda de San Salvador the previous May, which Reyes claimed and del Río initially denied but later admitted. Otherwise, both agreed that del Río had been a member of Calaxtrin's band less than a year and that he had never visited the band's main settlement in the Sierra del Rosario. In the summary of his deposition in Durango, del Río was characterized as a *mulato* or *lobo,*[3] twenty-eight to thirty years old, like Reyes a shepherd by occupation, but not married. He claimed that he had been captured by the "enemies" a month before on the hacienda of his birth, La Zarca, and taken to a nearby sierra. Later, after attacking the Hacienda de San Salvador, most of the band returned to Calaxtrin's main camp, but fifteen men, including Reyes and del Río, stayed behind to spy on the area's haciendas. Although he could have deserted the band upon arriving at the Hacienda de San Salvador, del Río said that he did not because the other band members threatened to kill him whenever they found him again if he escaped while spying. In his original confession to Carrera as well as in his deposition in Durango, del Río attributed the majority of his information on Calaxtrin's band to Reyes.

On June 26 Governor Fayni sent a brief report on his interrogation of Reyes and del Río to Antonio María Bucareli y Ursúa, the viceroy of New Spain, in Mexico City. The next day he began interrogating five more prisoners recently arrived from Real del Oro who also were accused of collaborating with the enemy. All five were Tarahumaras who spoke Spanish sufficiently well to be interrogated without an interpreter. They included Ignacio Tortuga, about forty years old, originally from the pueblo of Santa María de las Cuevas but more recently a resident of the pueblo of San Miguel de las Bocas; Ignacio Luis, between forty and fifty years old, and his wife María Petrona, described as "over thirty," both from the pueblo of Carichí; and Alexandro de Bustamante (alias Alexandro de Arenivar) and his brother Santos de Bustamante, both from the pueblo of Santa María de las Cuevas, around thirty and twenty-five years old respectively. All had been absent from their home pueblos for at least a year.

In early May 1773 a party of Indians allied with the Spanish had taken Ignacio Tortuga, Ignacio Luis, and María Petrona into custody at a remote spot called Tecolotes. At the same time, they captured an Indian woman who had been Ignacio Tortuga's companion for the previous three years, having abandoned her husband, an Indian man from the pueblo of San Miguel de las Bocas. This party had been ordered by Luis María Zatarain, *justicia mayor* of Real del Oro, to locate the raiding bands that had recently attacked haciendas in the jurisdiction of Real del Oro. The leader of the party, a Tarahumara known as Capitán Melchor from San Miguel de las Bocas (and an acquaintance of Ignacio Tortuga), suspected that the group had been spying for the raiding bands although they claimed that they were innocently baking mescal (presumably referring to the hearts of the agave plant). About the same time, Capitán Melchor's party arrested the brothers Alexandro and Santos de Bustamante at a ranch of the nearby hacienda of La Zarca, also on suspicion of spying for the enemy. Capitán Melchor then turned the prisoners over to Zatarain. On May 9, after sending Ignacio Tortuga's female companion to the Catholic priest in Las Bocas to be reunited with her husband, Zatarain placed the remaining five prisoners in jail.

Zatarain wanted to send the prisoners to Durango right away, fearing that their friends would attempt to free them from the local jail, but the danger of attack along the way and the weakness of the Spanish defenses delayed their transfer until late June. Immediately upon their arrival in Durango, Governor Fayni began interrogating them, basing his questions in part on accusations made against them by the prisoners Reyes and del Río and by the hacienda manager Carrera. Reyes and del Río identified Ignacio Tortuga (whom they called Luis Tortuga) as a captain of one of the raiding bands under Calaxtrin's control. Reyes claimed in fact that Tortuga was the head of the raiding party that had captured him fourteen months earlier, and he told del Río that Tortuga had once presented him with a bow and quiver for having gathered critical information while serving as a spy. Carrera went even further in his accusations, claiming that Tortuga commanded five or six raiding parties and that he operated under the loose control of Calaxtrin's son, who held Tortuga in high esteem for his bravery. Tortuga vehemently denied these accusations in his deposition of June 29, but the opportunity for further interrogation ended on July 13, when he mysteriously died in prison, his death officially attributed to "illness."

Del Río also identified Alexandro de Bustamante as a spy for Calaxtrin's band on the Hacienda de San Juan Bautista and testified that Bustamante had been involved in the attack on that hacienda in late March or early April, an accusation that Reyes also made but Bustamante denied. Later, as they were being taken back to the jail, Bustamante beat del Río for having testified against him, an offense for which he was flogged. After changing his story several times, Bustamante finally testified that, while he had not personally engaged in spying or raiding against the Spanish haciendas, his brother Santos was a member of a raiding band that included Ignacio Tortuga, Ignacio Luis, Ignacio Luis's son-in-law Vicente (an Indian from the pueblo of Chuvíscar), an Apache named Juan Antonio who had been raised by Spanish settlers, and another unnamed Apache.

According to Bustamante, members of this band had informed him that they had recently turned a herd of stolen horses over to a band of six *gente de razón* and previously had delivered horses to bands under Calaxtrin. Possibly in retribution for del Río's charges against him, Bustamante identified del Río as one of the six *gente de razón* who had received the horses from Tortuga's band and accused him of helping the Apache Juan Antonio escape from jail on a previous occasion. Although in their original testimonies Santos de Bustamante and Ignacio Luis denied any wrongdoing, they admitted their guilt when confronted by Alexandro de Bustamante's charges, acknowledging that his characterizations of their raiding activities and their involvement with bands under Calaxtrin's control were accurate.

These accounts of Calaxtrin's band, provided mainly by members or allies of this band, clearly reflect the divergent perspectives and interests of the witnesses, and they undoubtedly are colored by the atmosphere of coercion, manipulation, and physical deprivation that characterized the judicial context within which they were produced. Of all the testimonies those of Alexandro de Bustamante, Santos de Bustamante, and Ignacio Luis are most suspect. The fact that their brief and often redundant statements were elicited primarily while these prisoners confronted one another with accusations and counteraccusations suggests that their interrogators coerced consensus from them. In any case, they provided only limited information on Calaxtrin's band in contrast with José Reyes, whose account is both more detailed and seems more spontaneous. Also, Reyes's account is supported by the statements of José del Río, who, while reportedly deriving much of his information from Reyes, gave his deposition for the most part in private, away from Reyes.

The descriptions of Calaxtrin's band found in these documents are complemented by a report on life in the band's main camp provided by José Thomás de la Trinidad, the fifteen-year-old son of a shepherd (*vaciero*) from the Hacienda de San Salvador.[4] During a raid on the hacienda in early May 1773, members of the band captured Trinidad along with his brother, two other boys, and a girl and then took them back to Calaxtrin's main camp. They later killed Trinidad's brother and another boy while apparently distributing the other children among band members for whom they were forced to work. In early July, when his "owner" sent him to retrieve some livestock, Trinidad escaped, walking for three days until he arrived at the Spanish settlement of Mapimí. There he recounted his experiences to Andrés José de Velasco y Restan, a sergeant major in the local militia and owner of the haciendas of San Salvador and Ramos, both major targets of the raiding bands (cf. Navarro García 1964:411). Velasco y Restan summarized the boy's account in a report sent to Governor Fayni on July 8, 1773.

Despite the rigors of captivity—not to mention the horror of witnessing the murder of his brother—Trinidad provided a remarkable account of Calaxtrin's home base, so clear and detailed in fact that Viceroy Bucareli doubted its veracity as soon as he read it. In a letter to Hugo O'Conor, commandant-inspector of the northern presidios, Bucareli wrote that "it is hard for me to believe that a boy of such a young age who spent his time herding livestock would have such judgment and fearlessness to observe and learn the customs, government, and ideas and other operations of those who supposedly are in rebellion" (Bucareli y Ursúa 1773b:415v).

Although Bucareli surely underestimated the ability of a fifteen-year-old to observe and report his observations accurately, it is possible that Velasco y Restan embellished the boy's account with details of the raiding bands in the area with which he had had personal experience or about which he had learned from others. Rumors about these bands undoubtedly circulated along the frontier, and as owner of the Hacienda de San Salvador and the employer of Alexandro de la Carrera, Velasco y Restan also would have heard in detail the descriptions of Calaxtrin's band provided by Reyes and del Río the month before. Perturbed by the inadequacy of the Spanish colonial defense against the raiding bands, he perhaps linked the boy's account to that of the spies to create the spectre of a major organized threat to the survival of the frontier settlements. Nevertheless, the overlap between the two sets of accounts is minimal, and there are several inconsistencies between them, suggesting that they are largely independent.

Description of the Band

Taken together, these various accounts offer considerable information on the composition, organization, and activities of Calaxtrin's band. Here I provide a synthesis and evaluation of this information.

Membership

Estimates of the band's size vary considerably. According to del Río, Reyes told him that the band had grown to include 200 people, but the hacienda manager Carrera testified that Reyes had told him that the "enemy troops" in the nearby sierras alone numbered 600 men while the band as a whole included 1,700 men. Reyes himself testified that there were 1,000 people of all ages and both sexes living at the band's main camp. The fifteen-year-old captive, José Thomás de la Trinidad, estimated that there were 900 men in this camp, along with many women, children, and old people. Arriving at a precise count of the number of people in the band would have been quite difficult given the movement of people into and out of the main camp, but clearly the band was of substantial size, larger than any other single raiding band described in the late eighteenth century.

The band included individuals of diverse ethnic backgrounds. Of the Indians in the group, only a few were Apaches. Some of these may have been Apaches known as *criados,* a reference to their having been raised (*criado*) in Spanish households, presumably after being captured as children in Spanish raids against the Apaches. Carrera stated that the band included some Gileño Apaches, a term designating Apaches specifically from the Gila River area of Arizona and New Mexico as well as all Apaches from west of the Rio Grande (Griffen 1988a:4–5; Moorhead 1968:170; Opler 1983:388–389). He also identified the two principal leaders of the group—Calaxtrin and his son, also named Calaxtrin—as Apaches, although in the other reports they are characterized only as Indians.

According to Reyes and del Río, the majority of Indians in the band were said to be Tarahumaras from mission pueblos, rather than Tarahumaras who had not yet been incorporated into the mission system. Except for the former Jesuit mission of San Miguel de las Bocas, the pueblos of origin of the Tarahumaras are not given. Information is available, however, on the home pueblos of other Tarahumaras who were being arrested in 1773 by the *corregidor* of Chihuahua for suspected involvement in raiding activities (Queipo de Llanos 1773:404v, 408). These pueblos included the Franciscan missions of Babonoyaba, Santa Isabel, San Pedro, and Tapacolmes and the former Jesuit missions of Satebó, Guadalupe, La Joya, San Francisco de Borja, Santa María de las Cuevas, San Lorenzo, Santo Tomás, and Carichí. Some of these Jesuit missions had been taken over by secular clergy in the 1750s and the remainder in 1767, when the Jesuits were expelled from the Spanish empire (Griffen 1979; Alcocer 1958; Arlegui 1851; Revilla Gigedo 1966; Deeds 1981).

Most of these pueblos were located near major Spanish economic centers in the foothills and basin-and-range country of central Chihuahua, in or just east of the area known as the Upper Tarahumara (Tarahumara Alta). The conclusion that the majority of Tarahumaras in Calaxtrin's band were affiliated with these pueblos is reinforced by the report of commandant-inspector O'Conor to the effect that the Indians in the Upper Tarahumara were "restless" while those further south in the Lower Tarahumara (Tarahumara Baja) were loyal to the Spanish (Bucareli y Ursúa 1773e:10). At about the same time Franciscans reported that the Indians in their missions in the mountains of the Upper Tarahumara were at peace while those in their missions outside the sierra were involved in the raiding (Laba 1793; Barragán 1793).

By 1773 Tarahumaras from most of these pueblos had participated in the Spanish economy for more than a century as both draft and free laborers. Many of these Indians formed part of a floating labor pool that moved between the mission pueblos and the Spanish economic centers (Dunne 1948; Griffen 1979:46–49; Deeds 1981, 1989). Thus, those who joined Calaxtrin's band might have come by way of the Spanish haciendas and towns rather than directly from the missions.

Other than Tarahumaras, the only Indians mentioned by Reyes as members of Calaxtrin's band were Cholomes, although Governor Fayni claimed that Reyes and del Río testified that Tepehuan Indians from the Durango mission of Tizonazo were beginning to join the "rebels." The Cholomes appear periodically in the history of northern New Spain, but little is known about them other than that they were nomadic, lived in the more arid regions of northern New Spain, and raided Spanish settlements (Griffen 1979:14, 31–32). However, some Cholomes were present in Franciscan missions of central Chihuahua (Griffen 1979); according to Reyes, those in Calaxtrin's band came from such mission pueblos.

Calaxtrin's band also included many individuals of mixed Indian, African, and European ancestry. These people were designated generically as *gente de razón* or *castas* and distinguished more specifically in accordance with the colonial racial classification as *negros, mulatos, lobos, coyotes,* and *moriscos.* Each of these terms was intended to denote one of the infinite possible combinations of ancestry, but their exact significance varied considerably at different times and places. The documents clearly indicate that these people were mostly agricultural workers on local haciendas, members of the rural proletariat rather than mine workers, tradespeople, or small independent farmers or ranchers.

Only one European, who went by the name of Don Antonio de la Campa, was said to be a member of the band. Reyes identified him as a Spaniard (*Español*) but also stated that he did not know what country Campa was from and gave no further information on his background. He described him as tall and fair-skinned and reported that he typically carried small pistols and wore a linen cap, blue-striped pants, and a leather tunic like those used by the Spanish presidio soldiers (see Navarro García [1964], fig. 133, for an 1803 drawing of such a soldier).

The captive Trinidad indicated that there were many children in the band's base camp, suggesting that the band was reproducing itself. Its apparently rapid growth, however, seems to have derived primarily from the incorporation of new members from outside, either captives or people who voluntarily left their mission and hacienda communities to join the band. In some cases band members coerced captives into joining the band by threatening to kill them if they refused; in others they were enticed to join by the promise of a share in the spoils. Women captives, according to Trinidad, lost their desire to escape because they became so accustomed to the life of the band that they forgot their families and former homes. Terror also must have played a role in convincing them to conform to the band's demands. Reyes reported that women captives were distributed among the band's leaders, who raped and then killed them when they became sick because of their fear.

Reyes also reported that the band members did not mistrust the non-Indians in the band because they converted them to the band's cause through a special rite of incorporation. In this rite the band members administered the captives a drink prepared from peyote and other herbs for three days. Governor Fayni commented on the effectiveness of this ritual in his report to the viceroy of New Spain:

. . . although their union [with the band] derives from having been made prisoners or captives, they remain apostates voluntarily because upon their entry they are administered a decoction of the root called peyote mixed with other herbs, which disturbs their reasoning in the manner of intoxication [and] later, although they regain their senses, their spirits remain inclined toward the rebels' cause and they refuse or are hesitant to separate themselves from their company. (Fayni 1773:11)

Social and Political Organization

According to the fifteen-year-old captive, at the band's principal settlement the band members lived in four separate *rancherías* on either side of a lake or stream, each *ranchería* with its own leader. The residents of these *rancherías* were not segregated by ethnicity, although the leaders of all the rancherías were Indian men. The leader of the principal *ranchería* was the leader of the band as a whole; Trinidad reported that, although he was old and crippled to the point of having to be helped onto his horse, all the other band leaders obeyed his commands. Del Río said that Calaxtrin was treated as the "Captain General of the Interior Nations," while the hacienda manager Carrera described him as "Governor of the Hostile Nations, whom they recognize as their head." Both characterizations probably exaggerated the political influence that Calaxtrin enjoyed outside his band.

According to several of the accounts, Calaxtrin provided overall planning for the band's activities, especially deciding when and where they would raid. He also reportedly divided the food supplies among the band members according to need and controlled the distribution of cloth and other goods acquired in the raids, which he stored in a large buffalo-hide "tent," presumably a tipi. Calaxtrin's second in command was his son, called Calaxtrin the Younger (*el mozo*) to distinguish him from his father, Calaxtrin the Elder (*el viejo*). Calaxtrin the Younger was in charge of directing the band's military operations in accordance with his father's instructions. According to Reyes, he also supervised the distribution among his troops of the jewelry, clothing, and other luxury goods captured during the raids, saving the best for his father.

When they left the main settlement to raid, the band's warriors were divided into small parties. Each party, according to Carrera and Governor Fayni, was composed of twenty-two men led by a captain and one or two scouts. The raiding parties, like the *rancherías* at the band's main camp, were not segregated by ethnic group, and both Indians and non-Indians served as captains. The position of captain apparently was based on a fighter's military skill and valor in battle rather than his ethnicity or kinship relations with other members of the band.

Some Indian women, dressed as men, accompanied the raiding parties; Fayni identified them as Tarahumara women and reported that they "handled their weapons with equal inhumanity and furor" as the men (Fayni 1773:12). Reyes said these women were responsible for killing the women in the places they attacked. In addition, those men who, under the guise of workers, served as spies in the Spanish settlements appear to have been affiliated with specific raiding parties. In some cases these spies would sneak away from the settlements to join their compatriots just before a raid, but in other instances they lived permanently in the settlements—undercover, as it were.

The band's political organization thus displayed some hierarchy, with status achieved rather than inherited. Calaxtrin's son's high position may have reflected a tendency for band leadership to pass from father to son, but his own achievements probably were more important. There also was some differential access to resources, and several markers of status differences were reported. The captive Trinidad described the elder Calaxtrin's buffalo-hide tent as larger than the horsehide tents of the other band members, and Reyes reported that Calaxtrin had a small adobe house while the others had no "formal" housing. Further distinctions among band members are seen in the practice of giving the leaders of the raiding parties their pick of the female captives and probably a larger share of the booty as well. The choice, fatty strips of meat found along the spine under the horse's mane also were reserved for the leaders of the band and raiding parties; the others could eat only cuts from the remainder of the animal. According to Carrera, these distinctions were maintained at death, expressed in the types of food placed alongside a corpse.

Economy

The band's economy was mixed, based on raiding for livestock supplemented by some agriculture and presumably hunting and collecting of wild resources. Reyes reported that the band members planted maize, beans, and squash at their main camp. Trinidad said their fields were irrigated and added melons and watermelons to the crops listed by Reyes. He noted that the band had produced a surplus of maize in 1772, which they stored in horsehide bags, and ate buffalo meat, which they possibly acquired in trade with Indians farther north. He also mentioned that the band members prepared a beverage—probably brewed from agave since it was called *pulque*—which they consumed in large quantities as an intoxicant.

The mainstay of the band's diet was horse and mule flesh together with some beef. Trinidad stated that the band members owned no sheep or goats, presumably because these animals could not be driven rapidly away from Spanish settlements after raids. Livestock was crucial to the band's existence because, given the aridity of the area in which they lived, a band this large could not have survived on foods produced or collected locally. Nonetheless, the band members apparently were not concerned with maintaining and expanding their herds through natural reproduction, for Trinidad reported that they regularly ate the younger animals.

The quantity of livestock available on the Spanish haciendas during the second half of the eighteenth century was enormous. In 1777, the governor of Nueva Vizcaya reported that raiders had stolen more than 68,000 head of livestock in Nueva Vizcaya between 1771 and 1776, in addition to killing 1,674 people and capturing 154 others (Barray 1857). Of course, not all these animals would have been taken by Calaxtrin's band, but his band's share surely would have been more than sufficient for its members' survival. In fact, the possibility of acquiring large numbers of livestock through raiding was a primary factor allowing the formation of such a large raiding band. The growth of the band, in turn, enabled it to expand its raiding activities while simultaneously requiring that it do so to acquire the increasing amounts of food that it needed to survive.

In addition to eating the animals they took from Spanish settlements, Calaxtrin and his followers appear to have served as major intermediaries in a regional trade in stolen livestock, principally horses and mules. The animals they traded included those they stole themselves as well as those delivered to them by other, much smaller bands that raided independently. According to Reyes, during the dry season the band grazed its herds in a well-watered spot near the main settlement. Then in the rainy season, when pasturage and water were more widely available, they drove the herds north, where they exchanged them with Apaches and possibly other Indian groups for skins, hide bags, arrows, and lances. Del Río said that this exchange took place in a remote section of the Hacienda de Encinillas, located about 25 kilometers north of the large Spanish villa at Chihuahua and 400 kilometers north of the band's main settlement in the Sierra del Rosario. He added that he had heard of a European living among Indians farther north who also was involved in this clandestine livestock trade. It is not improbable that the animals captured by Calaxtrin's band in Nueva Vizcaya eventually were traded or sold to the French in Louisiana or possibly to Spanish settlers in Texas or New Mexico, with whom the Indians in Texas maintained a flourishing trade (Navarro García 1964:97, 105; Griffen 1988b:6–7, 151–162).

This regional trade apparently was paralleled by a system of exchange within the band. Velasco y Restan, who recorded the captive Trinidad's account, added at the end of his report that the band members maintained a trade among themselves in shoes, boots, vests (*cotones*), pants, and other things they produced from hides and skins that they themselves cured. Trinidad stated that both men and women typically wore such leather clothing, replacing it with finer cloth garments during their dances and in what possibly was their version of a formal promenade.

Raiding

The band reportedly undertook most of its raiding of Spanish settlements during the dry season, which in this area of northern Mexico falls at two times of the year—March to June and September to November. Before leaving their main camp, according to the captive Trinidad, they would bring out a statue of Nuestra Señora de los Dolores to inspire the fighting spirit of the men in the band, who went on their raids "dressed like Spaniards in trimmed pants, vests, etc. mounted on horses with iron-stirruped cowboy [*vaquero*] saddles and with weapons" (Velasco y Restan 1773:194). The band members kept this statue of the Virgin inside a glass case in a niche in a cave near their principal *ranchería*. They placed shawls, cloths, reliquaries, silver buckles, and other jewelry on and around the statue, taking care to burn candles there and keep the shrine clean by washing and sweeping it. They also danced at this shrine with a drum, flute, and a large flag decorated with ribbons.

According to Reyes, the band's raiding parties would leave the Sierra del Rosario a few days after the new moon, traveling together under the leadership of Calaxtrin the Younger to a spring called Juana's Tits (*Tetas de Juana*). There they would separate and move through the back country to positions adjacent to the settlements they intended to attack. Usually these positions were situated in the rugged hills or mountains scattered across this area where their presence would go unnoticed and where they could retreat if necessary.

Often before an attack the raiding parties would dispatch spies to the settlements to collect information or retrieve information from spies already in place. The band valued highly the intelligence gathered by these spies and, according to Carrera, had its agents in all the haciendas, presidios, and other major frontier settlements. According to del Río, the information they gathered sometimes was carried by messengers from one raiding party to the next and then ultimately back to Calaxtrin the Elder to aid him in planning the band's military strategy.

The raiding parties tried to time their attacks to coincide with the full moon. Del Río said that during the raids the Indians used bows, arrows, and lances. Reyes reported that two *gente de razón* worked fulltime at the main settlement manufacturing arrows and possibly bows and lances as well. The non-Indians in the band relied on lances, carrying hide shields and wearing leather tunics for protection. Whether they also used firearms is unclear. Governor Fayni reported to the viceroy that the individuals who knew how to use firearms did so, relying on guns, powder, and shot they had stolen, but the captive Trinidad indicated that even though the band members had many firearms as well as powder and shot, they did not know how to use them. Del Río said they failed to use their firearms not for lack of knowledge but for lack of powder. Because many band members had worked in the settlements they were attacking, they often wore masks that the Indians in the band made for them from hide taken from the heads of cattle. There also is evidence that some used *noms de guerre* to disguise their identities.

Calaxtrin the Younger apparently did not participate personally in most of the attacks, but according to Carrera he sometimes would appear with a drum and flag to lead the troops in his personal detachment to the aid of a raiding party in need of reinforcement. After an attack but before retreating with their captives and booty, the raiding parties would retrieve the bodies of any of their members who had been killed. They carried the corpses away to a safe location, where they buried them in a flexed position, placing food next to the bodies and covering the graves with earth and stones to prevent their discovery.

After a previously agreed-upon length of time—the reports state eight days—the various raiding parties would regroup at Juana's Tits and from there return to the Sierra del Rosario. As they approached the main settlement, the people who had remained behind would come out to meet them, carrying hide bags of agave wine (*pulque*), on which everyone would get drunk. Alexandro de Bustamante, perhaps confusing Juana's Tits with the band's main camp in the Sierra del Rosario, reported that Tortuga's band had turned horses over to Calaxtrin's band at Juana's Tits, "where there are great *rancherías* and [where] they celebrate many dances accompanied by drinking the peyote drink [*la Bevida de pellotes*] given them by the Apaches, with which they become inebriated" (Bustamante 1773:358v). Bustamante provides no further description of these dances, which appear to have been linked, like the drinking of agave wine, to victory celebrations.

The principal targets of these raids were the grazing lands and central settlements of three of the area's largest haciendas (San Salvador de Horta, La Zarca, and Ramos), located 80 to 125 kilometers from the Sierra del Rosario. The band also attacked smaller ranches they encountered on their way to their principal targets and occasionally raided mining centers. Like other raiding bands in the area, they probably attacked mission pueblos and presidios as well.

The raiding parties apparently did not discriminate among their victims, killing Indians and non-Indians alike. The majority of people killed or captured in the raids were non-Indian *castas,* presumably because these groups constituted the largest component of the hacienda populations and were more vulnerable since they cared for the haciendas' livestock and often lived in ranches outside the hacienda centers. Because no Spanish captives are mentioned in the accounts of Calaxtrin's band, it is possible that the raiding parties tended to kill rather than capture them. Spaniards presumably would have made less desirable captives since they would have been more reluctant than the *castas* to participate in the band's raiding activities. Also there were fewer Spaniards than *castas* in the haciendas, and as the elite they would have lived in the often fortified hacienda centers.

According to Reyes and del Río, Calaxtrin's band focused its attacks on these three haciendas because its members were angry with the haciendas' managers. Presumably many of the band members had worked for these managers in the past and had been mistreated by them. Vengeance, however, appears to have been a less important motive for the raiding than the desire and need to steal horses and mules for food and trade. Also, as Reyes pointed out, by killing or stealing these horses and mules they eliminated the settlers' principal mode of transportation and thus their ability to retaliate against the raiders. Reyes also stated that Calaxtrin ordered an attack on the Hacienda de San Salvador because he had heard that the mules there were especially good.

In addition to these rather specific motivations, the documents suggest that the band hoped to achieve a more revolutionary goal through raiding. Reyes said that their aim was to "destroy the land," and Carrera concluded that the band's strategy was to attack the settlements repeatedly until they had completely destroyed them. The most radical view was reported by the captive Trinidad, who said that the band's intention was to finish off the frontier settlements and make themselves owners of everything. The accounts do not reveal, however, whether Calaxtrin and his followers had formulated a comprehensive, long-range revolutionary program.

Banditry, Resistance, and Cultural Creativity

Of the many raiding bands operating in Nueva Vizcaya in the second half of the eighteenth century, Calaxtrin's band stands out because of its large size and the ethnic diversity of its members. The existing historical record unfortunately does not document the course by which this unusual band came into existence. Given its many similarities to Apache groups of the period, one can speculate that the band began as a much smaller and predominantly Apache band— possibly the band accused of raiding in eastern Nueva Vizcaya in 1770 under the leadership of Canastrín and two other captains (Navarro García 1964:193–194)— and then grew rapidly as people dissatisfied with their lot in the colonial society abandoned the Spanish missions and economic centers. This band's apparent control over much of the regional clandestine trade in livestock perhaps accounts for why it rather than some other band grew so large, a growth no doubt facilitated by the minimal Spanish military presence in the region at the time (Rubio Mañé 1959; Navarro García 1964:140; Moorhead 1968).

By 1773 Tarahumaras, not Apaches, were the dominant ethnic group in the band. Around 1770 Spanish colonial administrators began to realize that Tarahumaras, sometimes allied with Apaches, were responsible for much of the violence directed against the Spanish settlements in Nueva Vizcaya (Navarro García 1964:227ff.). Many regarded the Tarahumaras as their most dangerous enemy because they were able to live within colonial society under the guise of loyal Christians. By 1773 the *corregidor* of Chihuahua had jailed more than one hundred Tarahumaras suspected of participating in raiding activities (San Vicente 1773; Bucareli y Ursúa 1773a).

Some Spanish officials attributed the apparent upsurge in Tarahumara discontent to the impact on them of the 1767 expulsion of the Jesuits from the Spanish empire (Cuéllar 1768; Carrillo 1773; Nava 1794; Parrilla 1794).[5] In many instances representatives of the Spanish Crown confiscated the Indians' livestock and other properties under the mistaken assumption that they belonged to the Jesuits; in some cases the Indians were held liable for debts incurred by their former missionaries (Benedict 1972; Campo 1773). In addition, unlike in the more distant missions in the mountains and canyons of the Sierra Madre Occidental, the Jesuit missions closest to the Spanish economic centers were transferred to secular priests under the bishop of Durango rather than to Franciscan missionaries (Revilla Gigedo 1966; Alcocer 1958). The regulations governing the secularization of missions facilitated the settlement of mission lands by non-Indians, and the secular priests were often less than zealous in their defense of the Indian communities. As a result, the barrier that the Church traditionally had raised against the appropriation of the Indians' land and labor by the growing non-Indian population was substantially weakened (cf. Taylor 1988; Van Young 1988).

On the other hand, Tarahumaras from the Jesuit missions had been involved in raiding before the expulsion of the Jesuits (Braun 1764:17; Bargas 1762; Lizassoain 1763:6v–8). In addition, the Tarahumaras implicated in raiding after 1767 did not come exclusively from the ex-Jesuit missions but also from Franciscan missions and other Spanish settlements, which were not directly affected by the expulsion order. While the adverse effects of the expulsion and secularization undoubtedly contributed to Tarahumara discontent after 1767, the factors motivating their participation in raiding appear to have been linked to the structures of oppression and exploitation intrinsic to Spanish colonial society.

Because Calaxtrin's band depended for its survival on stealing Spanish livestock, it resembles the bandit bands that Hobsbawm and many others have studied (Hobsbawm 1959, 1981; Vanderwood 1982; Crummey 1986). In several other respects, however, it differed significantly from Hobsbawm's model of bandit bands. Hobsbawm (1981:20) indicated that these bands tended to average between ten and twenty members. In eighteenth-century Nueva Vizcaya, many raiding bands, including the raiding parties dispatched by Calaxtrin to attack Spanish settlements, fell within this range, but Calaxtrin's band as a whole clearly was many times larger, even if only the most conservative estimates of its size are accepted. Also, unlike typical bandit bands, Calaxtrin's was not a predominantly male group but a complete society that included males and females of all ages. It also operated largely independently of the local peasants, who often were victims of its attacks. Except for men sent to spy in the area's haciendas, the band's members did not move in and out of the local peasant and peon societies and did not rely on them for asylum or economic support. While livestock taken from haciendas constituted the band's principal food source, the band members appropriated these animals themselves rather than receiving them from the peasantry, and they acquired the remainder of their diet from hunting and gathering and from crops planted at their main base.

To my mind, Calaxtrin's band is more accurately regarded not as a bandit band at all but as a nomadic raiding version of the *cimarrón* (maroon) societies that developed during the colonial period in many parts of the New World (Price 1973). Viewing Calaxtrin's band in these terms facilitates an understanding of the type of cultural creativity associated with the band. As Kopytoff (1976) argues in her study of fugitive slave communities in Jamaica, the members of these maroon communities did not reconstitute any particular African society in their refuge areas. Rather they created out of diverse African traditions a society and culture that was distinctively New World, "in tune with the social realities that surrounded them" (Kopytoff 1976:46). Their orientation, in other words, was forward-looking, not backward-looking (Ranger 1968).

Such an orientation appears to have characterized the members of Calaxtrin's band. Given the band's ethnic and cultural heterogeneity, the option of establishing a purely Indian or for that matter a purely African or European culture would not have been available, but there is no evidence that this alternative would have been attractive to the band's members even if it were possible. Rather, the sense one gets from reading the accounts of the band is that its members were extremely flexible and open in cultural matters, incorporating beliefs and practices from a variety of sources.

Cultural creativity in this or any other setting never involves the invention of an entirely new culture out of thin air. Most elements of the band's culture undoubtedly could be traced to Indian, African, or European antecedents or to modifications of these antecedents that developed during the previous 250 years of the colonial period. While some of its cultural practices possibly can be considered innovations, the band's cultural creativity resided primarily in its dynamic modification, elaboration, and recontextualization of preexisting beliefs and practices in the process of adapting to the special circumstances in which it lived.

This creativity can be seen throughout the band's culture. One example is its appropriation of Catholic symbols, rituals, and artifacts, apparently for inspiration and protection in connection with its raiding activities. Another is its adaptation of the indigenous use of peyote to the new purpose of incorporating captives into the band by transforming their consciousnesses. Another example, which possibly involved more innovation than the others, was the creation of a network of spies in the Spanish settlements, a development that exploited weaknesses in the colonial system deriving from a chronic labor shortage that allowed workers to move easily and frequently from one economic center to another.

Of the various factors that promoted cultural creativity in the context of Calaxtrin's band, three were particularly important. The first was the need to incorporate and coordinate large numbers of individuals of diverse cultural backgrounds. The second was the necessity to adapt to new economic conditions, which involved the creation of a rather sophisticated military organization to exploit the resources on the frontier and a more complex political organization to supervise the distribution of these resources and coordinate the emerging regional market in stolen livestock. The third factor derived from the necessity to establish a base of operations a safe distance from the Spanish settlements yet within striking range of them. In this region of northern Mexico the areas that met these requirements were only marginally suitable for agriculture, yet the majority of people in Calaxtrin's band originally were sedentary agriculturalists. The band's survival thus depended on the members adopting a more nomadic, hunting, gathering, and quasi-pastoral way of life, based in part on the adaptation created by the Apaches and other Indian groups to this rugged, arid area.

The type of cultural creativity that characterized Calaxtrin's band is consistent with what I perceive to be its revolutionary or at least proto-revolutionary goals. In the literature on colonial Nueva Vizcaya, raiding of Spanish haciendas and ranches often is portrayed as motivated almost exclusively by economic rather than political considerations (e.g., Navarro García 1964:303, 340, 442; Moorhead 1968:14). In this view, raiding was a more or less straightforward adaptation of a traditional nomadic hunting-and-gathering subsistence pattern to the new set of resources introduced by Europeans. The raiders are regarded as parasites whose overall survival strategy required them to stop short of destroying the Spanish establishments in order to continue exploiting them.

Such an understanding of colonial raiding perpetuates the misconception that the members of these raiding bands were geopolitically naive savages or criminals. This view probably could not be legitimately applied to any of the raiding bands operating in Nueva Vizcaya in the eighteenth century, but it clearly is inappropriate in the case of Calaxtrin's band. The available evidence suggests that this band intended to eliminate the elite class that owned and managed Nueva Vizcaya's principal haciendas and transfer this elite's wealth to its own members, most of whom were drawn from the ranks of the local rural proletariat. These goals clearly exceed the limited reformist aims that Hobsbawm (1981:26) suggests is characteristic of bandit bands and also differ at least in part from those typically associated with primary resistance and revitalization movements. While such movements often aspire to the complete destruction of the segments of colonial societies that seek or achieve domination over them, they tend to be strongly nativistic in orientation. Calaxtrin's band, in contrast, did not reject wholesale the culture of the society to which it was opposed. Rather, it adapted some aspects of this culture to its own purposes and embraced its material products—including the luxury goods of its principal enemy, the colonial elite—to the point in some cases of imitating their use in Spanish colonial society. Despite its important cultural dimensions, the resistance of Calaxtrin and his band was primarily political, directed not toward destroying all vestiges of European culture but rather toward destroying Spanish colonial society in order to establish control over its resources.

In a letter dated August 10, 1773, commandant-inspector O'Conor (1773b) informed the viceroy of New Spain that the "spies" held in the royal prison in Durango were to be sent on to Guadalajara. Whether Reyes, del Río, and the others ever left Durango and what their eventual fate was is unknown. During the fall and winter of 1773 O'Conor and his troops scouted sections of the Bolsón de Mapimí, searching without success for Calaxtrin's main camp (Bucareli y Ursúa 1773d, 1773e). When notified of the negative results of these expeditions, the viceroy concluded that his doubts about the veracity of the fifteen-year-old captive's report were well-founded. Although skepticism about some details of the captive's account perhaps was warranted, the viceroy's near-complete dismissal of the report is puzzling, particularly because we know that he was notified about the same time that a Spanish expedition from Coahuila and a second young captive had reported the existence of a large camp with crops in the Bolsón de Mapimí (O'Conor 1773a; Bucareli y Ursúa 1773c).

During the next decade the Spanish colonial government pursued a military and political strategy designed to eliminate the Bolsón de Mapimí as a refuge for raiding bands and promote peaceful relations with the Indian people in the region. As a consequence, the level of violence diminished somewhat, but ethnically diverse raiding bands continued to attack Spanish settlements throughout the 1780s and into the 1790s (Navarro García 1964; Gálvez 1951; Ugarte y Loyola 1788; Florez 1788). In the spring of 1784, twenty-four Tarahumaras accused of raiding and collaborating with Apaches were hanged and quartered in Chihuahua, while many others languished in jails across eastern Nueva Vizcaya (Marley 1983:115–117).

In the final decades of the colonial period—from the 1790s to 1821—the Spanish government's program of appeasement combined with intimidation and retribution produced a dramatic reduction in raiding activities (Navarro García 1964, 1965). This period of near tranquility came to an abrupt conclusion in 1831, when the postcolonial Mexican government suspended ration payments to Apache people who had settled near some of the northern presidios. The frequency of raiding quickly rose to the levels found during the most violent periods of the previous century. Tarahumaras and non-Indians are reported to have acted as spies, trading partners, and members of some of these bands, but Apaches were unquestionably responsible for the majority of the raiding, and in 1842 the Mexicans resumed ration payments to them. The ensuing peace remained tentative, however, until near the beginning of the twentieth century, when a war of extermination eliminated the remaining raiding bands in Chihuahua (Griffen 1988b:28–32, 69–80, 156–157; Altamirano and Villa 1988: vol. 3, 745–867).

Notes

I am indebted to José Luis Mirafuentes Galván for sharing his knowledge of resistance movements in northern New Spain with me. His *Movimientos de resistencia y rebeliones indígenas en el norte de México (1680–1821)* (1975) guided my search for documentation on Calaxtrin and his band. I also am grateful to William Taylor for his insightful comments on the initial version of this paper, to Cecilia Troop for her help in translating the more intractable sections of the Spanish documents, to Pamela Ballinger for her assistance in compiling information on resistance and the history of northern New Spain, to Jake Homiak for information on maroon societies in the Caribbean, to Alice Kehoe for comparative material on Plains Indian societies, and to Luis González Rodríguez for data on Jesuit and Franciscan missions in colonial Nueva Vizcaya. I also thank Julie Perlmutter for preparing the map, the Smithsonian Institution for providing financial support for this research, and Luis González Rodríguez and the Instituto de Investigaciones Antropológicas of the Universidad Nacional Autónoma de México for their hospitality during the summer of 1990.

1. Standard historical works on late colonial Nueva Vizcaya, such as Navarro García (1964) and Moorhead (1968), mention such multiethnic bands in passing. Considerable primary documentation on these bands can be found in Mexico City in the Archivo General de la Nación, especially in *Jesuitas*, vols. 2–27, *Historia*, vol. 299, *Cárceles y Presidios,* vol. 9, and *Provincias Internas*, vols. 41, 42, 43, 47, 49, 69, 128, 132, 142, 154, and 162. Most of the relevant documents in these volumes are summarized in Mirafuentes 1975.

2. The documents I have consulted in preparing this overview of Calaxtrin's band are housed in the Archivo General de la Nación in Mexico City. The testimonies of the people suspected of involvement with Calaxtrin's band along with the statement of the hacienda manager Carrera are found in *Provincias Internas*, vol. 132, fols. 276–370. The young captive's account is located in *Provincias Internas*, vol. 43, fols. 192–196. Commentaries by Spanish officials on these accounts

and other related materials are found in *Provincias Internas*, vol. 43, fols. 6–6v, 11–14, and 312–313v; *Cárceles y Presidios*, vol. 9, fols. 163–168v, 289–292v, and 415–416; *Correspondencia de Virreyes, Primera Serie*, vol. 40, nos. 1,014–1016, fols. 11v–17v; *Correspondencia de Virreyes, Primera Serie*, vol. 41, nos. 1,054–1,056, fols. 14–17v; *Correspondencia de Virreyes, Primera Serie*, vol. 44, nos. 1,143–1,147, fols. 20–27; and *Correspondencia de Virreyes, Primera Serie*, vol. 46, nos. 1,220, fols. 8v–14.

3. *Lobo* was a colonial racial category probably indicating here mixed Indian, African, and European ancestry.
4. Trinidad did not identify Calaxtrin by name, but his portrayal of the band's leader so closely resembles descriptions of Calaxtrin provided by other witnesses that we can assume that the two were the same man.
5. It is possible that the level of Tarahumara raiding did not itself increase after 1767 but rather the official awareness and reporting of the violence did, especially after the appointment in 1771 of O'Conor as commandant-inspector of the northern presidios.

References

Alcocer, José Antonio. 1958. *Bosquejo de la historia del Colegio de Nuestra Señora de Guadalupe y sus misiones, año de 1788*. Edited by Rafael Cervantes. Mexico City: Porrúa.

Altamirano, Graziella, and Guadalupe Villa, comps. 1988. *Chihuahua: Textos de su historia, 1824–1921*. 4 vols. Mexico City: Gobierno del Estado de Chihuahua, Instituto de Investigaciones Dr. José María Luis Mora, and Universidad Autónoma de Ciudad Juárez.

Arlegui, José. 1851. *Crónica de la Provincia de N.S.P.S. Francisco de Zacatecas*. 2d ed. Mexico City: Cumplido.

Bargas, Gregorio Xavier. 1762. Letter to Nicolás de Calatayud, San Borja, June 13, 1762. Mexico City, Archivo General de la Nación, *Jesuitas*, vols. 2–27, n.p.

Barragán, Francisco Nepomuceno. 1793. *Relación de los conventos, vicarías, y misiones que el rey tiene encomendados al cuidado de esta Provincia de N.S.P.S. Francisco de los Zacatecas* and Letter to Conde de Revilla Gigedo, Monterrey, October 26, 1793, Mexico City, Archivo General de la Nación, *Provincias Internas*, vol. 5, exp. 13, fols. 345–353.

Barray, Felipe de. 1857. "Resumen general de las hostilidades cometidas por los indios enemigos. . . ." In *Documentos para la historia de México*, 4th series, vol. 4, pp. 90–91. Mexico City: Imprenta de Vicente García Torres.

Benedict, H. Bradley. 1972. "El saqueo de las misiones de Chihuahua, 1767–1777." *Historia Mexicana* 22:24–33.

Braun, Bartholomé. 1764. *Carta del p[adre] Bartholomé Braun visitador de la Provincia Tarahumara a los p[adres] superiores de esta Provincia de Nueva Es-*

paña sobre la apostólica vida, virtudes, y santa muerte del p[adre] Francisco Hermano Glandorff. Mexico City: Colegio de San Ildefonso.

Bucareli y Ursúa, Antonio María de. 1773a. Letter to Julián de Arriaga, Mexico City, June 26, 1773. Mexico City, Archivo General de la Nación, *Correspondencia de Virreyes*, Primera Serie, vol. 39, no. 975, fols. 15–19.

———. 1773b. Letter to Hugo O'Conor, Mexico City, August 4, 1773. Mexico City, Archivo General de la Nación, *Cárceles y Presidios*, vol. 9, fols. 415–416.

———. 1773c. Letter to Julián de Arriaga, Mexico City, August 27, 1773. Mexico City, Archivo General de la Nación, *Correspondencia de Virreyes*, Primera Serie, vol. 41, no. 1,054, fols. 14–17.

———. 1773d. Letter to Julián de Arriaga, Mexico City, October 27, 1773. Mexico City, Archivo General de la Nación, *Correspondencia de Virreyes*, Primera Serie, vol. 44, no. 1,143, fols. 20–24v.

———. 1773e. Letter to Julián de Arriaga, Mexico City, December 27, 1773. Mexico City, Archivo General de la Nación, *Correspondencia de Virreyes*, Primera Serie, vol. 46, no. 1,220, fols. 8v–14.

Bustamante, Alexandro de. 1773. Deposition, Durango, June 30, 1773. Mexico City, Archivo General de la Nación, *Provincias Internas*, vol. 132, fols. 355–359v.

Campo, Francisco Javier del. 1773. Letter to "Señor Comisionado de Temporalidades," Villa de San Phelipe el Real [Chihuahua], August 20, 1773. Mexico City, Archivo General de la Nación, Temporalidades, vol. 8, fols. 264–265v.

Carrillo, Francisco Antonio. 1773. Letter to Fernando José Manguino, Chihuahua, February 5, 1773. Mexico City, Archivo Histórico de Hacienda, vol. 304, exp. 6, n.p.

Crummey, Donald, ed. 1986. *Banditry, Rebellion and Social Protest in Africa*. London: James Currey Ltd.; Portsmouth, N.H.: Heinemann Educational Books.

Cuéllar, Lope de. 1768. Letter to Marqués de Croix, Chihuahua, January 6, 1768. Mexico City, Archivo General de la Nación, *Provincias Internas*, vol. 98, Primera Parte, exp. 1, fols. 65–65v, 67–68v.

Davidson, David M. 1966. "Negro Slave Control and Resistance in Colonial Mexico, 1519–1650." *Hispanic American Historical Review* 46:235–253.

Deeds, Susan M. 1981. "Rendering unto Caesar: The Secularization of Jesuit Missions in Mid-Eighteenth Century Durango." Ph.D. diss., University of Arizona.

———. 1989. "Rural Work in Nueva Vizcaya: Forms of Labor Coercion on the Periphery." *Hispanic American Historical Review* 69:425–449.

Dunne, Peter M. 1948. *Early Jesuit Missions in Tarahumara*. Berkeley: University of California Press.

Fayni, José. 1773. Letter to Antonio María Bucareli y Ursúa, Durango, June 26, 1773. Mexico City, Archivo General de la Nación, *Provincias Internas*, vol. 43, fols. 6–6v, 11–13v [incomplete].

Fehrenbach, T. R. 1974. *Comanches: The Destruction of a People*. New York: Alfred A. Knopf.

Florez, Manuel Antonio. 1788. Letter to Antonio Valdés, Mexico City, June 24, 1788.

Mexico City, Archivo General de la Nación, *Correspondencia de Virreyes*, Primera Serie, vol. 146, no. 390, fols. 442–448v.

Gálvez, Bernardo de. 1951. *Instructions for Governing the Interior Provinces of New Spain, 1786.* Translated and edited by Donald E. Worcester. Berkeley, Calif.: Quivira Society.

Gerhard, Peter. 1982. *The North Frontier of New Spain.* Princeton, N.J.: Princeton University Press.

Griffen, William B. 1969. *Culture Change and Shifting Populations in Central Northern Mexico.* Anthropological Papers no. 13. Tucson: University of Arizona.

————. 1979. *Indian Assimilation in the Franciscan Area of Nueva Vizcaya.* Anthropological Papers no. 33. Tucson: University of Arizona.

————. 1988a. *Apaches at War and Peace: The Janos Presidio 1750–1858.* Albuquerque: University of New Mexico Press.

————. 1988b. *Utmost Good Faith: Patterns of Apache-Mexican Hostilities in Northern Chihuahua Border Warfare, 1821–1848.* Albuquerque: University of New Mexico Press.

Hobsbawn, Eric. 1959. *Primitive Rebels: Studies in Archaic Forms of Social Movement in the 19th and 20th Centuries.* New York: W. W. Norton.

————. 1981. *Bandits.* Rev. ed. New York: Pantheon Books.

Katz, Friedrich, ed. 1988. *Riot, Rebellion, and Revolution: Rural Social Conflict in Mexico.* Princeton, N.J.: Princeton University Press.

Kopytoff, Barbara. 1976. "The Development of Jamaican Maroon Ethnicity." *Caribbean Quarterly* 22:33–50.

Laba, Ignacio María. 1793. Letter to Conde de Revilla Gigedo, Guadalupe, Zacatecas, October 24, 1793. Mexico City, Archivo General de la Nación, *Provincias Internas*, vol. 5, exp. 13, fols. 332–337.

Lizasoain, Ignacio. 1763. "Informe del padre Lizasoain sobre las provincias de Sonora y Nueva Vizcaya." Mexico City, Biblioteca Nacional de México, Archivo Franciscano, leg. 15/280, fols. 1–30v.

Marley, David, ed. 1983. *Gazeta de México (enero a agosto de 1784).* Facsimile ed. Mexico City: Rolston-Bain.

Mirafuentes Galván, José Luis. 1975. *Movimientos de resistencia y rebeliones indígenas en el norte de México (1680–1821).* Vol. 1, *Guía Documental.* Colección Documental, no. 3. Mexico City: Archivo General de la Nación and Archivo Histórico de Hacienda.

Mooney, James. 1898. *Calendar History of the Kiowa Indians.* Bureau of American Ethnology, Annual Report 17, 129–445. Smithsonian Institution: Washington, D.C.

Moorhead, Max L. 1968. *The Apache Frontier: Jacobo Ugarte and Spanish-Indian Relations in Northern New Spain, 1769–1791.* Norman: University of Oklahoma Press.

Nava, Pedro de. 1794. Letter to Juan Isidro Campos, Chihuahua, February 7, 1794. Mexico City, Archivo General de la Nación, *Temporalidades*, vol. 50, fols. 27–28v.

Navarro García, Luis. 1964. *Don José de Gálvez y la comandancia general de las*

Provincias Internas del norte de Nueva España. Seville: Escuela de Estudios Hispano-Americanos.

————. 1965. *Las Provincias Internas en el siglo XIX*. Seville: Escuela de Estudios Hispano-Americanos.

O'Conor, Hugo. 1773a. "Diario de la marcha . . . a fin de conseguir la pacificación de los indios tarahumares, Atotonilco, June 23, 1773." Mexico City, Archivo General de la Nación, *Cárceles y Presidios*, vol. 9, fols. 163–168v.

————. 1773b. Letter to Antonio María Bucareli y Ursúa, Chihuahua, August 10, 1773. Mexico City, Archivo General de la Nación, *Cárceles y Presidios*, vol. 9, fols. 289–292v.

Opler, Morris E. 1983. "The Apachean Culture Pattern and Its Origins." In *Southwest*, edited by Alfonso Ortiz, 368–392, vol. 10 of *Handbook of North American Indians*, edited by William C. Sturtevant. Washington, D.C.: Smithsonian Institution Press.

Parrilla, Luis. 1794. Letter to Conde de Revilla Gigedo, Mexico City, April 10, 1794. Mexico City, Archivo General de la Nación, *Provincias Internas*, vol. 15, exp. 4, fols. 4–4v.

Porras Muñoz, Guillermo. 1980. *La frontera con los indios de Nueva Vizcaya en el siglo XVII*. Mexico City: Fomento Cultural Banamex.

Powell, Philip W. 1952. *Soldiers, Indians and Silver: North America's First Frontier War*. Berkeley: University of California Press.

Price, Richard, 1973. *Maroon Societies: Rebel Slave Communities in the Americas*. Garden City, N.Y.: Anchor Books.

Quiepo de Llanos, Pedro Antonio. 1773. Letter to Antonio María de Bucareli y Ursúa, Chihuahua, April 20, 1773. Mexico City, Archivo General de la Nación, *Provincias Internas*, vol. 42, fols. 404ff.

Ranger, T. O. 1968. "Connexions between 'Primary Resistance' Movements and Modern Mass Nationalism in East and Central Africa. Parts I and II." *Journal of African History* 9:437–453, 631–641.

Revilla Gigedo, Conde de. 1966. *Informe sobre las misiones—1793—e instrucción reservada al marqués de Branciforte—1794—*. Edited by José Bravo Ugarte. Mexico City: Editorial Jus.

Rubio Mañé, J. Ignacio. 1959. "El teniente coronel don Hugo O'Conor y la situación en Chihuahua, año de 1771." *Boletín del Archivo General de la Nación* 30:353–391.

San Vicente, Juan de. 1773. Letter to Antonio Bucareli y Ursúa, Chihuahua, March 30, 1773. Mexico City, Archivo General de la Nación, *Provincias Internas*, vol. 41, fols. 379–379v, 381.

Spicer, Edward H. 1962. *Cycles of Conquest: The Impact of Spain, Mexico, and the United States on the Indians of the Southwest, 1533–1960*. Tucson: University of Arizona Press.

Taylor, William B. 1988. "Banditry and Insurrection: Rural Unrest in Central Jalisco, 1790–1816." In *Riot, Rebellion, and Revolution: Rural Social Conflict in Mexico*, edited by Friedrich Katz, 205–246. Princeton, N.J.: Princeton University Press.

Ugarte y Loyola, Jacobo. 1788. Letter to Manuel Antonio Florez, Arispe, February 7, 1788. Mexico City, Archivo General de la Nación, *Provincias Internas*, vol. 112, exp. 2, fols. 182–186.

Vanderwood, Paul. 1982. "Bandits in 19th-Century Latin America: An Introduction to the Theme." *Bibliotheca Americana* 1:1–27.

Van Young, Eric. 1988. "Moving toward Revolt: Agrarian Origins of the Hidalgo Rebellion in the Guadalajara Region." In *Riot, Rebellion, and Revolution: Rural Social Conflict in Mexico*, edited by Friedrich Katz, 176–204. Princeton, N.J.: Princeton University Press.

Velasco y Restan, Andrés José de. 1773. Copy of report to José Fayni, Mapimí, July 8, 1773. Mexico City, Archivo General de la Nación, *Provincias Internas*, vol. 43, fols. 193–196.

Santiago's Horse: Christianity and Colonial Indian Resistance in the Heartland of New Spain

William B. Taylor

Violent conquest and, especially in the recent literature, peasant resistance have been compelling themes in the history of rural Mexico. Millenarian movements have captured the imagination of colonial historians lately (Barabas 1987; Florescano 1987; Gruzinski 1989; Van Young 1986, 1989), and for the national period Reed on the Caste War of Yucatán, Friedrich on the agrarian revolt of Tarascans in the Zacapu Valley of Michoacán in the early 1920s, and Womack and Warman on the valiant defense of their lands and communities by country people of Morelos offer unforgettable depictions of epic struggle and confrontation.[1] They "came to object," as Warman says, borrowing a phrase that village leaders have sometimes used in their petitions to the state during and after the colonial period. But there is much more to Mexico's rural past since the sixteenth century than conquest and armed resistance occasionally punctuating long intervals of political inactivity. Slower, less dramatically episodic histories and unobtrusive changes were occurring that reveal more about the

153

process of change and endurance. Concentrating on epic struggle and dramatic confrontations tends to polarize the long history of first encounters into exalted native resistance at one end and destruction or abject submission to the oppressor's ways at the other.

This polarization applies to colonial religious history as well. The literature is rich in works that emphasize what Spanish friars did to and for natives in the "Spiritual Conquest" and describe the sweeping replacement of native forms with Spanish forms in religious buildings during the sixteenth century as a metaphor of cultural change (Kubler 1961; Ricard 1933; Kobayashi 1974; Trexler 1984). Hartz called Catholicism "an effective weapon for imposing the European feudal ethos on men who had never known it"—people who were fundamentally submissive, if not passive (Hartz 1964:25,49). At this pole of the literature, Catholic priests were preeminent figures in their parishes, followed without much question by "the masses" (Brading 1973, 1983). At the other pole, Indians maintained a triumphal idols-behind-altars resistance, only pretending to convert and doing everything they could to avoid contact with the colonial government. Here priests appear to be insignificant players in local religious practice and the church is hardly worth mentioning as a factor in the social history of colonial Indian communities.[2]

These polarities do not account for much of the varied history of local religious practices and institutional relationships in the heartland of Mexico toward the end of Spanish colonial rule—a void that leads me to doubt the metaphor of conquest for colonial history and the separation of colonial encounters into violence perpetrated by Europeans and open resistance by natives. "Conquest" is the standard term for Spanish impositions in various parts of Latin America early in the sixteenth century. It rightly implies great changes and domination from outside. But it also implies a single, decisive act of destruction or domination and an early crystallization of colonial Indian culture that misses (1) the need for repeated acts of repression long after the first encounters, (2) continuities, reciprocities, and colonial Indian appropriations across the Conquest even in areas where Spanish control was greatest, and (3) the possibility of important changes in Indian communities throughout the colonial period.[3]

The violence-resistance polarity is a convenient place to begin a discussion of the earliest history of Europeans and Native Americans in the Mexican heartland, because there *was* collision. There was violence, terror, and destruction and some determined confrontation and resistance. But it is not a good place to end the discussion. Focusing too sharply on this distinction passes over most of the history of the old central areas of Spanish rule in which violent imposition and epic resistance were not directly involved. In Mexico's heartland most native subjects did not respond to the new religion with a sly rejection; nor did they flatly submit to subjugation.[4] Open resistance, accommodation, submission, and consent were not mutually exclusive or necessarily antithetical responses to Spanish rule and the official representation of Christianity. Resistance often was oblique; intending to construct a more satisfying world, it could manipulate the government's own logic while reinforcing the legitimacy and stability of Spanish rule.

This essay considers, through two examples, how local communities of Indians actively manipulated both the symbols and the institutions of Catholicism and how such symbols and institutions have multiple meanings for the colonial history of the descendants of Native Americans in Mexico. One example is Santiago—Christ's apostle, St. James the Greater; the other is a series of disputes between the priests and parishioners of a central Mexican parish in the 1760s and 1770s.

The emphasis is on local practices without separating localities from the wider colonial society or viewing local religion as neatly separable from the state religion or subject to change mainly in great transformations. This is not an entry into "popular" religion in the sense that local practices would have little to do with beliefs and formal organization. My intention is to follow Christian's view of local religion as providing "ways to deal with the local natural and social world, as well as the wider social, economic, and political network of which they are a part." For Christian the "practical impingement of the institutions of a central religion on the religious life of peasants" is as much a part of this history as the ways in which local practices may have departed from and challenged doctrine (Christian 1981, 1987:372).

Santiago and His Horse

Santiago is the saint who stood most clearly for the violence done by Spaniards to Native Americans in the conquest period of the sixteenth century yet continued to hold their attention long after the imposition of Spanish rule. In Spain Santiago stood for the *Reconquista*—Christianity on the march, the holy war against Islam in Iberia.[5] In the sixteenth century he crossed the Atlantic as a central image also in the Spanish expeditions into mainland America, was invoked for his aid and protection against Indian armies, and was claimed by the Franciscans as patron of their evangelical province of Xalisco and by the Dominicans in their province of Mexico.[6] For Spaniards he represented their destiny to rule and the Indians' destiny to submit. He was eagerly promoted by Spanish evangelizers as a personification of Christian conquest and widely accepted by Indians as a force to be propitiated and invoked.

The Humilladero chapel in Pátzcuaro, Michoacán, was known as one of the colonial monuments to this meaning of the saint and memory of the conquest. According to the Spanish Capuchin Fray Francisco de Ajofrín, who traveled in New Spain during the early 1760s, this "chapel of submission" commemorated a pivotal event in the conquest of Michoacán. At the site of the chapel Santiago appeared to the Spanish forces two hours before dawn on the day of battle. The Spaniards awoke "invigorated and full of courage," while the Indians awoke "confused and scared. Then, without raising their weapons, they gave up, humble and submissive."[7]

Images of Santiago and human impersonators of the saint were important props in the dramas of mock combat that Spaniards staged for themselves in America and promoted among Indian neophytes during the sixteenth and seventeenth centuries. In the Dance of the Moors and Christians, a standard form for these ritual military engagements, Indians reenacted the *Reconquista*, with Santiago leading the Christians into glorious victory over the infidel (Warman 1985:20, 60). The parallel with the Spanish conquest of Indian America would not have been lost on the native spectators and participants. As Trexler suggests, these early spectacles were intended as instruments of Spanish political control, "conquest through behavioral control," as he puts it, that "conjured a world safe for Hispanicism."[8] Through Santiago as fierce patron of the Spaniards, the memory of violent conquest remained alive, and villagers might welcome the sting of his sword at fiesta time as penance for their sins.[9] But Indian understandings were far from carbon copies of Spanish intentions.

Even the intentions were not so simple. In a late sixteenth-century account of missionary activity in the Franciscan province of Xalisco, Fray Francisco Mariano de Torres spoke of a similar association between Santiago and Indian submission but with the added implication that Indians might also share in the saint's protection. He reported that the Indians of the province, especially at Tonalá, were well disposed to the friars because the Apostle Santiago had fought there for the Spaniards,

showing himself to be a true son of thunder by conquering and frightening the Indians . . . and brandishing lightning to illuminate them. As soon as the venerable Padre

Segovia arrived, they recounted the events for him with astonishment. And taking advantage of this, this holy man began to preach to them of Christ's fidelity to Christians. (Torres 1960:47)[10]

As Padre Segovia understood, although Santiago was a primary symbol of the Spanish empire, the saint's patronage also conveyed the idea that Christian Indians might share in his formidable power.[11] Exemplifying this dual message, Santiago grew into an important if ambiguous symbol in colonial pueblos. Especially during the seventeenth and eighteenth centuries his representations in sculpture and painting—dressed in armor and mounted on a white horse with his sword raised to strike the infidels arrayed at the horse's feet[12]—were acquired and carefully preserved by villagers all over the heartlands of Spanish America.[13]

From the beginning of Christianity in the New World the ambiguities that made devotion to the images of Santiago more than cults of Indian humiliation went beyond this mixed Spanish message to the gulf between official explanations and Indian understandings. Before the 1560s there were few friars and secular priests in the Mexican heartland, and however energetic their efforts they were hampered by their small numbers, faulty understanding of native conceptions, and limited ability to communicate the subtleties of Catholic dogma in the local languages. Not surprisingly, colonial Indian Christians elaborated on the new religion in their own terms.[14]

Santiago's attraction to Indian neophytes was due partly to his horse. Judging by the monumental representations of fanged serpents and the intimate associations between eagles or jaguars and the most esteemed warriors, large and fierce animals close at hand were very important in prehispanic cosmologies as agents of divine power and representations of authority.[15] According to Clendinnen (1991b:82–83), native warriors regarded the Spaniards' horses not as obedient brutes or emblems of the owners' social standing but as courageous, powerful animal warriors that may have acted in unison with their riders but were independent of them. In the *Relación de Michoacán*, a 1541 account of native history and ceremony for western Mexico, during the Conquest Aztec emissaries and their Tarascan rivals shared this conception of horses as powerful, independent agents. They thought of the horses as armored deer with manes and long tails, possibly even as gods in their own right. The horses were said to talk to their Spanish riders and wield deadly firearms. They were worthy of the same tribute in food as the Spaniards (*Relación de las ceremonias* 1977:238, 241, 264–266).

Indians of Mexico had no large domesticated animals and thus might well have perceived trained responses as expressions of the animal's will. Even at a distance, the sight and sounds of a cavalry charge left lasting impressions of the horses' strength and ferocity—the ground rumbling under their hooves, metal shoes flashing and kicking up dust and bits of earth, eyes rolling, nostrils dilated, big teeth showing behind foaming lips, and unearthly whinnying and panting—that were epitomized in Santiago's mount.[16] Writing after 1620, Francisco de San Antón Muñón Chimalpahín C., the Indian chronicler from Amecameca, reportedly recorded a local tradition about the conquest of Mexico in which Santiago's horse killed and wounded as many of the enemy with his mouth as the saint did with his sword.[17]

A pervasive native belief that also would have been folded into early colonial understandings of Santiago was that animals were agents of greater forces working upon human destiny. An animal could be the manifestation of divinity; it could be infused with the migratory spirit of a *nagual* (wizard); and it could be the protective yet vulnerable associate (*tona*) that every human individual had (Aguirre Beltrán 1963:98–112; Musgrave-Portilla 1982). As manifestations of the divine, animals could directly injure and destroy. They could also signal an impending disaster, as in the belief that when an owl's hoot was heard or a large fly called the Miccarayoli was seen circling a house, someone inside would soon die (Ribadeneira y Barrientos 1771:251–265).[18]

Precisely how beliefs in animal associations with the spiritual welfare of humans affected Indian attraction to and understandings of Santiago remains uncertain. Was the saint regarded as a Christian wizard exercising great power through the horse? Could he, like a precolonial deity-impersonator, transform himself into the horse? Did the horse's whiteness suggest the color's ominous associations with death and uncertainty in Nahuatl thought and thereby reinforce the message of defeat and humiliation? Were colonial Indians in central Mexico inclined to an Indo-European mythology of equine ambivalence in which horses represented rebirth as well as death, freedom as well as a taming of the wild (Doniger 1987)? Could the horse, as a partly domesticated animal that protected Christians, be separated from the saint and appropriated by Indians? As the seventeenth- and eighteenth-century examples that follow suggest, over time there would certainly be local departures from the Spaniards' use of Santiago to symbolize Indian defeat and humiliation.

The dances of Moors and Christians introduced by Spaniards in the first colonial generation were reworked by parishioners and priests.[19] By the late sixteenth century Santiago's providential aid to Christians in battle was being transferred to mock engagements between mounted Indian townspeople and impersonators of wild, heathen Chichimecs. Well before the Europeans' arrival, nomads of north-central Mexico were regarded by sedentary communities and states to the south as Chichimecs, or barbarous invaders and looters.[20] By the late sixteenth century the Moors-and-Christians theme sometimes was rescripted with "Chichimec" interlopers being dislodged by local heroes. For instance, in 1590 the Franciscan Fray Alonso Ponce was welcomed into the village of Patamba (Michoacán) by about twenty Indian guards on horseback (one on a white horse, like Santiago), dressed as Spaniards and armed with wooden swords and pikes, who beat the roadside trees and brush shouting "Santiago, Santiago" and skirmished with ten or twelve "Chichimecs" who came out of the woods on foot (Warman 1985:81). In another spectacle enacted in Michoacán on the Day of the Holy Cross in 1643, the engagement of Christian Indians and "Chichimecs" followed the Moors-and-Christians scenario more closely. The Christian Indians assaulted a "castle" defended by "Chichimecs." The spectacle culminated in the arrival of Santiago, who vanquished the enemy and recovered the cross (Warman 1985:97–98). Like the Moors-and-Christians pageants, these new spectacles represented the triumph of Christianity over paganism in America and warned settled Indians about barbarousness and backsliding. But they could carry another, more indigenist message that was less apparent in the mock battles between Moors and Christians: Santiago protects local places against their enemies. This message would have been appealing in Michoacán, which provides the two examples. Like the territory of modern Jalisco, Querétaro, and Hidalgo, in parts of Michoacán Chichimec incursions were known to sixteenth-century villagers as much more than legends.

Although the dances of Moors and Christians came to be Indian events in the eighteenth century (Warman 1985:100), in middle- and late-colonial *pueblos* Santiago was not mainly a symbol of the Conquest or, at least, not mainly a terrifying or paralyzing signal to submit to the force of Spanish authority. He became more a local patron or a foil to the sense of community autonomy. Even where he was not the community's patron saint, Santiago's power was being harnessed to local purposes—to heal, protect, and fertilize. In 1624 at Ixmiquilpan in central Hidalgo, where nomadic Chichimecs still threatened colonial peace, an Indian named María reportedly claimed that her renowned curing powers resulted from having had intercourse with an invisible Spaniard who came, like Santiago, on a white horse. In María's vision the power of this man was transferred to her directly, without mediation or supplication.[21] Here the Spanish conquest was turned on its side: By union with the phantom Spaniard, she was magically empowered. Her vision contained a radical independence that is a short step from the idea that Santiago's power could be acquired and directed against one's enemies, individual or collective.[22]

More commonly, Santiago was called upon for help with the weather because of his association with thunder and lightning.[23] According to Jacinto de la Serna, who had ministered in the Tenango del Valle district early in the seventeenth century, an Indian shaman there tried to alter the direction of clouds and storms as the corn harvest approached by appealing to Christ, the Blessed Virgin, and Santiago. His supplication to Santiago referred to the saint's virility, courage, and military might and begged for empowerment: "Santiago, young man, help me, virtuous man, strong conqueror, and courageous man, make me powerful and help me so that the works and deeds of God Almighty are not lost."[24]

In the eighteenth century, while the old images of Santiago in the parish church were approached by Indian villagers for the same favors, attention increasingly was drawn to the horse, as if the animal had become the saint. According to Antonio de Ribadeneira y Barrientos in the commentaries he prepared for the Fourth Provincial Council's meetings in 1771, if a pregnant Indian was unable to give birth, an offering of corn would be made to Santiago's horse (Ribadeneira y Barrientos 1771:no. 54). In 1769 Indians of Tescala in the district of Huixquilucan near the Valley of Mexico were reported to have danced the forbidden dance of the Santiaguitos, in which a pony was adorned, incensed, and venerated. The saint, again, had left the spotlight.[25]

As with Tescala's pony, the late colonial examples generally express a shift away from the saint himself and suggest community more than individual practices. Community fiestas centering on Santiago appear quite often in the written record from the 1760s, perhaps largely because colonial authorities at that time intended to eliminate what they regarded as uncontrolled village celebrations generally and the dance of the Santiaguitos in particular.[26] This dance may also have become more popular in the preceding years, although that is less certain. In any case, prelates attending the Fourth Provincial Council were particularly worried about the pagan and anticolonial implications of the dance as they understood it, especially the song that accompanied the dancing. The Franciscan provincial said he had heard from reliable witnesses that the song was a lament by the Indians over their conquest by the Spaniards. The *cura* of Otumba added that he "had not been able to comprehend the language [of the song]." When he asked the Indians what the words meant, "they replied that they meant the same as arrogant or haughty, which referred to the sainted Apostle."[27]

The dances of the Santiaguitos may not have been as threatening as the church leaders imagined in 1771, but in an 1815 celebration at San Andrés, in the district of San Pedro Tlaquepaque (outside Guadalajara), Santiago was the focal point for what appeared to be both symbolic submission and resistance to colonia authority. In August of that year the Indian officials of San Andrés unsuccessfully petitioned the high court in Guadalajara for permission to hold their traditional dance of the Tastuanes on the day of San Pedro (September 8). According to the district governor, a local man dressed as Santiago would ride through the plaza hitting masked Indian pedestrians with the flat of his sword. Explaining that the dance ended with the people surging forward to pull down and manhandle the "saint," he concluded that "the worst of the matter" is "the many obscenities that they mutter both in Spanish and Nahuatl, and also their indecent actions once they turn to 'stripping the skin' from the one who acts as Santiago."[28]

This ending may have been doubly disturbing to a district governor: It appears to be, first, an inversion of the Moors-and-Christians scenario in which Santiago appears at the decisive moment to rout the Moors and, second, an echo of precolonial rituals such as the festival of Toxcatl described by Sahagún for Tenochtitlan, which ended with the deity impersonator (*ixiptla*) of Tezcatlipoca being assaulted and stripped of his mask and regalia and then sacrificed.[29] What had begun in sixteenth-century Jalisco as a commemoration of Santiago's timely aid to Spaniards under attack at Guadalajara by thousands of hostile Indians in 1541 and had grown into an annual reenactment of the miracle in Indian pueblos of Nueva Galicia by the early seventeenth century[30] was strangely twisted in this late colonial performance from the same region.

There were, then, multiple meanings and a growing ambivalence in Santiago's significance to Indians of central Mexico in the late colonial period. His various meanings were rooted not only in the official Spanish messages about conquest and conversion but also in native understandings of animals and the sacred and in adjustments to colonial rule at the local level. Even in the sixteenth century, when the performances were more often directed by and performed for colonial authorities, Santiago's official significance was mixed. The early message of Indian submission and Spanish power included the problematical (to colonial governors, at least) idea that Indian converts could also be protected by the Spaniards' patron saint of war. Santiago remained an armed avenger, but his enemies were the enemies of Christ, not Indians in particular.[31]

The notion of protection would become more complicated and localized as it grew in importance toward the end of the colonial period. The saint could be propitiated and invoked for his protection[32]; crop failures and other misfortunes could be lamented as his punishment for individual and collective sins; or he could be attacked and insulted in spectacles of inversion that also separated him from his horse. In some cases the saint virtually disappeared or became the horse, a force of nature and potential protector physically more powerful than a man but possibly harnessed to its master's uses. These variations from the original messages suggest that, in spite of the continuing interest in Santiago, the way was prepared for his demotion, unless he was the patron saint of the community, or for his transformation into an animal benefactor with mainly local meaning.[33] In all these cases, whether regarded as a source of special favor or as an object of ridicule, Santiago was a focal point of *local* expression, attached to pueblos, neighborhoods, and individual believers. Father Serna's shaman apparently was little concerned, if it occurred to him at all, that his appeal to Santiago to move the rain clouds might deprive another community of life-giving moisture.

Indians and the Arancel of 1767

Santiago makes an attractive case study in the contested cultural history of Spanish rule, but he is harder to document and contextualize than some less eye-catching institutional aspects of local religion and politics such as the relations between parish priests (*curas*) and their Indian parishioners. From the beginning of Spanish colonization, *curas* were royal appointees, located at sensitive intersections between Indian subjects and higher authorities. In the Hapsburg conception of the state, which envisioned two majesties—the Crown as father and the Church as mother—no clear line divided secular and religious life. Until the mid-eighteenth century an energetic *cura* might operate quite freely as keeper of public order and morals, punishing adulterers, gamblers, and drunkards and reporting more serious offenses to royal judges. He and his assistants (*vicarios*) also were expected to report to the higher levels of royal government on agricultural conditions, natural disasters, local disturbances, and other political news; record the population; supervise the annual elections of village officers in communities within the parish; and help maintain social control in other ways. He could be a patron in times of illness and want. As a moral and spiritual father and healer and a literate local resident often able to speak the native language of his parishioners, the *cura* was well placed to represent the requirements of the state to rural people and interpret their obligations, as well as intercede for them with higher authorities.

One protracted dispute, between the priests and Indian parishioners of Ozoloapan in the jurisdiction of Temascaltepec (Estado de México) from 1767 to 1776—an important juncture in the high politics of church and state—will serve to illustrate some of the complexity of village Indian resistance and accommodation to colonial pressures in the eighteenth century (AGN Clero Regular y Secular 23 exp. 6, Clero Regular y Secular 68 exp. 2). The Ozoloapan dispute, which centered on the fees and services the parish priest could properly collect for baptisms, marriages, funerals, blessings, and the like, was also understood by all its participants to involve his wider authority to direct the public life of the parish. The two priests who served at Ozoloapan over the dispute's nine-year course repeatedly complained about the Indians' refusal to pay the proper fees and perform the customary services and their disrespect for clerical authority. The Indians, for their part, complained that the priests were behaving oppressively—imposing excessive fees and using unwarranted violence. Both parties appealed to colonial superiors, especially the *audiencia* (the high court in Mexico City), to define the limits of colonial authority and local autonomy within the parish.

The record begins with a complaint in 1767 by the *cura*, Mariano Ruis Coronel, against the Indians of San Juan Atexcapan. Father Ruis reported that within a few weeks of his appointment to the parish, in December 1766, the Indians of this outlying village had secured an order from the archbishop's attorney general that the new priest must follow the *arancel* (a schedule of fees for sacramental services approved and published by the archbishop). The Indians presented the *arancel* to Father Ruis in a haughty manner, saying that they had secured it only for their pueblo, not for the parish as a whole. Now, in his words, "under cover of this order" and on the "frivolous pretext of the litigation" and their alleged poverty, the Indians were "behaving in such an insolent and disorderly way that they are paying none of the parish duties" and refusing to perform all the customary services agreed to in writing in 1758. The *cura* felt personally injured by the Indians' "malice": They intended "to do damage to my personal reputation and station" even though, he said, he had always acted "in a benign, loving, and impartial way."

In response to the priest's complaint, the *audiencia* ordered the *teniente* (deputy) of the district governor in Ozoloapan to see that the Indians paid their fees according to the *arancel*. Father Ruis replied with thanks but lamented that because of "the isolation of this place, the broken terrain, the insolence of the Indians, and difficult access to the markets" there was no one he could count on to help him hold the Indians to their obligations.

Both the date and the form of this opening salvo are significant. Before 1767 sacramental fees in most parishes were determined by custom and local agreement rather than by the *arancel* of 1637, with its various amendments. There was great variation from parish to parish, and for a long time there were only occasional formal complaints in which Indian parishioners requested enforcement of the old *arancel* instead of customary fees and services. During the 1750s, however, uncertainty about the proper fees increased as parishes administered by the regular orders were secularized. The new secular *curas* often were said to have disregarded or revised customary fees, and Indians sometimes responded by withholding payment, refusing to abide by the customary fee schedule, failing to attend Mass, or pressing for division of the old parish territories. *Curas* sometimes retaliated by withholding services. And both sides went to court in record numbers.

Intended, as Archbishop Lorenzana put it, to "cut the habit of litigation at its roots," establish a "fixed rule," and provide a decent living for *curas* who lacked other resources, the new *arancel* of July 1767, issued a few months after the Ozoloapan litigation began, mainly added to the confusion. Indians could ask for the *arancel* to be applied or could choose to follow customary obligations. Because local interests and customary obligations varied, there was considerable uncertainty over which course would be most advantageous to the Indian parishioners. The revised fee schedule of the 1767 *arancel* listed little of what villagers customarily paid and none of the labor service they performed. Whatever the cause, formal disputes over *aranceles* were numerous throughout the period 1767 to 1810, far more numerous than before 1767. Many were lodged by Indians to force the *cura* to abide by the published schedule, but many others were initiated by *curas* who complained that Indian pueblos demanding the *arancel* complied only with those provisions that suited them. Of course some *curas* wanted the *arancel*, too, even if it meant temporary confusion and a small reduction in income, for it produced cash rather than a welter of goods, cash, and services and was easier for the priest to administer. But even where the *cura* and parishioners both wanted the *arancel*, bitter disputes could arise. One reason is that *curas* began pressing to perform more of the services that required fees, especially Sunday Mass outside the parish seat, elaborate funerals, and processions and feast day celebrations in the main church.

Whether the *cura* preferred custom or the *arancel*, he was likely to regard his clerical fees as a right, to be defended as the essence of his authority. As one *cura* put it in an aggressive letter to his Indian lay assistant (*fiscal*) in an outlying village,

Tell the sons of that *pueblo* that the clerical fees are by order of natural law, divine law, ecclesiastical law, and royal law. It is not a voluntary contribution, as you and the others seem to think. Just as I am obliged to give you spiritual care, you are obliged to care for my material needs, as St. Paul says. (AGN Clero Regular y Secular 75 exp. 5, fol. 326, Br. Francisco de la Cueva, *cura* of San Luis de las Peras, April 29, 1786)

Verbal intimidation, physical punishment, and ceremonies of deference were familiar instruments of the priest's power. However, in resorting to the power of the written word, this *cura* found his pen turned against him. His letter survives because the Indian recipient saved it to use as evidence of the priest's unfatherly conduct.

By 1768 the Atexcapan *arancel* dispute had bubbled over into the three other villages of the parish of Ozoloapan, and the four pueblos together secured a court order that required the *cura* to follow the new *arancel*. On December 8, 1768, as Father Ruis was preparing to leave for Atexcapan to celebrate the Feast of the Immaculate Conception, an Indian of the head town died. The priest sent his Indian deputy, the *fiscal*, to the mourners with a message that the fee would be four pesos for the burial. Before leaving town he authorized his notary to permit the burial once the fee was paid. According to Father Ruis, the next day the entire village council, including the *fiscal*, buried the body in the church with full honors and the cross raised on high—ignoring the notary who had confronted the mourners at the church door, saying he would allow them to proceed once the fees were paid. On December 13 Ruis wrote a complaint to the *audiencia* and added that the Indians of the parish were not showing him or the holy Church proper respect; for example, Indian officials had pulled a parishioner out of church by the hair during Mass on the eve of the Immaculate Conception feast and whipped him just outside. Ruis repeated that he could do nothing because there was no one to help. He asked for a judicial order that the Indians of the four pueblos must obey the first *audiencia* decree ordering the Indians of Atexcapan to pay their fees according to the *arancel*. The Indian officials of the head town replied that they had waited for the *cura*'s return to start the burial and that after they had paid three pesos he had authorized them to proceed.

Widening application of the new *arancel* after 1767 moved the relationship between *cura* and communicants toward a financial transaction. In a way this is what many Indians from outlying pueblos, like the Atexcapans, would have wanted: It reduced or eliminated labor service to the *cura* and people of the parish seat and other inconvenient and disagreeable acts of subservience that had been customary.[34] The desire of remote villagers to loosen the bonds of customary service to the parish priest echoes the tension between subject villages and head towns apparent in the late eighteenth-century attempts by many subordinate pueblos to gain the legal status of head towns or parish seats or at least get their own resident priest. After the 1767 *arancel*, which raised the fee for Mass in the outlying villages to twice that of the head town, the *cura* or his itinerant *vicarios* could find the church doors locked against them when they traveled outside the parish seat to perform the service of the Eucharist.

In early 1769 Indians of one of the pueblos complained to the *alcalde mayor* (district governor) that his lieutenant for Ozoloapan had arrested two of their officials at the *cura*'s request for not paying the customary fees. The *audiencia* responded that the Indians were to be released if the *arancel* dispute was the only reason for the arrests. It added that the *cura* was to obey the *arancel*. Apparently the claims in court were suspended at this point, although the dispute itself had not been resolved. Ruis left Ozoloapan in 1770, having won a more desirable parish in the periodic competitions for vacant posts.

The judicial record picks up again in August 1771, when the Indian *alcalde* of Atexcapan accused the new *cura*, Simón de Castañeda, of using "loathsome force" in violation of royal laws and in disregard of the *arancel*: of whipping Indians, including the *fiscal*, who was whipped in public with his pants down, and of not permitting confession at Easter until the fees for Mass in the outlying pueblos were paid. The *alcalde* went on to complain of the villagers' "life of oppression" under this *cura* who, he said, claimed to be the king of the parish. The *audiencia* responded with the standard terse order for all parties to follow the *arancel*.

In the late eighteenth century Indian pueblos often greeted new parish priests with a lawsuit—if not over clerical fees then over local elections or control over the treasuries of lay brotherhoods. This tendency was abetted by the rapid turnover of parish priests, especially after the last round of secularization of parishes starting in the 1750s. Among other things these suits provided a means for village leaders to put some distance between themselves and the *cura*, show him where local authority was to reside, and assert the autonomy of the local community without challenging the authority of the Crown. These were contests in which there were winners and losers. Both sides used the verb *ganar* (to win) for verdicts that did not obviously favor the other party.

Some *curas* observed that their Indian parishioners believed that the *arancel* had freed them from obedience to the priest in other matters. Many suits that began as disputes over clerical fees became more general, looping complaints against the *cura*. Indian parishioners in these disputes were remarkably reluctant to compromise with the *cura* and settle with him extrajudicially (where the *cura* was intransigent, compromise would have been all but impossible in any case). In some cases they were simply determined to go directly to higher authorities in Mexico City, bypassing the *cura*'s traditional authority as mediator and judge. The villagers' growing inclination to avail themselves of the high courts in disputes with the parish priest enhanced the mediating role of the *audiencias* and the Indians' attorneys in Mexico City and Guadalajara, who often were retained permanently to look after whatever legal actions the community might have pending. Indeed, there were well-known cases of attorneys encouraging pueblos to litigate. And the *audiencia* itself must have been aware that the Indians' new litigiousness with their priests by the 1760s was encouraged by—and took advantage of—the royal decrees secularizing parishes and expelling the Jesuits and other administrative attempts to redefine parish priests as spiritual specialists.

In August 1772 Father Castañeda wrote a blistering reply to the Indians' complaint, emphasizing what he called their "perverse nature." He knew that trouble awaited him when he first arrived because, although it was "customary for the entire village council to meet me and accompany me to the head town, none of the officials except the *fiscal* did so." The Indians, he added, resisted the new *arancel*'s fees for Mass in the outlying pueblos, and the Indian *alcalde* ignored his call for the establishment of a school. During the ceremony in which the *cura* formally invested the village officials with their staffs of office, he had exhorted the *alcalde* to fulfill his obligations, to which this Indian retorted: "The *cura* should stick to giving Mass and confession, and only when he is called. Otherwise he should stay in his house."

The Indian official's *vara*, or staff of office, was apt to be featured in dramatic confrontations involving both threats and the kind of violence that left bruises and broken bones. Defiant Indians brandished their *varas*; priests responded by striking out with their own silver-tipped canes and angrily seizing the officials' staffs. One priest who was particularly fond of minatory gestures imprisoned the Indian council's staffs. Such physical conflict involving these symbols of office points to the wider assault at that time on the judicial role of parish priests that was part of the Spanish Bourbons' reformulation of church-state relations in the late eighteenth century.

Father Castañeda went on to recount how the same *alcalde* came to the parish seat escorted by his village councillors during Easter week in 1772. The *cura* rebuked him for his disobedience in not attending church in the head town and not making other Indians from his pueblo do so. According to Castañeda, the *alcalde*'s reply was so heated and offensive that he had to order up twelve lashes. At this point one of the councillors rose to the *alcalde*'s defense, shouting to the other Indians to help him, and "they threw themselves upon me, shoving their staffs of office in my face and saying they would defend themselves with the staffs, for the king had given these to them for that purpose."

In August the *alcalde* had gone to Mexico City, promising to obtain another *cura* for the parish. In the meantime the Indians were not fulfilling their Christian duties. They went elsewhere for baptism and did not call him to administer the last rites so that, "thanks to their depraved character and addiction to a brutal licentiousness, they have gone to eternity without the slightest spiritual aid." The *alcalde*, he had heard, had been collecting small contributions of a *real* (one-eighth of a silver peso) or two from all households to continue the lawsuit against the *cura*. Castañeda blamed the "malevolence of the Indian *alcalde*" and the administrator of a nearby hacienda, Don Francisco Maroto. Indians in general were easily taken in by outside agitators, he said, and some of the recalcitrants were Maroto's sharecroppers and thus under his control. The *cura* continued his litany of complaints against Maroto, especially that he buried Indians in the hacienda chapel without the priest's permission, saying he was the lord of the chapel as well as of the hacienda and "in both, he alone gives the orders." Castañeda also blamed the Indians' attorney in Mexico City, an "unprincipled defense counsel and source of discord between *curas* and their parishioners." Castañeda said he had complained to the deputy district governor but had received no help. Later in 1772 the *audiencia* issued yet another short decree for the parish of Ozoloapan: The *cura* was to follow the *arancel* and the Indians were to do their Christian duties.

The record ends with a document dated October 6, 1776, in which the attorney for the Indians of Atexcapan petitioned for better spiritual care, claiming that Father Castañeda had been cruel to his clients, levying excessive charges and not obeying the *arancel* despite two *audiencia* verdicts to this effect won by the Indians. Castañeda, the petition alleged, had imprisoned the *alcalde* when payments were not to his satisfaction, had failed to confess anyone at Easter, did not celebrate Mass in Atexcapan, and rarely came to confess the dying. When asked to do so, he had allegedly replied, "Let the devil take them." No reply from the *audiencia* or further action by the priest or parishioners is recorded in these files.

After failing to win a clear victory at court, the Ozoloapan *curas*, previously so energetic in defense of their local interests, withdrew from the fray. Father Ruis Coronel found another post as quickly as he could; Father Castañeda spent less and less time in the outlying pueblos. Both were familiar career patterns: Parish priests, and especially their *vicarios*, often remained in a parish for only a few years, or they became rooted in the head town or stayed away from the parish for months at a time. But for these two *curas* the prolonged *arancel* disputes also lengthened the emotional distance between pastor and parish. The formal disputes hardened their feelings of isolation, fear, loneliness, and helplessness, as well as their worst judgments of Indians as cunning imbeciles who were adept at using their protected legal position to win unjust orders from the *audiencia*. *Curas* in such circumstances often spoke of Indians as "this ignorant rabble," "Moors without a lord," "deceitful and lazy," and people of "small hearts and lowly spirits." Indian towns were "seminaries of disputes." The Ozoloapan priests' failure to gain more than minimal support from the *teniente* when local defiance peaked in 1767 and 1772 and the disappointing verdicts from the *audiencia* added to their frustration over the challenges to their traditional duties as father, judge, and enforcer in the moral life of the parish.

The immediate answer to why so many formal complaints over clerical fees were made by Indian parishioners and priests after 1767 would seem to be the encouragement of the Crown, the archbishop, the *audiencia*, and licensed attorneys. But in every parish involved there were other reasons as well. Incoming *curas*, especially in newly secularized parishes, depended on the sacraments for a living and might well violate local practices to increase their income from fees, or parishioners might treat the arrival of a new pastor as a chance to change the customary fees to their advantage. A parish priest might be opposed for personal immorality, excessive use of force, demands for labor service, business interests, and control over community property and elections during this time of population growth, land shortages, new administrative demands, and declining real wages.

The Ozoloapan case documents two other kinds of brokers and men of influence in late colonial villages who contributed to the suits against parish priests. One was the hacienda administrator, who used his association with Indian sharecroppers to feed the conflict. The other was the local Indian who took up a collection from fellow villagers to launch lawsuits in the name of the community. In the Atexcapan example he was a village official, but often he was a self-appointed legal agent with connections to a lawyer in Mexico City—a political entrepreneur who had been left off the ladder of community offices. If he succeeded in court at the priest's expense, his reputation soared and the path was cleared for his election to community office and further enrichment. Leaders of this kind often were the product of intense factionalism within villages, and a successful litigation against the *cura* could signal the rise of a new group to local influence.[35]

But even in this case of estrangement and hostility toward the *curas* it is clear from the Atexcapan Indians' desire for a priest and the sacraments that they were not leading a pagan revival or a separatist movement. They accepted the dogma of the church as it was taught to them; they were concerned with salvation in Christian terms, with the "welfare of our souls," as they put it. Even when their feelings toward him ran more to fear and anger than to love and respect, the *cura* was clearly an important spiritual figure for them, not an object of indifference or simply an adversary or hired hand.

It would be a mistake to speak of *curas* in these circumstances only as they described themselves—as isolated, lonely, defenseless servants of God—or only as the Indians described them to colonial judges—as omnipotent tyrants. These descriptions are important social facts in themselves, but they are too much like the bad priest–good priest antinomy that streaks the literature on the Church in Mexican history—from Fernández de Lizardi's greedy, alienated *curas* in *El periquillo sarniento*, "who make a profit from living and dead parishioners alike," to apologies that treat *curas* generally as selfless community leaders of unquestioned paternal authority. Few of the *curas* documented in late colonial records, including those of Ozoloapan, were poised to be tyrants or martyrs. As intermediaries and specialists in rites of passage for individual believers and the community and in the mysteries of a powerful state religion, they possessed instruments of influence, well-being, and terror; and their contacts outside the community, their traditional part in policing public life, their economic interests, and their command of the written word gave them added access to power. They were rarely the unquestioned local leaders, however, and their effective influence, always contingent, was under sharp attack in the late colonial period.

The elusive Santiago and his horse and the more readily located confrontations between the priests and parishioners of Ozoloapan suggest that Indian responses in the Mexican heartland to late colonial political pressures focused on local rule and protection against more demands from Spanish authority without challenging that authority or contributing much to Indian class identity. Both the patronage of Santiago's horse and the independence contained in the *alcaldes'* staffs of office reflect a localized Christian identity that interpreted and adjusted to the received beliefs and expectations of priests and other colonial officials. As Weismann has written about popular art in the late eighteenth century, colonial Indian culture was "not so much disrespectful of [official] tradition as untamed by it, surmounting it" (Weismann and Sandoval 1985:198).

The priest in these Indian parishes supplied the framework for Catholic practice. He was central to rites of the life cycle, weekly Mass, annual confession and communion, the periodic feast days and blessings, and the administration of church affairs. He also might exercise considerable influence through his economic interests and political activities, but in general he appears to have been a good deal less important to the religious aspects of everyday life, especially outside the parish seat. The fact that local religious practices focused on parishioners' earthly life did not directly challenge the priest and his concern for Christian souls. They could be congruent and overlapping in ways that confirmed the Christianity of Indian villagers and explain their desire for a resident priest. These eighteenth-century villagers generally had come to regard themselves as good, even superior Christians, but theirs was an "applied" Christianity marked in the priests' minds by drunkenness, animistic propitiation, a possessive materialism, and a less than sufficient regard for sin and individual salvation that was likely to dishearten and sometimes repel their Catholic ministers.

From an image widely disseminated by early colonial authorities as a primary symbol of their destiny to rule a Christian empire and deliver the gift of God's protection to converts, Santiago became a saint attached to local meanings (including the old ones intended by the authorities). As colonial authorities suspected, there were subversive if not pagan implications in these departures from the original message of the conquerors, but only in the seventeenth-century vision of María, the healer from Ixmiquilpan, was Santiago's sword poised to

challenge the colonial order. When a widespread struggle for political and social liberation swept Mexico in 1810, his sword was sheathed. Santiago was not
the symbol to activate that national cause, any more than he could much hearten
early nineteenth-century royalists in their defense of New Spain.[36]

The litigiousness of the Ozoloapan pueblos and Indian officials there shak-
ing their royal staffs of office at the *cura* resisted the acts of one kind of colonial official while validating colonial authority at a higher level. This chain of
disputes over clerical fees and election procedures took its cue from recent royal
and archiepiscopal decrees to standardize the schedule of fees and limit the
curas' local authority in favor of royal governors. While expressing a determined opposition to labor service, externally imposed alterations of clerical
fees, and other perceived injustices, these late colonial lawsuits and protests
were framed as supplications for the king's favor. Their petitions and complaints
to the colonial courts more often began with "Venimos a pedir" ("We come to
request") than "Venimos a contradecir" ("We come to object"). And the *audiencia's* mechanical rulings that all parties must follow the *arancel* seem to have
been a sufficient victory for most Indian litigants.

Although these lawsuits were always presented in the name of the community, resistance of this kind did not simply express communal solidarity against
intrusive outsiders. They could also express personal ambitions, factional divisions, and other kinds of local dissension. And written evidence of religious and
ceremonial practices tends to highlight corporate community behavior, whether
directed from above or originating from below, leaving the misleading impression of little conflict within communities.

In the Ozoloapan disputes and the Santiago performances, colonial Indians
did not regard themselves as agents of a precolonial revival or enemies of the
colonial state and its religion. True, where Indians who believed that they were
chosen Christians went on to make invidious comparisons to their social bet-
ters and distinguish between Christianity and the Church, millennial dreams of
a new order could have revolutionary possibilities. Such dreams rarely were
acted upon—rarely, at least, beyond the local level, where they had helped define
a colonial identity.

If political tradition has much to do with the disunity of Mexico as a nation
in the nineteenth century, these examples of religion and resistance in central
and western Mexico (where the majority of future Mexicans resided at the end
of the colonial period) suggest an interpretation that differs from Hartz's
(1964:chaps. 1–3). Hartz portrayed colonial Spanish America as a feudal, au-

thoritarian society whose servile masses had no experience in self-government. Political peace depended upon the iron grip of the *encomienda* (grant of Indians, mainly as tribute payers), landless Indian subjects, a tradition of "Indian absolutism," "popular submissiveness," and "the incapacity of the people to assume Enlightenment responsibilities." Once the legitimacy of the imperial government was challenged after 1808, the social and political order inevitably collapsed into anarchy.

The Indian resistance and accommodations documented in this essay suggest that the weakness of Mexican national governments in the nineteenth century had less to do with popular submissiveness, Indian absolutism, and a lack of political mobilization than with the longstanding political strength and experience of localities and regions. Political participation was much greater than one would expect from Hartz's summary. The *curas* of Ozoloapan certainly felt the weight of local political initiative that was not simply the product of a petty tyrant's machinations. The observation of David Wells, a late nineteenth-century North American commentator (1887:84–85), that a "native spirit of independence" was the principal source of Mexico's disunity comes closer to the militant myopia of districts and pueblos such as Ozoloapan, Atexcapan, and Tlaquepaque. This political strength of localities and, to a lesser extent, regions should not be regarded only as a prehispanic legacy or a function of spatial separation, as Brand (1966:40) suggested. It was also promoted by the Indians' position in colonial society as laboring, producing, tribute-paying subjects of the Crown. As members of corporate *pueblos de indios*, they fitted into the Hapsburgs' idea of a mediated, patrimonial state. For the future national state a major problem was the weakness of territorial and institutional loyalties between localities and the Crown's *audiencias* and viceroy. With the decline of the court system and the old legitimacy of the highest political leaders after independence, comparatively few rural constituencies thought their interests were well served by state and national governments.

Notes

I am grateful to David Carrasco, Ramón Gutiérrez, Peggy Liss, Nancy Mann, Scarlett O'Phelan, and William Merrill for good advice and especially to Inga Clendinnen for enlarging my view of Indian perceptions of the saint and his horse in the early sixteenth century.

1. Chapter 8 of Frye's doctoral dissertation (1989) reflects on the epic quality of Warman's and Friedrich's books, which gave me pause to consider why I still

assign them, Womack, and Reed (plus Luis González's *San José de Gracia* and Agustín Yáñez's *The Edge of the Storm*) to my Mexican history classes many years after publication. Epic or not, I still regard them as the best, most accessible works in English on the thought and action of rural people that are located in time, place, and political and economic context.

Katz (1988) has edited and provided valuable connecting essays for a recent book on the history of armed resistance in rural Mexico since prehispanic times.

2. This is the view of Aguirre Beltrán (1963). While not holding to an idols-behind-altars view, the Spanish American chapters of Lockhart and Schwartz's social history of colonial Latin America (1983) in effect leave out the Church and priests as factors in Indian communities.

   Some recent approaches that lean toward one of the poles consciously seek to consider the other. Van Oss (1986:36, 105, 156, 183) concludes that "a new Christian community was formed" among highland Indians of Guatemala and that the parish clergy were a rich, powerful, dominating elite there, but he accepts that this was a "synthetic rural Catholicism" in which colonial Indians considered themselves devout Catholics on their own terms. Klor de Alva (1982) favors the idea of pervasive Indian resistance to conversion in central Mexico rather than a "true spiritual conquest," at least in the sixteenth century. He acknowledges the possibility of conversion but concludes that "the majority of urban and rural natives . . . simply borrowed from Christianity whatever elements were necessary to appear Christian . . . without changing their religious convictions."

3. The idea of a crystallization of culture shows up near both poles of the literature on Spanish domination and Indian resistance; see, for example, Aguirre Beltrán (1963:102, 263–64) and Morse in Hartz (1964:127, 141).

4. Recent contributions to alternative views of Indian religious practices in New Spain include Clendinnen (1980, 1987a, 1987b, and especially 1991b), Farriss (1984), Miller and Farriss (1979), Frye (1989), Gutiérrez (1990), P. Carrasco (1975), Nutini (1988), Musgrave-Portilla (1982), and Gruzinski (1985, 1986, 1988).

   This is not the place to review at length the differences in emphasis within this literature, but there are many. Most authors lean toward the idea that colonial Indian religious beliefs and practices have local rather than higher and more official origins, but some emphasize continuities across the Conquest, either in community practices or private beliefs and acts. Others emphasize departures that followed lines "already established" or adhere to the outside imposition–native resistance formula. Some insist on the formation of a single, syncretic belief system that can be labeled folk Catholicism but that has a "pagan" core. Others question the appropriateness of the concept of syncretism for colonial Indian peasants. Still others see these people operating comfortably in two religious traditions at the same time. The ways in which colonial Indian religious practices were at once local and an integral part of the state religion have not received much attention.

5. According to local tradition he had visited Spain and preached the gospel there.

Later his martyred remains were believed to have been transported from Jerusalem to northwestern Spain for burial. A great pilgrimage cult began in the ninth century at Compostela with the discovery of the relics and subsequent stories of the apostle's personal appearance in a decisive victory over the Moors near Logroño. For an engaging introduction to the "creed" of St. James in Spanish history and his position as the patron saint of Christian Spaniards, see Kendrick (1960).

6. Weckman (1984:vol. 1, 149–51) lists eleven instances in which Santiago was invoked in battles against Indians in Mexico during the sixteenth century.

   An early Spanish tradition of Santiago appearing at a decisive moment in Cortés's expedition to Mexico to blunt Indian assaults is recorded in the account by his secretary, Francisco López de Gómara, who never visited America (1943:vol. 1, 92–93). During a fierce Indian attack on Spaniards at Tabasco, a mysterious man on horseback appeared and vanished three times, turning the native armies back until Cortés and reinforcements came to the rescue. Some of the men believed that the unknown cavalryman was "the apostle Santiago, patron saint of Spain." Cortés preferred to think it was St. Peter, his special guardian. Either way, says López de Gómara, it was judged a miracle. In the preceding chapter (p. 85) López de Gómara says Cortés invoked Santiago as well as God and St. Peter in another engagement with coastal natives. This apparition episode was commemorated in Gabriel Lobo Lasso de la Vega's epic poem *Mexicana* (1970:94). Bernal Díaz del Castillo, who took part in this battle, wrote that if Santiago had appeared there, he had not been privileged to witness the apparition (Díaz del Castillo 1982:63–64).

   Another tradition of a decisive appearance by Santiago during the Conquest comes from the city of Querétaro. The parish church there was dedicated to Santiago in honor of his reputed intervention in the battle against Otomí and Chichimec Indians in 1531 (Alcedo 1967:vol. 3, 265).

   Valle (1946), the most extensive work on this saint, written from an ardently Catholic and hispanophile viewpoint, identifies fourteen reports of Santiago apparitions in Spanish America from 1518 to 1892. New Spain in the sixteenth century figures in seven of these cases (including the Tabasco and Querétaro incidents mentioned earlier). Valle reports none for New Spain in the seventeenth and eighteenth centuries. His interpretation for the sixteenth century is similar to Trexler's in that he has Indians interpreting Santiago as "the new telluric force, invincible, irresistible . . . the Son of Thunder . . . with his message of terror" (Valle 1946:15).

7. Ajofrín (1964:vol. 1, 221). The Spaniards awoke "esforzados y animosos"; the Indians "confusos y asustados; y luego, sin venir a las armas, se entregaron humildes y rendidos."

8. Trexler (1984:208, 216). I disagree here with Trexler's view that this was in fact as well as in intent the function of mock battles. He implies a more thoroughgoing Spanish control over Indian communities than I think is justified.

In contrast with Trexler, Baumann (1987) describes Tlaxcalan nobles scripting the early post-Conquest *moros y cristianos* events to impress the viceroy and enhance their prestige in the colonial world as loyal, courageous Christian subjects.

9. Lumholtz (1902:vol. 2, 329) found a similar belief about Santiago at Zapotlán el Grande, Jalisco, in the late nineteenth century: Santiago "is a good deal of a liar and has made himself rich at the expense of the Indians. Though the people do not like him he always has his way because he frightens them."

The interpretation of Santiago as a symbol of defeat and submission to colonial Indians is developed by Choy Ma (1979:333–437; only pp. 421–437 deal with Santiago in America). Choy Ma is primarily concerned with the Spaniards' intentions and their message to Indians that the Conquest was punishment from God and that Santiago was God's agent in this affair. While he holds out the possibility of an Indian reworking of Santiago's meaning as a liberating force, little evidence is offered from a colonial Indian perspective, especially little for Mexico after the sixteenth century.

One of Choy Ma's few examples of Indians in Mexico accepting the Spanish version of Santiago—which he describes as Santiago trampling an Aztec warrior (1979:431)—is a Europeanized conquest scene illustrated in Diego Durán's *Historia de las Indias de Nueva España* (probably drawn in the 1560s or 1570s). The passage in Durán's text that corresponds to this illustration says only that the rider invoked the name of Santiago before engaging the enemy. What made the episode remarkable to Durán and worthy of an illustration was that the rider was a woman who had led a bold assault on Indian forces in a seemingly impregnable location outside Tetlan (perhaps Tetela del Volcán, Morelos) when Cortés was on the point of turning away (Durán 1967:vol. 2, 573–574 and pl. 62).

Choy Ma (1979:432) believes that the idea of Santiago as "Indian-slayer" rather than "Moor-slayer" is supported also by a change in colonial images of the saint in which prostrate Indians replaced turbaned Moors under the horse's feet. An inventory of images of Santiago with their makers, dates, and owners would be needed to test this hypothesis fully. For Mexico the colonial images I know from published sources and visits to parish churches in Jalisco, Michoacán, and the Estado de México and to the Franz Mayer Collection in Mexico City show exotic Moors rather than Indians as Santiago's victims. One Santiago *mata-indios* from Santa María Chiconautla, Estado de México, is described in the exhibition catalogue *Mexico: Splendors of Thirty Centuries* (1990:346).

Santiago in either guise seems to have been a more captivating character in Indian parishes of Peru during the colonial period. He was more often *mata-indios* in Peruvian representations. Of the twenty-one colonial Santiagos illustrated in Macera's *Pintores populares andinos*, two appear to be *mata-indios* and seven others show llamas or alpacas (native cameloids) near the horse's raised front feet. Macera (1979:xlii) posits a change in representations of Santiago at Cuzco during the colonial period, from mainly *mata-indios* at the beginning to a mounting preference for *matamoros* in the seventeenth and eighteenth centuries. For a brief discussion of Santiago in colonial Peru and two more illustrations of *mata-indios*, see Gisbert (1980:195–198 and the illustrations facing p. 198 and following p. 210).

10. According to an eighteenth-century account, Padre Segovia also promoted the cult of Santiago at Tetlan, an Indian pueblo between Guadalajara and Tonalá, after learning from local Indians that Santiago had protected the forces of Nuño de Guzmán during a battle there (Valle 1946:chap. 2).

    Felipe Guaman Poma de Ayala, the early seventeenth-century Peruvian Indian author, also associated Santiago's power with thunder and lightning (Guaman Poma 1980:vol. 2, 376–377). Santiago is widely known in central Mexican villages today as the "son of thunder" (Warman 1985:113–135). Did Indians universally make the association on their own, learn it from other Indians, or learn it mainly from Spaniards? The answers are not clear, but for colonial Peru, where Santiago was often associated with Illapa, lord of lightning, the precolonial basis seems strong.

11. In his interpretation of the politics of oppression in sixteenth-century New Spain, Trexler (1984:194) presents the messages of the "military theatre of the conquest" as Indian obedience and the honor of being a Spaniard. He describes no ambiguity, only Indian submission and Spanish destiny to rule. I am suggesting that the cult of Santiago conveyed the honor of being a Christian as well as the honor of being a Spaniard. As Christians, colonial Indians might also enlist his support. Carrillo y Gariel (1950:12) makes this point when he notes that the Indian *cacique* Nicolás Montáñez attributed his victory against Chichimec enemies in 1531 more to the aid of the Apostle Santiago than to the courage of the many Indian warriors who fought under his command.

    That Santiago was a common Christian name for Indian nobles in the sixteenth century also suggests his patronage of Indian Christians, as does the popularity of Santiago as the patron saint of pueblos. In his tabulation of patron saints for 2,156 *ciudades*, villas, pueblos, and barrios, Carrillo y Gariel (1950:13–24) found Santiago to be second only to Mary in popularity with 207 namings (9.6 percent).

12. This was also the standard attire and posture in Spanish accounts and images of Santiago before and after the colonial enterprise in America began (Kendrick 1960:42 and pls. IIa and Xa).

13. Weismann (1950:58) thinks that most of the Mexican Santiagos were made in the seventeenth century. For Peru, Macera (1979:xlii) and Gisbert (1980:197–198) suggest that Santiago was often represented in American-made images during the sixteenth century, although few examples survive.

    A spiritual geography is needed for Santiago in New Spain. My examples come from rural communities of central and western Mexico, where he continues to be venerated. Warman (1985:113–135) finds the current veneration to be centered in the states of Veracruz, Puebla, Morelos, Jalisco, Zacatecas, Mexico, and the Distrito Federal.

14. Clendinnen (1987b, 1990, 1991a) sheds new light on questions of communica-

tion across cultures, syncretism, and the practice of religion in sixteenth-century Mexico.

15. The Tenocha-Mexica are the best known of native state-holders at the time of the Conquest, thanks to their aggressive expansion then, the archaeological record, Bernardino de Sahagún's *Florentine Codex*, other accounts of early missionaries, and a large secondary literature.

16. Horses appear prominently in sixteenth-century Indian pictorials of the Conquest. In Book 12 of the *Florentine Codex* they are depicted as restless, always in motion, with legs raised, kicking up dust. Sometimes they are massed for a charge, their mouths open and their teeth showing (Anderson and Dibble 1978:29, 30, 65, 69, 82). In the *Códice de Tlatelolco* (ca. 1564) and the *Lienzo de Cuauhquechollan* (Puebla, sixteenth century) horses appear in battle rearing up on their hind legs, their mouths and large eyes wide open and their ears pulled back (Glass 1964: pls. 41, 45). In the *Lienzo de Tlaxcala* they appear in nearly all the fighting scenes as solid, outsized, branded creatures. Some are shown rearing up like Santiago's mount or with big teeth, tongue, and penis showing. Sometimes the neck of the charging horse is stretched well forward as if the animal were about to attack with its mouth. The artist of the *Lienzo de Tlaxcala* and other makers of sixteenth-century pictorials such as the *Códice Osuna* were particularly impressed by horses' capacity for food and frequently show them eating (e.g., Glass 1964: pl. 49).

17. Cited in Bustamante (1810). See Gibson and Glass (1975:331).

    In nearly the same words and claiming to paraphrase Indian testimony, Juan de Torquemada (1943–44:vol. 1, 496 [libro 4, cap. 69]) wrote that Santiago's horse "with his mouth, forelegs, and hindlegs did as much damage as the horseman with his sword" during the Spaniards' battle with the Aztecs in Tenochtitlan shortly before the Noche Triste. Unless Bustamante borrowed without attribution from Torquemada rather than Chimalpahín, these two early seventeenth-century accounts of the warrior horse may have come from a common oral tradition in and near the Valley of Mexico.

18. In prehispanic belief the personal association between an animal and an individual apparently took two distinct forms, the *nahualli* and the *tonalli*. López Austin (1980:vol. 1, 427–430) regards both as spiritual entities that could separate from the human body. The *tonalli* resided in the head and in association with an animal counterpart (known in Spanish as the *tona*), which was identified shortly after birth. The *tonalli* could escape the body during dreams, drunkenness, or coitus. If it was lost or if the animal counterpart died, the individual also would die soon. The *nahualli* resided in the liver. Only wizards (known in Spanish as *naguales* because of their association with this spiritual entity) could release this spirit into a powerful animal that would act out the wizard's will. Everyone had a *tona* or animal counterpart, but not everyone was a *nagual*. The prehispanic wizards were elite men associated with the fiercest animals.

    If López Austin is correct about this sharp distinction between *nahualli* and *tonalli*, sometime during the early colonial period the distinction declined. By the seventeenth century *naguales* were said to transform themselves (not just release their liver-spirit) into animals, often domesticated animals such as dogs and goats, perhaps indicating that these colonial wizards were commoners who could not claim the most powerful animal counterparts; on the idea of transformation, the increasing importance of dogs, and a decline in the distinction between *tona* and *nagual* in the colonial period, see Aguirre Beltrán (1963:98–112) and Musgrave-Portilla (1982:45, 57). Also during the colonial period a native conception in which particular divine forces both nurtured and destroyed may have given way to a more Christian notion of black magic in which the wizard was essentially malevolent and often took the form of a small black dog (see Musgrave-Portilla 1982).

19. Warman (1985) and Baumann (1987) explore this idea of a culture of conquest and its "other face"—Indian reworkings.

20. The literal meaning of *chichimec* is not certain, but all the renderings suggest an unwelcome outsider. Siméon (1977) says it means "those who suck milk from the breast" (from *chichi,* "to suckle")—that is, those who prey on others. Robelo (1940) derives the term from *chichiman* (unknown region). And Santamaría (1942) says it means "dog on a leash" (from *chicho* for "dog" and *mecatl* for "rope"); or perhaps the meaning is dog who punishes (dog *with* a rope).

21. AGN Inquisición 303 fols. 69–71, the Augustinian guardian's short report on Indian idolatry in the vicinity of Ixmiquilpan, 1624. The description of María's dream is not full enough to establish whether she regarded intercourse with the Spaniard as submission rather than a more neutral or reciprocal communication. In either case his power was transferred to her without mediation or supplication.

    Similar seventeenth-century cases of young non-Indian men appearing to Indian *curanderas* and diviners in their dreams or in a drug-induced state and giving them secret powers and incantations are recorded in Ponce (1953: vol. 1, 379, *cura* of Zumpahuacan in the early seventeenth century) and Ruiz de Alarcón (1953: vol. 2, 52, *cura* of Atenango in 1629). In Ruiz de Alarcón's description, an Indian woman named Mariana "consulted" *ololiuhqui* (psychedelic morning glory) for advice about a wound that had not healed. A young man, whom she judged to be an angel, appeared to her and told her not to worry, that God saw her poverty and would favor her. That night the young man crucified her and taught her his powers of curing. Ponce mentions diviners using *ololiuhqui* and having a young black man, Christ, or angels appear and tell them what they wanted to know.

22. Indians from Ixmiquilpan in the seventeenth century were alive to the possibility of collective assaults on Spanish masters and alliances with Chichimecs. In August 1642 a struggle between two Indian factions over control of the governorship turned into an assault on Spanish authority when the *alcalde mayor* and his militia tried to intervene. A group of *macehuales* (Indian commoners) decorated with Chichimec markings and armed with bows and arrows reportedly menaced the *alcalde mayor* when he arrested their favorite and threatened death to all

Spaniards. The *alcalde mayor* feared that they would form an alliance with Chichimec Indians from the nearby Cerro Gordo to overthrow Spanish rule (AGN Criminal 55 fols. 122ff.).

For the anticolonial visions of another Indian witch in a Chichimec setting farther north, see Behar (1987).

23. Given the prominence of lightning and clouds in native religions of Mesoamerica (e.g., Chance 1989:160), Santiago's association with thunder and lightning must have added greatly to his appeal as a source of power and fertility. Taggart (1983: chaps. 6–9) provides detailed evidence of lightning bolts as the central metaphor of the mythology of two Nahua communities in the Sierra de Puebla. Santiago turns out to be the patron saint of both.

24. Serna (1892:38): "Santiago el mozo, ayudadme, varón fuerte vencedor y hombre valeroso, valedme y ayudadme, que [no] se perderán las obras y hechuras de Dios todo poderoso."

    Other seventeenth-century accounts by parish priests of local religious practices in central Mexico pueblos also mention conjurers of the clouds and the belief that the clouds and winds are angels and gods (Ponce 1953: vol. 1, 379; Ruiz de Alarcón 1953: vol. 2, 23–24). In Ponce's description, presumably for Zumpahuacan, conjurers called *teciuhpeuhque* made many hand signals and blew at the clouds and winds.

25. AGN Criminal 120 exp. 25 fol. 286v. Horses and riders were admired by all classes in colonial Mexico. De la Mota y Escobar (1966:34), writing at the turn of the seventeenth century, observed Indians' particular love of horses (and trees). The many robberies of single horses recorded in eighteenth-century Indian districts suggests both the presence of horses in Indian pueblos and their value.

    Evidently Spaniards and Indians both associated the horse with power, albeit perhaps different kinds of power—social and military for Spaniards, mystical as well as social and military for Indians. The rider's position above pedestrian onlookers, coupled with his trappings, his horsemanship, and the quality of his mount, suggested superiority, virility, and wealth, not to mention mobility. Horses were luxury transport, faster but not as durable on the rough and mountainous roads as mules and donkeys and rarely used as draft animals.

    Indians and horses, pageantry, and the Conquest come together in Joel R. Poinsett's observation from his travels in central Mexico in 1822 that

    there is no country in Europe, where the superstitious forms of worship are more strictly observed than in Mexico. . . . [The Indians] are fond of pageants and processions. . . . The Indians are particularly fond of appearing in processions, clothed in the armor and other habiliments of the followers of Cortes. This dress is associated, in their minds, with majesty and power, and they delight to ride on a war horse, armed from head to heel with helmet and mail. (1824:87)

    Although Poinsett leaves the reader to wonder whether the Indian conquistadors he saw were saluting the Spaniards' power in this exchange of roles or felt they had become, at least for the moment, Santiago's lieutenants, his observation is consistent with the popularity of mock battles and Indian men playing at soldiers in community religious fiestas in the eighteenth century.

26. I am not certain when the Dance of the Santiaguitos was forbidden by the Crown. The secular *cura* of Zacualpa (Cuautla district) complained in 1763 that the pueblo of Temoac—which he regarded as a lawless, idolatrous place—resisted his attempts to end the dance even though other pueblos in the district had complied with the prohibition (AGN Clero Regular y Secular 156 exp. 9, fols. 366ff). On February 11, 1769, Archbishop Lorenzana and his provisor published a pastoral letter calling for an end to the dances of Santiaguito, the Nescuitiles, and the Palo del Bolador and live representations of the passion of Christ (Moreno de los Arcos 1982:28–34).

    Because of Santiago's association with the *Reconquista*, the Dance of the Santiaguitos could have been a variation on the old *moros y cristianos* pageants. But probably there was not one standard Dance of the Santiaguitos. At least, celebrations on his day or in which his image appeared varied (several variations are described in the text). At Tecali (Puebla), where Santiago was the patron saint, Indians danced the Hahuixtle ("dance from before the Conquest") on the Day of Santiago; dancers arrayed around a *teponastle* (hollowed log drum) and some "dressed as Chichimecs" pursued captive deer in a mock hunt. See AGI Mexico 839–841 (1735). Various modern versions of the dances of Santiago are mentioned in Warman (1985:113–135).

27. Bancroft M-M 69–70, *diario* of the Fourth Provincial Council, 1771, fols. 200v–201r. The Dance of the Santiaguitos came up in the council's discussion of Indian idolatry.

    José Miguel Guridi y Alcocer (1799:81v), the scholarly priest of Acaxete, Puebla, also regarded this dance as evidence of Indians' pagan spirit. In one of his rare references to Mexico in this treatise, Guridi spoke of the old pagan spirit being encountered only in small, unimportant Indian pueblos, in such dances as the *torito* (little bull) and Santiagos, "which is the main one."

28. AJANG Civil, bundle labeled 1800–1819, leg. 3 (109), August 21, 1815, petition by the officials of San Andrés and the *subdelegado*'s report:

    . . . tiene el nombre de Tastuanes y se contrahe a vestirse varios indios muy ridiculamente con máscara y que montado uno de ellos a caballo y con espada en mano que es el que llaman Santiago comienza a darles a los demás de sintarazos que resisten con un palo que trae cada uno en la mano, pero ya despues que se embriagan los que eran antes sintarazos se buelven cuchilladas de suerte que cada año resultan de su danza uno, dos o más heridos aunque de esto ni dimana queja alguna pues los pacientes sufren aquello por decir que viene de Santiago. No es lo más lo que llevo espuesto a Vuestra Excelencia sino es que así en castellano como en mexicano son muchas las obsenidades que hablan y también las ac-

ciones indecentes que hacen al tiempo que manifiestan estarle quitando la piel al
que hace de Santiago.

Drawing on Santoscoy (1889), Warman (1985:108–110) describes the dance of
the *tastoanes* (a corruption of *tlatoani*, meaning "Indian lords") in this same
town, San Andrés, plus three others near Guadalajara in 1889. The 1815 and
1889 descriptions are not exactly parallel or equally detailed, but the same basic
structure of the performance is recognizable in both: A mounted Santiago engaged masked pedestrians in combat. He escaped many times but eventually was
captured, taken off the horse, and humiliated. The apparent differences in the
1889 version are that the saint was killed; the *tastoanes'* struggle against him was
sanctioned by the judgment of kings; the dance was held on the Day of Santiago
rather than (or perhaps in addition to) the Day of San Pedro; and the *tastoanes*
were not represented only as Moors (several of the names of *tastoanes* indicate
that they were infernal characters (for example, Barrabas and Satan).

    The differences between the descriptions, if they are real differences between the
performances, suggest changes in degree rather than kind. The inversion of the
saint's power is common to both. (Warman suggests that the traditional message of
good triumphing over evil had been inverted in 1889. But given that the *tastoanes*
were the kings' subjects, measured the community's lands, and executed the saint
on royal orders, the performance seems to confirm the integrity and legitimacy of
the community more than it signified the victory of evil over good. Following Musgrave-Portilla's interpretation of the devil and nagualism after the Conquest, perhaps the Barrabas figure and his compatriots were understood as not exactly evil.)

    Warman treats this dance in 1889 as an example of radical change within the
original *moros y cristianos* tradition after Mexico's national independence and as
evidence of a more independent popular culture and diminishing influence of the
priesthood that emerged during the anarchy of Mexican political life before and
during the Reform Period. Judging by the 1815 description, the "radical" change
in this case occurred before national independence. The *subdelegado* did not say
how old the earlier dance of the *tastoanes* may have been, but he gave no indica-
tion that it was a new practice.

    For additional information about past and present *tastuanes* dances in pueblos
of the Zapopan and Tonalá districts near Guadalajara, see Mata Torres (1987).

29. The Toxcatl festival is described and richly interpreted by Carrasco (1991) and
    Clendinnen (1991b).
30. Valle (1946:30–33), citing Tello's *Crónica miscelánea*, recounts the pious tradi-
    tion of 1541 and Tello's comment that "Indians in the pueblos of Galicia reenact
    this miracle each year."
31. McKinley (1948:368–373) describes this conception of Santiago's violence in a
    modern Dance of the Santiagos at Xalacapan in the district of Zacapoaxtla, Puebla.
32. Valle (1946:53) recounts an oral tradition from Janitzio, an island pueblo on
    Lake Pátzcuaro, about Santiago as village protector during the Independence

War. When royalists tried to take the pueblo, Santiago came down from the hill, whereupon the local patriots multiplied and scattered the enemy. Valle describes the modern *moros y cristianos* dance at Janitzio as a representation of reciprocity and community responsibility.

33. As Carrillo y Gariel notes (1950:11), the faces of many of Santiago's horses have an almost human expression.

    One of the best-known village Santiagos, from Tupátaro, Michoacán, seems tame and approachable, like the friendly little images of Mary described by Weismann (1950); a photograph of it by Edward Weston is reproduced in Gruening (1928: facing p. 249) and in Brenner (1929: facing p. 68). Weston wrote a memorable description of this Santiago when he went to see it in the 1920s:

    Here in Tupátaro the villagers were more than hospitable, and excited as children when I asked permission to photograph their Santiago. Santiago wears a childlike expression. They must feel more than mere reverence for a saint, he must be like them—one of them. So Santiago was. He could have been displayed in any American department store amongst the toys—a super toy. All details have received careful, tender attention. He was booted and spurred, over his neck hung a little sarape, around his waist a real faja, and his spirited hobby horse had been branded! Because of a recent fiesta the horse was still wreathed with roses. (Weston 1961:vol. 1, 176)

34. Two striking patterns in the records of *arancel* disputes are the ability of rural villagers to make cash contributions to village leaders who carried on the lawsuits against *curas* and their willingness to replace customary services with cash payments.

35. Factionalism within villages and larger rural communities receives attention in my forthcoming book, *Magistrates of the Sacred: Priests and Parishioners in Eighteenth-Century Mexico.*

    The hacienda administrator and the legal entrepreneur are two examples of how the power of a *cacique* (local boss) was built in the period of transition from colonial rule to national independence. It remains to be seen how important factionalism was to the rise of local bosses generally.

36. In the usual way Santiago occasionally was on the lips of fighters in the Independence War. During the siege of Cuautla in 1812, for example, some insurgents reportedly invoked Santiago before an assault (Morelos 1927:vol. 1, 265).

References

Archives and Manuscript Collections
Archivo General de Indias, Seville (AGI)
   Audiencia de México

Archivo General de la Nación, Mexico (AGN)
    Clero Regular y Secular
    Criminal
    Inquisición
Archivo Judicial de la Audiencia de la Nueva Galicia, Guadalajara (AJANG)
    Civil
Bancroft Library, University of California, Berkeley Mexican Manuscripts
    (Bancroft M-M)

Books and Articles

Aguirre Beltrán, Gonzalo. 1963. *Medicina y magia: El proceso de aculturación en la estructura colonial.* Mexico City: Instituto Nacional Indigenista.

Ajofrín, Fr. Francisco de. [1763] 1964. *Diario del viaje que por orden de la Sagrada Congregación de Propaganda Fide hizo a la América septentrional en el siglo XVIII.* Mexico City: Instituto Cultural Hispano Mexicano.

Alcedo, Antonio de. [1786–1789] 1967. *Diccionario geográfico histórico de las Indias occidentales o América.* 4 vols. Madrid: Atlas.

Anderson, Arthur J. O., and Charles E. Dibble, eds. 1978. *The War of Conquest: How It Was Waged Here in Mexico.* Salt Lake City: University of Utah Press.

Barabas, Alicia. 1987. *Utopías indias: Movimientos socioreligiosos en México.* Mexico City: Editorial Grijalbo.

Baumann, Roland. 1987. "Tlaxcalan Expression of Autonomy and Religious Drama in the Sixteenth Century." *Journal of Latin American Lore* 13, no. 2:139–153.

Behar, Ruth. 1987. "The Visions of a Guachichil Witch in 1599: A Window on the Subjugation of Mexico's Hunter-Gatherers." *Ethnohistory* 34:115–138.

Brading, David A. 1973. "Government and Elite in Late Colonial Mexico." *Hispanic American Historical Review* 53:389–414.

————. 1983. "Tridentine Catholicism and Enlightened Despotism in Bourbon Mexico." *Journal of Latin American Studies* 15:1–22.

Brand, Donald. 1966. *Mexico: Land of Sunshine and Shadow.* Princeton, N.J.: Van Nostrand.

Brenner, Anita. 1929. *Idols Behind Altars.* New York: Payson and Clarke.

Bustamante, Carlos María. 1810. *Memoria principal de la piedad y lealtad del pueblo de México, en los solemnes cultos de Nuestra Señora de los Remedios desde su llegada hasta su regreso al santuario de Tototepec.* Mexico City: ñ.p.

Carrasco, David. 1991. "The Sacrifice of Tezcatlipoca: To Change Place." In *To Change Place: Aztec Ceremonial Landscapes,* 31–57. Boulder: University Press of Colorado.

Carrasco, Pedro. 1975. "La transformación de la cultura indígena durante la colonia." *Historia Mexicana* 25:175–203.

Carrillo y Gariel, Abelardo. 1950. *Imaginería popular novoespañola.* Mexico City: Ediciones Mexicanas.

Chance, John K. 1989. *Conquest of the Sierra: Spaniards and Indians in Colonial Oaxaca.* Norman: University of Oklahoma Press.

Choy Ma, Emilio. 1979. *Antropología e historia*. Lima: Universidad Nacional Mayor de San Marcos.

Christian, William. 1981. *Local Religion in Sixteenth-Century Spain*. Princeton, N.J.: Princeton University Press.

———. 1987. "Folk Religion: An Overview." In *The Encyclopedia of Religion*, edited by Mircea Eliade, vol. 5, 370–374. New York: MacMillan.

Clendinnen, Inga V. 1980. "Landscape and World View: The Survival of Yucatec Maya Culture under Spanish Conquest." *Comparative Studies in Society and History* 22:374–383.

———. 1987a. *Ambivalent Conquests: Maya and Spaniard in Yucatán, 1517–1571*. Cambridge: Cambridge University Press.

———. 1987b, "Franciscan Missionaries in Sixteenth-Century Mexico." In *Disciplines of Faith: Studies in Religion, Politics, and Patriarchy*, edited by Jim Obelkevich et al., 229–245. London: Routledge & Kegan Paul.

———. 1990. "Ways to the Sacred: Reconstructing 'Religion' in Sixteenth-Century Mexico." *History and Anthropology* 5:105–141.

———. 1991a. " 'Fierce and Unnatural Cruelty': Cortés and the Conquest of Mexico." *Representations* 33:65–100.

———. 1991b. *Aztecs: An Interpretation*. Cambridge: Cambridge University Press.

Díaz del Castillo, Bernal. 1982. *Historia verdadera de la conquista de la Nueva España*. Madrid: Instituto Gonzalo Fernández de Oviedo, C.S.I.C.

De la Mota y Escobar, Alonso. 1966. *Descripción geográfica de los reynos de Nueva Galicia, Nueva Vizcaya, y Nuevo León*. Guadalajara: Instituto Jalisciense de Antropología e Historia.

Doniger, Wendy. 1987. "Horses." In *The Encyclopedia of Religion*, edited by Mircea Eliade, vol. 6, 463–468. New York: MacMillan.

Durán, Diego. 1967. *Historia de las indias de Nueva España e islas de la Tierra Firme*. 2 vols. Mexico City: Porrúa.

Farriss, Nancy M. 1984. *Maya Society under Colonial Rule: The Collective Enterprise of Survival*. Princeton, N.J.: Princeton University Press.

Florescano, Enrique. 1987. *Memoria mexicana: Ensayo sobre la reconstrucción del pasado*. Mexico City: Editorial Joaquín Mortiz.

Friedrich, Paul. 1970. *Agrarian Revolt in a Mexican Village*. Englewood Cliffs, N.J.: Prentice-Hall.

Frye, David. 1989. "Culture, Population, and Rural Economy in a Mexican Town: An Ethnohistorical Account." Ph.D. diss., Princeton University.

Gibson, Charles, and John B. Glass. 1975. "Prose Manuscripts in the Native Historical Tradition." In *Handbook of Middle American Indians*, edited by Robert Wauchope, vol. 15, 311–400. Austin: University of Texas Press.

Gisbert, Teresa. 1980. *Iconografía y mitos indígenas en el arte*. La Paz: Gisbert.

Glass, John B. 1964. *Catálogo de la colección de códices*. Mexico City: Instituto Nacional de Antropología e Historia.

Gruening, Ernest. 1928. *Mexico and Its Heritage*. New York: The Century Co.

Gruzinski, Serge. 1985. "La 'segunda aculturación': El estado ilustrado y la religiosidad indígena en Nueva España (1775–1800)." *Estudios de Historia Novohispana* 8:175–201.

———. 1986. "Normas cristianas y respuestas indígenas: Apuntes para el estudio del proceso de occidentalización entre los indios de Nueva España." *Historias* 15:31–41.

———. 1988. *La colonisation de l'imaginaire: Sociétés indigènes et occidentalisation dan le Mexique espagnol, XVI–XVIII siècles.* Paris: Gallimard.

———. 1989. *Man-Gods in the Mexican Highlands: Indian Power and Colonial Society, 1520–1800.* Stanford, Calif.: Stanford University Press.

Guaman Poma de Ayala, Felipe. 1980. *El primer nueva corónica y buen gobierno.* Edited by John V. Murra and Rolena Adorno. 3 vols. Mexico City: Siglo XXI.

Guridi y Alcocer, José Miguel. 1799. "Discurso sobre los daños del juego." Manuscript in Sutro Library, California State Historical Society, San Francisco.

Gutiérrez, Ramón. 1990. *When Jesus Came, the Corn Mothers Went Away: Marriage, Sexuality, and Power in New Mexico, 1500–1846.* Stanford, Calif.: Stanford University Press.

Hartz, Louis, ed. 1964. *The Founding of New Societies: Studies in the History of the United States, Latin America, South Africa, Canada, and Australia.* New York: Harcourt, Brace & World.

Heyden, Doris. 1987. "Caves." In *The Encyclopedia of Religion*, edited by Mircea Eliade, vol. 3, 127–133. New York: MacMillan.

Katz, Friedrich, ed. 1988. *Riot, Rebellion, and Revolution: Rural Social Conflict in Mexico.* Princeton, N.J.: Princeton University Press.

Kendrick, T. D. 1960. *St. James in Spain.* London: Methuen.

Klor de Alva, Jorge. 1982. "Spiritual Conflict and Accommodation in New Spain: Toward a Typology of Aztec Responses to Christianity." In *The Inca and Aztec States, 1400–1800: Anthropology and History*, edited by George A. Collier, Renato I. Rosaldo, and John D. Wirth, 345–366. New York: Academic Press.

Kobayashi, José María. 1974. *La educación como conquista: Empresa franciscana en México.* Mexico City: El Colegio de México.

Kubler, George. 1961. "On the Colonial Extinction of the Motifs of Pre-Columbian Art." In *Essays in Pre-Columbian Art and Archeology*, edited by Samuel K. Lothrop. et al., 14–24. Cambridge, Mass.: Harvard University Press.

Lobo Lasso de la Vega, Gabriel. [1588] 1970. *Mexicana.* Madrid: Atlas.

Lockhart, James, and Stuart Schwartz. 1983. *Early Latin America: A History of Colonial Spanish America and Brazil.* Cambridge: Cambridge University Press.

López Austin, Alfredo. 1980. *Cuerpo humano e ideología: Las concepciones de los antiguos nahuas.* 2 vols. Mexico City: Universidad Nacional Autónoma de México.

López de Gómara, Francisco. 1943. *Historia de la conquista de México.* Mexico City: Editorial Pedro Robredo.

López Lara, Ramón. 1984. *Zinapécuaro: Tres épocas de una parroquia.* 3d ed. Morelia: Editorial Fimax.

Lumholtz, Carl. 1902. *Unknown Mexico*. 2 vols. New York: Charles Scribner's Sons.

Macera, Pablo. 1979. *Pintores populares andinos*. Lima: Fondo del Libro del Banco de los Andes.

McKinley, Arch. 1948. "The Account of a Punitive Sentence." *Tlalocan* 2:368–373.

Mata Torres, Ramón. 1987. *Los tastuanes de Nextipac*. Guadalajara: Unidad Editorial del Gobierno de Jalisco.

Mexico: Splendors of Thirty Centuries. 1990. New York: The Metropolitan Museum of Art.

Miller, Arthur G., and Nancy M. Farriss. 1979. "Religious Syncretism in Colonial Yucatán: The Archaeological and Ethnohistorical Evidence from Tancah, Quintana Roo." In *Maya Archaeology and Ethnohistory*, edited by Norman Hammond and Gordon R. Willey, 223–240. Austin: University of Texas Press.

Morelos, José María. 1927. *Documentos inéditos y poco conocidos*. 3 vols. Mexico City: Secretaría de Educación Pública.

Moreno de los Arcos, Roberto, ed. 1982. "Dos documentos sobre el arzobispo Lorenzana y los indios de Nueva España." *Históricas* 10:27–38.

Musgrave-Portilla, L. Marie. 1982. "The Nahualli or Transforming Wizard in Pre- and Postconquest Mesoamerica." *Journal of Latin American Lore* 8, no. 1:3–62.

Nutini, Hugo. 1988. *Todos Santos in Rural Tlaxcala: A Syncretic, Expressive, and Symbolic Analysis of the Cult of the Dead*. Princeton, N.J.: Princeton University Press.

Poinsett, Joel R. 1824. *Notes on Mexico, Made in the Autumn of 1822*. Philadelphia: H. C. Cary and I. Lea.

Ponce, Pedro. 1953. "Breve relación de los dioses y ritos de la gentilidad." In *Tratado de las idolatrías, supersticiones, dioses, ritos, hechicerías y otras costumbres gentílicas de las razas aborígenes de México*, vol. 1, 369–380. Mexico City: Ediciones Fuente Cultural.

Reed, Nelson. 1964. *The Caste War of Yucatan*. Stanford, Calif.: Stanford University Press.

Relación de la ceremonias y ritos y población y gobierno de los indios de la provincia de Michoacán. [1541] 1977. Morelia: Balsal Editores.

Ribadeneira y Barrientos, Antonio Joaquín. 1771. "Disertaciones que el Asistente Real Dn. Antonio Joaquín de Rivadeneira escribió sobre los puntos que se dieron a consultar por el Concilio Quarto Mexicano." Spanish Codex 52, John Carter Brown Library, Providence, R.I.

Ricard, Robert. 1933. *La "Conquête spirituelle" du Mexique. Essai sur l'apostolat et les méthodes missionaires des ordres mendicants en Nouvelle-Espagne de 1523–24 a 1572*. Paris: Institut d'Ethnologie.

Robelo, Cecilio. 1940. *Diccionario de aztequismos*. 3d ed. Mexico City: Ediciones Fuente Cultural.

Ruiz de Alarcón, Hernando. 1953. "Tratado de las supersticiones y costumbres gentílicas que oy viven entre los indios naturales desta Nueva España." In *Tratado de las idolatrías, supersticiones, dioses, ritos, hechicerías y otras costumbres gentíli-*

cas de las razas aborígenes de México, vol. 2, 17–180. Mexico City: Ediciones Fuente Cultural.

Santamaría, Francisco J. 1942. *Diccionario general de americanismos*. Mexico City: Editorial Pedro Robredo.

Santoscoy, Alberto. 1889. *La fiesta de los tastoanes, estudio etnológico-histórico*. Guadalajara: S. G. Montenegro.

Serna, Jacinto de la. 1892. "Manual de ministros para el conocimiento de sus idolatrías y extirpación de ellas. . . ." In *Colección de documentos inéditos para la historia de España,* vol. 104, 1–267. Madrid: Imprenta de la viuda de Calero.

Simeón, Rémi. 1977. *Diccionario de la lengua nahuatl o mexicana*. Mexico City: Siglo XXI.

Taggart, James M. 1983. *Nahuat Myth and Social Structure*. Austin: University of Texas Press.

Toor, Frances. 1947. *A Treasury of Mexican Folkways*. New York: Crown.

Torquemada, Juan de. 1943–44. *Monarquía indiana*. 3 vols. Mexico City: S. Chávez Hayhoe.

Torres, Fr. Francisco Mariano de. 1960. *Crónica de la Sancta Provincia de Xalisco*. Mexico City: Colección Siglo XVI.

Trexler, Richard. 1984. "We Think, They Act: Clerical Readings of Missionary Theatre in Sixteenth-Century New Spain." In *Understanding Popular Culture: Europe from the Middle Ages to the Nineteenth Century*, edited by Steven Kaplan, 189–227. Berlin: Mouton.

Valle, Rafael Heliodoro. 1946. *Santiago en América*. Mexico City: Editorial Santiago.

van Oss, Adriaan. 1986. *Catholic Colonialism: A Parish History of Guatemala, 1524–1821*. Cambridge: Cambridge University Press.

Van Young, Eric. 1986. "Millennium on the Northern Marches: The Mad Messiah of Durango and Popular Rebellion in Mexico, 1800–1815." *Comparative Studies in Society and History* 28:385–413.

―――. 1989. "Quetzalcoatl, King Ferdinand, and Ignacio Allende Go to the Seashore; or, Messianism and Mystical Kingship in Mexico, 1800–1821." In *The Independence of Mexico and the Creation of the New Nation*, edited by Jaime Rodríguez, 109–127. Los Angeles: UCLA Latin American Center.

Warman, Arturo. 1978. *. . . Y venimos a contradecir: Los campesinos de Morelos y el estado nacional*. 2d ed. Mexico City: Centro de Investigaciones Superiores del Instituto Nacional de Antropología e Historia.

―――. 1985. *La danza de Moros y Cristianos*. 2d ed. Mexico City: Fondo de Cultura Económica.

Weckman, Luis. 1984. *La herencia medieval de México*. 2 vols. Mexico City: Fondo de Cultura Económica.

Weismann, Elizabeth Wilder. 1950. *Mexico in Sculpture, 1521–1821*. Cambridge, Mass.: Harvard University Press.

Weismann, Elizabeth Wilder, and Judith Hancock Sandoval. 1985. *Art and Time in Mexico from the Conquest to the Revolution*. New York: Harper and Row.

Wells, David A. 1887. *A Study of Mexico*. New York: D. Appleton and Co.

Weston, Edward. 1961–68. *Daybooks*. 2 vols. Rochester, N.Y.: George Eastman House.

Womack, John. 1969. *Zapata and the Mexican Revolution*. New York: Knopf.

Part 3
Living
History:
Contemporary
Issues
and
Historical
Context
in the
United States

▲▲▲

Maintaining
the
Road
of
Life

Alice B. Kehoe

Life as a road to be traveled, as the sun travels around the earth, is a popular metaphor among Plains Indians (e. g., DeMallie 1984:86; in Peyote meetings the leader is the Road Man). We see the road of human life in the Americas continuing from the late Pleistocene to the present. Many have been the obstacles in the road—perhaps the most difficult of all was the massive invasion of America from Europe—but no obstacle has been insurmountable. The descendants of the early people remain walking the road of life here in America.

Time Frame

By the most conservative estimates, humans have been in the Americas at least since the terminal Pleistocene, thirteen thousand years ago (Kehoe 1992:chap. 1). Controversial although soundly argued archaeological interpretations would extend this human history back to eighteen to thirty thousand years ago. Spiri-

193

tual knowledge in some American Indian communities describes these peoples as truly indigenous, having come from realms within our earth. Scientific or spiritual, those who study the history of the Americas agree that we are looking at many millennia of human life here, and these millennia have been fraught with crises, from shifts in climate to wars of conquest.

About nine thousand years ago agriculture began, evidenced in remains excavated in Oaxaca, Mexico (Schoenwetter 1974). A road of life built on the cultivation of plants and management of animal resources came to be followed by all American peoples except those in the harsh northern and southern extremes of the continents (Kehoe 1981). The pervasiveness of agriculture in the Americas has been obscured by European observers' expectations of monocrop fields and fully domesticated animals, so that multicrop cultivation systems and range management programs have been assumed to be natural conditions. The prevalent American Indian ethic of living with, in mutual respect, rather than dominating other forms of life has been another element in the European failure to recognize the full extent of indigenous agriculture.

By the second millennium B.C.E., cities existed in Meso- and South America. As with agriculture, the presence of cities has not been acknowledged as it ought to have been, in part because many American cities were what Arensberg (1968:7–9) terms "green cities," which incorporated homesteads with gardens, and not the familiar European compact "stone city" inside a boundary wall. Thus the Olmec cities of the first millennium B.C.E. in Mexico and the great Mississippian city of Cahokia, which filled the bottomlands at the confluence of the Mississippi and Missouri rivers from about A.D. 900 to 1300, have been said to be "ceremonial centers" with hamlets. Other forms of relatively complex societies, such as those formerly agricultural Plains tribes whose complex structure was latent most of the year and activated during the summer rendezvous, have similarly been misjudged. To some degree the failure to recognize indigenous American development was due to European efforts to legitimatize their capitalist economies' extensions overseas (cf. Meek 1976; Wood 1983, 1984). Jennings (1975) bluntly calls this the "cant of conquest."

By 1492 aboriginal trade networks stretched from Siberia across northernmost America into Greenland, where for nearly five centuries they had fed into Norse trade into Europe. Another trade network circled the North Pacific, reaching to San Francisco Bay, meeting there with the route southeast into the Pueblo country and central Mexico. From the mouth of the Columbia River the route

Lewis and Clark were to take went inland across the Rockies to the Missouri headwaters and thence to the Midwest. Routes from the Atlantic shores went inland along the St. Lawrence and through the Great Lakes, along river systems through the Appalachians into the Ohio country and Tennessee or up along the Mississippi from the Gulf. Maya traded throughout the Caribbean, highland Mexicans both overland and along the Pacific into northern South America, South American merchants all along the Pacific coast from Chile to Ecuador, and Andean caravans between the west coast, the mountains, and the eastern lowlands, where boats plied both inland and along the continent's east coast. For nearly four millennia nations had flourished and fallen—what we now call the Olmec, Monte Albán, Hopewell, Teotihuacán, Toltec, Maya, Mississippian, Aztec, Kotosh, Moche, Nazca, Tiwanaku, Chimu, Inca, and Marajoara. Life in America was neither primitive nor particularly peaceful.

Change

That American Indian societies changed through time is incontrovertible. This seems a truism now, but through the 1950s American Indians were pictured as static. Radin, for example, wrote in 1952:

One of the fundamental traits of these major [Eurasian] civilizations was their essential instability, the frequent social-economic crises through which they passed and the amazing vitality of . . . fictions . . . that stability existed eternally, but in the afterworld not in this. . . . Contrasted with these major civilizations, there have always existed other civilizations, those of aboriginal peoples, where societies were fundamentally stable, where no basic internal social-economic crises occurred. . . . Here we have an amazing antithesis which it is of fundamental importance to remember if we wish to understand the civilizations of aboriginal peoples and to see them in their proper perspective. (Radin 1952:7–8)

That "proper perspective" was the perspective of colonizing conquerors. It dominated anthropology no less than government agents and missionaries.

As Radin reiterated the traditional antithesis, a revolution in anthropology was occurring (Tax 1954:972; Clemmer 1969). The comfortable premise of European superiority "scientifically" explained by Comte and Spencer as the law of progress was battered by waves of assaults, Darwinian adaptationism, Dewey's Progressivism (Bolt 1987:107), the horrors of the two world wars, and capitalism's catastrophic collapse in the Great Depression. Hallowell wrote in 1944, "There is no reason to assume . . . that the societies of non-literate peoples whether past or present are intrinsically more static or conservative than the literate, historic, or so-called 'advanced' peoples" (1945:172), and Herskovits wrote in the same volume that "no living culture is static" (1945:143). In 1953 at an eight-week seminar prominent American anthropologists declared, "All the evidence leads to the conclusion that any autonomous cultural system is in a continuous process of change" (Siegel et al. 1954:984).

Change had to be accepted as intrinsic, and in 1956 Wallace offered a model of societal change that overcame what until then had been a central problem in explaining change (e.g., Hallowell 1945:177–178)—how institutional changes are effected by the individuals who are the actual loci of "culture." Wallace called his model one of "revitalization" (1956:268–270), a step beyond the analysis of "nativistic movements" published by Linton (1943). I would like to call Wallace's model one of cultural *reformulation*. It succinctly outlines the process through which societies have adapted to changed circumstances, thereby maintaining the road of life.

Using Wallace's model as a framework, we can describe the process of cultural reformulation in this manner:

1. Period of increasing individual stress—While the majority of members of the society find satisfaction in the accustomed patterns of behavior, changes in the society's situation cause an increasing number of people to become frustrated when they try to follow accustomed behavior.

2. Period of cultural distortion—Changes in the society's situation have become so pervasive or drastic that the majority of people find accustomed behavior leads only to frustration.

3. Period of reformulation—A "prophet" appears who articulates the ills of the society and proposes modifications in behavior. Disciples join the prophet, adapt the message to promote its acceptance by greater numbers of people, and proselytize it.

4. Reformulation of the culture—The message is comprehended in newly routine behavior.

This model places the individual as the effective but not the final cause of cultural change. It asks us to look at the circumstances that stimulate the call for change and at the same time acknowledge the leaders whose insight and dedication have been instrumental in effecting change.

The Ghost Dance

The classic case of American Indian cultural reformulation has been the Ghost Dance of 1890. It has been superbly documented in one of the greatest anthropological studies, James Mooney's *The Ghost-Dance Religion and the Sioux Outbreak of 1890* (1896). Mooney interviewed the prophet of this new doctrine, Jack Wilson (Wovoka), a Tövusi-dökadö Paiute in Walker River Valley, Nevada. Mooney observed the practice of this doctrine in Walker River Valley, among the Arapaho, and on other reservations. He carefully sifted through the assorted letters, memos, and published accounts of the Ghost Dance and the conflicts with Lakota Sioux that climaxed in the massacre at Wounded Knee Creek. He compared Wilson's doctrine to other religious doctrines and established its fit with the general pattern of prophets' religions that includes Christianity. At the end of his massive study Mooney (1896:927) stated that Wilson's doctrine continued to spread among Indians during the 1890s, "has become a part of the tribal life and is still performed at frequent intervals" in 1896. In the 1960s both Kehoe (1968) and Howard (1984) interviewed members of a Wahpeton Dakota congregation that followed Wilson's religion, and Vander (1986, 1988:11–27) has recorded the Ghost Dance religion (*Naraya*) of a contemporary Wind River Shoshone woman.

Scholars from Mooney through Vander who have known practitioners of Wilson's teachings have been impressed with their power to be a road of life for Indians on reservations. Wilson was born about 1860, the year the first U.S. Army post was built in his territory. He grew up in a period of increasing individual stress as Euro-American ranchers moved into Walker River Valley, destroying the valley's beds of *tövusi* (a papyrus with edible bulbs) and disrupting its fish runs with irrigation canals. To subsist the Paiute had to work for wages for the ranchers in addition to hunting and gathering in uncolonized areas; Jack had worked since his teen years for a rancher named Wilson, who gave him his English name. Most of the Paiutes, including Jack Wilson, amalgamated traits from both cultures, choosing to live in Paiute wickiups but dress in American clothes. In 1883 a rail line was built into the valley, encouraging more intensive colonization and bringing in Chinese laborers, who competed with the Paiutes for wage work. By the end of 1888 Wilson saw clearly an impending crisis. Federal courts had extended their jurisdiction into the valley in 1883, and a school had come in 1887. Tövusi-dökadö Paiutes could no longer think themselves a free people.

On January 1, 1889, while Wilson lay ill with fever, the sun was eclipsed. As a weather doctor, Wilson was obliged to rescue his people from the threat of unnatural darkness. Under the stress of his illness and extraordinary obligation, he lapsed into trance and believed his soul had been transported to heaven, where God instructed him to carry a gospel to the people. Awakening, he began preaching this New Tidings, as the Saskatchewan Dakota called it:

God told him he must go back and tell his people they must be good and love one another, have no quarreling, and live in peace with the whites; that they must work, and not lie or steal; that they must put away all the old practices that savored of war; that if they faithfully obeyed his instructions they would at last be reunited with their friends in this other world, where there would be no more death or sickness or old age. (Mooney 1896:771)

In the period of cultural distortion that began around 1889, Wilson articulated the crisis and formulated a modified behavior pattern that would permit his people to survive without forfeiting their heritage. A communal dance and beautiful songs expressed the joy and value of this heritage without jeopardizing compliance with the invaders' demands. His doctrine and its ritual appealed to thousands of other Indian people recently deprived of their autonomy and best lands. The "Ghost Dance" was enthusiastically performed on many reservations, including those of the Lakota, throughout 1890. Jack Wilson remained a successful and highly respected doctor and leader of his community until he died in 1932. The Paiute are still in Walker River Valley and are still Paiute.

These historical facts notwithstanding, a myth about the Ghost Dance appeared and is sustained:

The Ghost Dance among the Plains tribes lasted little more than a year or two, coming to a sharp end as a result of the suppression of the so-called "Sioux outbreak" with which it adventitiously had become connected in the minds of the whites. (Barber 1941:667)

Among primal peoples all over the world there is a sense of failure similar to that of those Native Americans who saw the massacre of a band of Ghost Dancers at Wounded Knee in 1890. Despite the protection of their Ghost Dance costumes, which the last Indian prophet Wovoka promised would make them invulnerable against the invaders' bullets, they were utterly destroyed. The Plains Indians' spiritual vision in which they might remain sovereign and free was demolished. Indians have never fully recovered a crucial aspect of their worldview since that terrible day at Wounded Knee. (Highwater 1981:xii)

Why should Barber, a respected social scientist, and Highwater, a purported Indian, purvey a falsehood scotched at the source by Mooney and scotched again a generation later by Lesser (1933a, 1933b), whom Barber cited? The myth of a quickly killed Ghost Dance is part of the legacy of conquest. It fit the vision of America's manifest destiny to overcome all opposition until the continent was its own.

What really happened "that terrible day at Wounded Knee," December 29, 1890, was that U.S. Army troops attempted to confiscate all the guns owned by the Mnikowoju band of Lakota camped at Wounded Knee Creek near the Pine Ridge Indian Agency. The Mnikowojus' leader, the aged diplomat Big Foot, had brought his people to the agency to participate in negotiations over the United States's·unilateral abrogation of the 1868 treaty. Some of the younger Mnikowoju objected to uncompensated loss of their means of defense and subsistence, Army troops fired upon the camp, and Big Foot and many women and children were killed. The surviving Mnikowojus slowly retreated fighting up the ravine as Oglala and Brulé reinforcements rode over the ridge from Pine Ridge Agency to salvage what they could of the battle. Lakota forces held a butte north of Pine Ridge Agency until they agreed to make peace on January 15, 1891. The U.S. Congress restored the cuts in appropriations (though not in territory) that had brought the Lakota to protest at Pine Ridge Agency, and twenty-five Lakota leaders taken prisoner by Gen. Nelson Miles were released to Buffalo Bill Cody, to join his Wild West Show. The Lakota families returned to their villages. Their great-grandchildren are there and are still Lakota.

No dispassionate observer, Barber sought influence—control—over others. He revealed his agenda in his 1952 book, *Science and the Social Order*. He claimed that "the social sciences, like all science, are primarily concerned for analysis, prediction, and control of behavior and values" (1952:259). In his 1941 paper he contrasted the "autistic fantasy" of the Ghost Dance with "the Peyote Cult," which he described as "completely nonviolent and nonthreatening to the white culture . . . an alternative response . . . crystallized around passive acceptance and resignation . . . better adapted to the existing phase of acculturation" (Barber 1941:668). In other words, the only good Indian is an emotionally dead Indian. Although in 1941 Barber was only a twenty-three-year-old graduate student and his paper included no original data, the essay soon became a standard citation and was reprinted twenty years later in Lessa and Vogt's *Reader in Comparative Religion*. Barber's paper parroted America's ideology of dominance.

Strategies of Persistence

The mythical Indian created to legitimatize European conquests (Dippie 1982; Bolt 1987:42) was no more than an animal, part of the native fauna, as William Douglass noted in 1755:

> *America* . . . no Civil Government, no Religion, no Letters; the *French* call them *Les Hommes des Bois*, or Men-Brutes of the Forrest: They do not cultivate the Earth by planting or grazing: Excepting a very inconsiderable Quantity of *Mays* or *Indian Corn*, and of *Kidney-Beans* . . . which some of their *Squaas* or Women plant; they do not provide for To-Morrow, their Hunting is their necessary Subsistence not Diversion; when they have good luck in Hunting, they eat and sleep until all is consumed and then go a Hunting again. (Meek 1976:137)

Such "Men-Brutes" could no more resist the advance of civilization than could the other animals of the forest. So Thomas Jefferson could insist that " 'in leading them . . . to agriculture, to manufactures, and civilization . . . in preparing them ultimately to participate in the benefits of our Government, I trust and believe we are acting for their greatest good' " (Prucha 1984:139).

Given such an argument for paternalistic domination, an obvious strategy to maintain self-determination would seem to be the demonstration of mastery of the components of civilization. This was the course followed by the Muskogee, or Creeks (Green 1982), and the Cherokee (McLoughlin 1986), who reformulated their cultural patterns to accommodate plantation agriculture, elected representative government, and literacy. In each of these features these Indian nations achieved widespread success and were fully comparable to the European-descended settlements in the early nineteenth-century Southeast. The tragic story of the removal of the Five Civilized Tribes from their homelands and the dispiriting tale of their never-ending fight in Oklahoma to continue their own civilized nations amply and forcefully indicates the futility of simply trying to disprove the myth of the ignoble savage.

For most American Indian groups, reformulation proceeded in small measures. Clothing and tools were readily taken from the invading culture because these were often cheaper, in time and labor, than native manufactures. Exchanging a deerhide for a yard of cloth, for example, is a cheaper way to obtain a soft, comfortable shirt than the older method of working the hide over and over to attain comparable softness. Similarly, steel knives last so much longer than stone knives that steel usually was in the long run cheaper. Other substitutions were made out of necessity, as when the bison herds disappeared and canvas tipis, the first substitution for bison hide lodge covers, proved less satisfactory than wood cabins.

The most significant changes were spurred by the dominant governments outlawing native languages, rituals, economic practices, social institutions, and residential patterns. Because the assimilationist policies were applied after the segregation of Indians onto reservations (or, in Latin America, *comunidades*), their effect was blunted by the governments' de facto perpetration of closed Indian communities. Many Indian institutions, such as the Sun Dance and the Lakota *tiospaye* community structure, went underground. Others, such as languages, were often drastically modified so that they appeared to have been replaced by their American analogs, although analysis of "Indian English" on a number of reservations shows retention of much of the native syntax and phonology and nonstandard meanings attached to many words (Leap 1982:150). Governments and private agents provided new arenas where a Pan-Indian, as distinguished from the diverse historic Indian, identity could be fostered. These new centers included pageants and schools. In the pageants put on by entrepreneurs from Buffalo Bill Cody to Wisconsin Dells developers, Indians, including even the famous Black Elk (DeMallie 1984:7–9, 63–66), standardized the cliché Indian, while the government schools for Indians embodied "separation from White society and unification with other Indian people . . . acceptance of those values or experiences which are interpreted as crucial for survival, and resistance to those values which are deemed as opposed to the 'Indian way'" (McBeth 1983:116–117). The net result of the paradox of policies segregating Indians in the avowed pursuit of assimilation was the strengthening of Indian identities. Diverse as their heritages were, the children—stripped of their parents' customs and languages, dressed alike, and compelled to speak English—learned that they were put together because they were "Indian." What does an "Indian" look like? The Wild West shows and then movies exhibited the type. "Indians" were a distinct "race," different from that of their conquerors.

The reformulated cultural patterns that came out of this early reservation period of cultural distortion were built on well-articulated opposition between whites and Indians. For a century or more both the dominant American and the various Indian societies have maintained what Schwimmer (1972), following the social psychologist Peter Blau, called "opposition ideology": Indians are communal, egalitarian, respectful of nature, spiritual, and physically superior; whites are individualistic, dominating, callous toward nature and other persons, materialistic, and physically soft. Generosity and sharing are the mark of the

Indian, exhibited in the ritualized giveaway (Kehoe 1980). As a number of observers have documented (e. g., Crumrine 1981; Dunnigan 1981; Larsen 1983; Lithman 1984), the rhetoric of opposed values signifies the existence and worth of the Indian community and allows individuals to declare affiliation.

Oppositional ideology solves the paradox of assimilationist policy and segregationist practice. The failure to assimilate is laid to the Indians' commitment to "Indian" values, a commitment that in the nineteenth century was seen as a racial characteristic (Hinsley 1979; Bieder 1986) and in the twentieth as a positive choice, a counterculture (Kelly 1983:120). The simplistic opposition of white to Indian, mirrored in the legal difference between ordinary citizen and Indian, has promoted a pan-Indian consciousness and alliances. Blurring the distinctiveness of the hundreds of aboriginal Indian nations, these alliances assisted particular groups through crises. An increasingly powerful element in ongoing reformulations of "Indian culture," oppositional ideology has been instrumental in the articulation of values held to characterize Indian communities. Prominent among these values is solidarity with fellow "Indians."

Today, strategies of persistence center on maintaining a core community, usually but not inevitably on reservations (or *comunidades*) and, within that community, a recognized group believed to be knowledgeable about traditional culture. Allied with these "traditionalists" are the intermediaries, who are respected as true Indians but delegated to deal with the opposition, the Outside (Fowler 1982; but see Deloria and Lytle [1984:242] for a somewhat different emphasis on "moralists" versus "pragmatists"). Because they must work within the established states represented within the United Nations, contemporary Indian communities ally regionally, nationally, and internationally—for example, in the Assembly of First Nations of Canada and the World Council of Indigenous Peoples. Indian politicians use the press and television to present the claims of their allied communities to a world audience whose moral sensibilities they hope to awake.

To illustrate, we may look at the little expatriate Wahpeton Dakota village in the Canadian province of Saskatchewan, which continued to celebrate Jack Wilson's Ghost Dance religion into the 1960s. These people had struggled to earn a bare living since settling there in 1878 (Elias 1988:203). In the 1970s, following the Canadian government's ill-advised 1969 White Paper calling for the abolishment of special status for Indians, an urban Indian man with family ties to the Wahpeton village joined colleagues from other Saskatchewan Indian groups to restructure the provincial Indian treaty rights proponents' organization. This restructured Federation of Saskatchewan Indians pressured the Canadian government, embarrassed by the Indians' media-reported outcries against the White Paper, to give it the monies allocated for Indian community development in the province. Thus funded, the organization had for the first time some real, worldly power. The Federation activist with Wahpeton Dakota ties ran for band chief of the reserve to legitimize his leadership position in the Federation and also to aid his family's impoverished community. New homes were built, as well as a decent road across the river to the city and a large community hall with a gymnasium for safe recreation, and a Dakota language instruction program was inaugurated. (The band chief himself, who was reared off the reserve and thus had little fluency in Dakota, took lessons.)

The outcome was similar to what has happened in many rural villages throughout the world—the transformation of the village into a bedroom community where residents could commute to jobs and shopping in the city but one where the retired elderly and the few families able to make a living by farming are seen as the core of the community's ethnic singularity. The Federation of Saskatchewan Indians, together with allied provincial Indian organizations, in the early 1980s changed the name of the National Indian Brotherhood of Canada to the Assembly of First Nations. This change to a markedly more striking title attests to the political sophistication of the leaders, including the Wahpeton Dakotas' band chief, who grew up "assimilated" into urban and national institutions. Whereas his grandparents had struggled against dire poverty, flagrant discrimination, and paternalism to follow Jack Wilson's injunction to lead "a clean, honest life," the contemporary Wahpeton Dakota leader shares a reformulated cultural pattern integrating a basic national material pattern with an interpretation of traditional Dakota beliefs and social values. The treaties signed by nineteenth-century Indians are now an instrument to maintain the distinction of these First Nations and hold the allegiance of the younger people.

The oppositional dualism that frames Western thinking and the American legal system perpetrated and sustained the segregated Indian communities now reasserting their sovereignty as indigenous nations. Underlying the segregation, as the Muskogee and Cherokee so unforgettably discovered, is the implacable insistence of the European colonists and their descendants on possessing American land and resources. For five centuries the real policy has been to get the Indians off the good land, have them give over their resources, and then let them fend as they might. This policy has caused terrible cultural distortions, but its narrow focus on land also has given that modicum of leeway needed for cultural reformulation. Thus a large number of Indian groups have persisted, adapting to the harsh conditions imposed upon them; some have perished, at least as viable societies, often when colonizers' policies of forced relocation coincided with epidemics of European diseases—for example, the Ciboney of the Antilles and the Timucua of Florida (Deagan 1985).

Can we acknowledge that the native peoples of the Americas practiced agriculture everywhere it is practiced today, that their manufactures exhibit technological intelligence and impressive skills in execution, that their governments in their great variety reflect the statesmanship of many renowned leaders? Can we acknowledge that Indian nations in 1492 had as many thousands of years of development and change as any European nation, that the Indian nations had weathered many crises? If so, then we should not assume that the decimation in Indian populations resulting from unprecedented epidemics coupled with the disruptions caused by invasions (Aaby 1985) was a fatal crisis.

James Mooney, who was from a poor Irish immigrant family, felt empathy not with the English but with the Indians. In his monograph on the Ghost Dance religion, he chronicled a series of Indian prophets such as Jack Wilson, leaders who reformulated guides to the road of life. Many other Indian leaders have operated primarily through political strategy, though often in conjunction with spiritual counsel, as in the classic pairing of Tecumseh, the Shawnee general in the War of 1812, and his brother, the prophet Tenskwatawa. The "Bureau Machine," as Charles Eastman called it (Iverson 1982:148), has often nearly strangled their efforts, but Indians have never lacked for insightful and canny men and women dedicated to keeping open the road of life.

The formidable odds posed by five centuries of immigrating millions have not gutted the resilience of Indian nations. If we can drop the myth of the vanishing red child of nature, we can recognize that Indians, like other humans, adapt their cultural patterns of behavior to circumstances, retaining as much as feasible of what still seems precious, dropping and adding to accommodate both outside demands and their own new ideas. No more and no less than other societies, Indians reformulate their cultures over time. Thus they, like the rest of us, maintain their roads of life.

References

Aaby, Peter. 1985. "Epidemics among Amerindians and Inuit: A Preliminary Interpretation." In *Native Power*, edited by Jens Brøsted, Jens Dahl, Andrew Gray, Hans

Christian Gulløv, Georg Henriksen, Jørgen Brøchner Jørgensen, and Inge Kleivan, 329–339. Bergen, Norway: Universitetsforlaget AS.

Arensberg, Conrad M. 1968. "The Urban in Crosscultural Perspective." In *Urban Anthropology: Research Perspectives and Strategies*, edited by Elizabeth M. Eddy, 3–15. Southern Anthropological Society Proceedings, no. 2. Athens: University of Georgia Press.

Barber, Bernard. 1941. "Acculturation and Messianic Movements." *American Sociological Review* 6:663–669.

———. 1952. *Science and the Social Order*. Glencoe, Ill.: The Free Press.

Bieder, Robert E. 1986. *Science Encounters the Indian, 1820–1880*. Norman: University of Oklahoma Press.

Bolt, Christine. 1987. *American Indian Policy and American Reform*. London: Allen & Unwin.

Clemmer, Richard O. 1969. "Truth, Duty, and the Revitalization of Anthropologists: A New Perspective on Cultural Change and Resistance." In *Reinventing Anthropology*, edited by Dell Hymes, 213–247. New York: Random House.

Crumrine, N. Ross. 1981. "The Dramatization of Oppositions among the Mayo Indians of Northwest Mexico." In *Persistent Peoples*, edited by George Pierre Castile and Gilbert Kushner, 109–131. Tucson: University of Arizona Press.

Deagan, Kathleen A. 1985. "Spanish-Indian Interaction in Sixteenth-Century Florida and Hispaniola." In *Cultures in Contact*, edited by William W. Fitzhugh, 281–318. Washington, D.C.: Smithsonian Institution Press.

Deloria, Vine, Jr., and Clifford Lytle. 1984. *The Nations Within*. New York: Pantheon Books.

DeMallie, Raymond J. 1984. *The Sixth Grandfather*. Lincoln: University of Nebraska Press.

Dippie, Brian W. 1982. *The Vanishing American*. Middletown, Conn.: Wesleyan University Press.

Dunningan, Timothy. 1981. "Ritual as Interethnic Competition." In *Persistent Peoples*, edited by George Pierre Castile and Gilbert Kushner, 132–150. Tucson: University of Arizona Press.

Elias, Peter Douglas. 1988. *The Dakota of the Canadian Northwest: Lessons for Survival*. Winnipeg: University of Manitoba Press.

Fowler, Loretta. 1982. *Arapahoe Politics, 1851–1978*. Lincoln: University of Nebraska Press.

Green, Michael D. 1982. *The Politics of Indian Removal*. Lincoln: The University of Nebraska Press.

Hallowell, A. Irving. 1945. "Sociopsychological Aspects of Acculturation." In *The Science of Man in the World Crisis*, edited by Ralph Linton, 171–200. New York: Columbia University Press.

Herskovits, Melville, J. 1945. "The Processes of Cultural Change." In *The Science of Man in the World Crisis*, edited by Ralph Linton, 142–170. New York: Columbia University Press.

Highwater, Jamake. 1981. *The Primal Mind*. New York: Harper and Row.

Hinsley, Curtis M., Jr., 1979. "Anthropology as Science and Politics: The Dilemmas of the Bureau of American Ethnology, 1879 to 1904." In *The Uses of Anthropology*, edited by Walter Goldschmidt, 15–32. Special publication no. 11. Washington, D.C.: American Anthropological Association.

Howard, James H. 1984. *The Canadian Sioux*. Lincoln: University of Nebraska Press.

Iverson, Peter. 1982. *Carlos Montezuma*. Albuquerque: University of New Mexico Press.

Jennings, Francis. 1975. *The Invasion of America*. New York: W. W. Norton.

Kehoe, Alice B. 1968. "The Ghost Dance Religion in Saskatchewan, Canada." *Plains Anthropologist* 13:296–304.

———. 1980. "The Giveaway Ceremony of Blackfoot and Plains Cree." *Plains Anthropologist* 25:17–26.

———. 1981. "Revisionist Anthropology: Aboriginal North America." *Current Anthropology* 22:503–509, 515–516.

———. 1989. *The Ghost Dance: Ethnohistory and Revitalization*. New York: Holt, Rinehart and Winston.

———. 1992. *North American Indians: A Comprehensive Account*. 2d ed. Englewood Cliffs, N.J.: Prentice-Hall.

Kelly, Lawrence C. 1983. *The Assault on Assimilation*. Albuquerque: University of New Mexico Press.

Larsen, Tord. 1983. "Negotiating Identity: The Micmac of Nova Scotia." In *The Politics of Indianness*, edited by Adrian Tanner, 37–136. St. John's: Institute of Social and Economic Research, Memorial University of Newfoundland.

Leap, William L. 1982. "Semilingualism as a Form of Linguistic Proficiency." In *Language Renewal among American Indian Tribes*, edited by Robert St. Clair and William Leap, 149–159. Rosslyn, Va.: National Clearinghouse for Bilingual Education.

Lesser, Alexander. 1933a. "Cultural Significance of the Ghost Dance." *American Anthropologist* 35:108–115.

———. 1933b. *The Pawnee Ghost Dance Hand Game*. Columbia University Contributions to Anthropology, no. 16. New York: Columbia University Press.

Linton, Ralph. 1943. "Nativistic Movements." *American Anthropologist* 45, no. 2:230–239.

Lithman, Yngve Georg. 1984. *The Community Apart*. Winnipeg: University of Manitoba Press.

McBeth, Sally J. 1983. *Ethnic Identity and the Boarding School Experience of West-Central Oklahoma American Indians*. Washington, D.C.: University Press of America.

McLoughlin, William G. 1986. *Cherokee Renascence in the New Republic*. Princeton, N.J.: Princeton University Press.

Meek, Ronald L. 1976. *Social Science and the Ignoble Savage*. Cambridge: Cambridge University Press.

Mooney, James. [1896] 1973. *The Ghost-Dance Religion and the Sioux Outbreak of 1890*. Fourteenth Annual Report, pt. 2, Bureau of Ethnology, Smithsonian Institution. Washington, D.C.: Government Printing Office. New York: Dover Publications.

Prucha, Francis Paul. 1984. *The Great Father*. Lincoln: University of Nebraska Press.

Radin, Paul. 1952. *The World of Primitive Man*. London: Abelard-Schuman.

Schoenwetter, James. 1974. "Pollen Records of Guila Naquitz Cave." *American Antiquity* 39, no. 2:292–303.

Schwimmer, Erik G. 1972. "Symbolic Competition." *Anthropologica* n.s. 14, no. 2:117–155.

Siegel, Bernard J., Evon Z. Vogt, James B. Watson, and Leonard Broom. 1954. "Acculturation: An Exploratory Formulation." *American Anthropologist* 56, no. 6:973–1,002.

Tax, Sol. 1954. "This Issue, and Others." *American Anthropologist* 56, no. 6:972, 1,166.

Vander, Judith, 1986. *Ghost Dance Songs and Religion of a Wind River Shoshone Woman*. Monograph Series in Ethnomusicology, no. 4. Los Angeles: UCLA.

———. 1988. *Songprints*. Urbana: University of Illinois Press.

Wallace, Anthony F. C. 1956. "Revitalization Movements: Some Theoretical Considerations for Their Comparative Study." *American Anthropologist* 58, no. 2:264–281.

Wood, Neal. 1983. *The Politics of Locke's Philosophy*. Berkeley: University of California Press.

———. 1984. *John Locke and Agrarian Capitalism*. Berkeley: University of California Press.

Change,
Continuity,
and Variation
in Native
American
Societies
as a
Response to
Conquest

Duane Champagne

If we are to speak of the destruction of Indian culture, then it would be helpful to know what Native American cultures were like before the arrival of Europeans. Then we would have a base line for comparing these cultures in the post-Columbian period. Our knowledge of early Indian societies and culture, however, is fragmentary because the written record is sparse. Furthermore, European observers and writers usually did not understand the intricacies of the social structures and cultures they described. This latter problem continues to plague the social sciences five hundred years after the landing of Columbus. Social scientists tend to make simplifying assumptions about the organization of indigenous societies. Therefore we do not get a full appreciation of the cultural, normative, political, and economic variation among Native American societies. The tendency has been to place indigenous societies on an evolutionary scale as early forms. Most classifications present American Indian societies in one-dimensional terms: primitive, simple, hunters and gatherers, horticultural, tribal, animistic, acephalous, or chieftain (Lenski 1969; Morgan 1877; Durkheim 1984; Spencer 1971; Parsons 1977). These classifications are helpful, to be sure, but limited. Their abstractions obscure variations in the empirical sociocultural orders that have existed in the Americas.

In this essay I critique several ways in which social scientists conceptualize social order, social interaction, and social change among native North American societies. I argue that many researchers view Indian societies as one-dimensional and therefore do not sufficiently account for the variation in institutional orders and processes and the variation of change. The concept of assimilation, I believe, is reductionist and should be replaced by more multidimensional conceptualizations. The general observation of endemic factionalism in Indian societies made by many students of Indian history and societies does not distinguish between routine conflict, which is played out within the bounds of the normative and political order, and factionalism, in which groups contest the fundamental rules of cultural, normative, or political order. I suggest ways of conceptualizing and analyzing the variation in Indian cultures (and by implication other cultures) and institutional orders and understanding the variation in their institutional responses to Western contact.

Culture and Institutional Relations in Iroquois, Creek, and Cherokee Societies

Rather than one-dimensional or broad evolutionary classifications, a more multidimensional approach will expand our understanding of social order and change in Native American societies. Indian societies are analytically complex, reflecting considerable variation in world view, culture, normative order, political organization, economic organization, and the institutions of social and political solidarity. What is more important, however, and perhaps most widely overlooked is that they vary considerably with respect to the internal relations among and within the major societal institutions. Conceptualizing and empirically describing the variation in institutional orders is a preliminary stage for any analysis of social change. Anthropologists have done some of this work, but they usually have only a secondary interest in change or the comparative analysis of change. Nevertheless, social scientists do not yet understand how to analyze variation systematically within and among the major institutional realms of polity, culture, social and political integration, kinship, and economy. Strides toward explaining societal variation and the conditions and possibilities of change seem especially promising in the sphere of cultural and institutional order.

The relations among kinship, polity, and culture, for example, vary among the Cherokee, the Creek, and the Iroquois. In Iroquois society the demigod Dekanawidah, a spokesman for the Great Spirit, supplied the constitutional charter of the Iroquois Confederacy. The organization and rules were divine and not subject to change and negotiation by humans (Wilson 1960). The divine institutionalization of the Iroquois Confederacy helps account for its continuity and Iroquois conservatives' strong defense for its preservation. After southern colonists drove the Tuscarora north between 1710 and 1720, the Iroquois chiefs refused to modify the confederacy to include the Tuscarora, even though they were a kindred nation. Since the Great Spirit created the confederacy with five nations, the chiefs upheld the ordained confederate order (Wilson 1960).

A primary purpose of the early five-nation confederacy was to create peace and harmony among the nations. Clans within each of the five nations managed judicial relations involving personal injury and murder. The confederacy extended the kin-based judicial system to include all five nations and managed judicial issues among them. Clans and lineages, however, were the primary political units in the nations and the confederacy (Morgan 1877, 1901; Wallace 1972). Binding decisions depended on consent from all lineages, clans, and nations. If a lineage dissented from the majority, it need not conform to the majority's will. At the confederacy's founding by Dekanawidah, forty-nine lineages attended. Each lineage present gained a place in the confederation council, while those lineages that chose to boycott the meeting were not allowed to have confederation chiefs. The nations and clans do not have equal numbers of confederation chiefs, but each lineage votes in clan meetings and unanimous consent is necessary for a clan decision. Similarly, a binding vote for an entire nation has required unanimous consent by all its constituent clans. Kinship groups have constituted the primary units of political organization, and their rights and obligations follow the divine commandments of the confederate constitution. This particular institutional configuration composed of mythically ordained kin-based polity has proven strongly resistant to change.

Creek society shows both general similarities and particular differences when compared with Iroquois society. Creek society was similar to Iroquois society in that Creek traditions foreordained the organization of the polity. The specific organizational details of the Creek polity, however, differ significantly from the Iroquois, and these differences turn out to be of considerable importance in understanding the function and history of Creek society. Creek polity comprised two groups of symbolically ordered towns, red and white, which reflected Creek views of a cosmic struggle between forces of the upper world and the lower world. Creek myths designated town colors, which were associated with a division of political duties; the red towns, for example, ruled in time of war and performed police duties. As far as we can now tell, the early Creek myths tell of migration from the west toward the east. In one myth the Creek, or perhaps more accurately the Muskogee, nation migrated east on a sacred mission to find the abode of the sun. After reaching the shores of the Atlantic, the Creek broke up into small villages and nations (IPH: vol. 9, 432). The Creek myths tell of four leading towns of the nation, whose names and details differ. It seems that as prominent towns rose and fell in influence the Creek reinterpreted the early myths to legitimate the ascendant towns' leadership. A case in point is Tucka-batchee, which in some early myths is not mentioned as one of the four central towns. Tuckabatchee became a leading red town after 1800, and some myths then recorded Tuckabatchee as a mythical central town. Of the four central towns, two are white and two are red. The two primary geographical divisions in Creek society each have a central red town and a central white town. Both districts are thus symbolically and politically complete, and throughout history the two districts often acted independently of each other. A long-standing political cleavage ran along the two geopolitical districts between the upper and lower towns, as the English called the two Creek divisions (Swanton 1928:25–472; Payne n.d.: vol. 9, 93–98; Grant 1980:326; Hewitt 1939:126–127).

In contrast with Iroquois myths, Creek myths have emphasized the hierarchy and history of the leading towns. For the Iroquois, kinship groups were the main political unit; in Creek society, towns were the primary political unit. Creek towns were particularistic religious centers. Each town with a ceremonial square had a separate relationship with the Great Spirit. The Great Spirit gave the town its sacred objects, its rituals, and its ceremonial organization. Individual Creek derived their social, ceremonial, and political identity from the ceremonial square or village of their mother. In each town, red and white clans formed the village polity. Ideally, though not always historically, a chief from a red clan led in a red town, while a chief of a white clan led in a white town. Again, the red and white symbolism reflected the antagonistic relations between red and white clans and between red and white towns. This antagonism reflected the dualistic cosmic struggle between red and white forces or spirits. White forces designated stability, order, harmony, and well-being; red forces designated malevolent underworld forces that caused change, disease, infertility, and ill health (Hudson 1976). The Creek social-political order reflected the dualistic cosmic order and the struggle for balance between the opposing cosmic forces. The institutions of the Creek polity, like those of the Iroquois, were a foreordained feature of the cosmic order and therefore not changeable by humans under normal circumstances. Thus the members of both societies viewed their polities in a strongly traditionalistic way, but the Creeks' national polity was formed by villages while the Iroquois' was formed by lineages and clans. Village delegations formed the Creek confederate council and were both ceremonial and political centers to a degree not found in Iroquois society. The differences between the Creek and Iroquois in social-political structure alone indicate different rules and traditions for most social and political decision making.

A comparison of the Creek and Iroquois with the Cherokee reveals even wider variation in institutional order. Cherokee creation myths have focused on validating a priesthood and the seven Cherokee clans. According to one creation myth, the seven sons of the Great Spirit formed seven clans. The sons of the Great Spirit also chose clan leaders (IPH: vol. 9, 492–500; Hudson 1976:136). Several sources say that the Great Spirit designated a principal priest who conducted national ceremonies in a heptagon-shaped arena at a central village. Cherokee from all villages in the nation gathered at the central village for the annual national festivals. Each clan had its assigned seating space within the heptagon, and the priests selected members from each clan to perform ceremonial and logistical tasks for the national festivals. A council of priests assisted the head priest. Each village had priests, and the priests made most of the political and ceremonial decisions in the society. The authority of civil leaders, or village headmen, was subordinate to the priest councils. Several oral accounts tell of the overthrow of the theocratic priesthood because of oppressive and immoral leadership (Payne n.d.: vol. 1, 9, 24, 28; vol. 3, 55–56, 125, 131ff; vol. 4, 15–20, 53, 55, 60, 85, 189, 235, 519; vol. 6, 5–6; Corkran 1957:363–364; Longe 1969:10–16). After the overthrow of the priesthood, village headmen and warriors assumed more prominent roles in Cherokee political affairs.

In contrast with the Creek and Iroquois, Cherokee myths divinely ordain seven Cherokee clans but not the political order. Many important Cherokee ceremonies also include the seven clans as part of their procedures. This institutional configuration gave the Cherokee a stronger sense of ceremonial and national kinship than was true among the more decentralized and segmentary kinship societies of the Iroquois and Creek. In contrast with both the Creek and

Iroquois, Cherokee political order was subordinate to the religious-ceremonial sphere. Cherokee myths did not directly dictate the structure and rules for political relations. Thus the Cherokee did not have a strong traditionalistic orientation toward maintaining a specific or foreordained political order. This allowed the Cherokee to experiment with different political arrangements without challenging their society's cultural world view and mythical commands.

In addition, Cherokee clans were important in village politics but were not significant in regional or national political organization. In Cherokee society the fundamental political unit was the village. Regional councils and the national council consisted of coalitions of village leaders. When village delegations attended the occasional national gatherings, they represented village communities and not their national clan. As in Creek society, the Cherokee national polity did not consist of kinship groups. Thus, clan or kinship prerogatives were not obstacles to change and decision making in national Cherokee political relations as they were among the Iroquois. Furthermore, while Cherokee social identity derived from the kinship-ceremonial complex, the latter organization was relatively unaffected by action in the political sphere. For most well-socialized Cherokee, whatever happened in the political sphere was minor compared with the continuity of kinship-ceremonial relations. This configuration of institutional relations provided the Cherokee with strong traditionalistic orientations toward national preservation and social solidarity but greater flexibility within the political sphere. Cherokee ceremonies and mythology fixed the seven clans as the primary institutions of national social solidarity but left the political sphere undefined and subordinate to the cultural sphere.

The Cherokee, the Creek, and the Iroquois represent three different societies and three different institutional configurations. The variation among the societies is of more than antiquarian interest since they contributed to shaping the possibilities of change and cultural survival. The Cherokee, with their socially solidary and relatively unencumbered institutional order, adopted major changes in political organization. They adopted a constitutional government in 1827. Under similar conditions, the less solidary and symbolically organized Creek strongly resisted change during the 1820s. When the Creek formed a constitutional government in 1867, the new government met considerable resistance from conservatives who wished to maintain the old institutional order. Similarly, the Iroquois, with their mythically constituted and decentralized kin-based polity, were strongly resistant to change. Major change in Iroquois society resulted from Handsome Lake's revitalization movement during the period 1799–1815. His movement introduced new religious views that legitimated change from a hunter–fur trade economy to settled agricultural communities. The movement did not create significant change in political relations, however. After 1817, when Christian Iroquois tried to introduce U.S. political models, Iroquois society split into pagan and Christian factions for the rest of the century. As a collective society, the Iroquois did not agree to accept U.S. political models.

Institutional order and culture inform social action—that is, historical events and group and individual actions take place within cultural and institutional contexts. Unless explanations of historical events take into account the understandings and contextual interpretations of the participants, analysts risk imposing their own views or culture on those events. Institutional order and culture not only inform social action but also create parameters for societal change and adaptation to new political and economic conditions. Thus, to understand processes of social change it is imperative to understand and analyze the culture and institutional relations of Indian societies.

Institutional relations indicate possibilities of change. According to sociological theory, societies with more specialized and solidary institutional relations have greater possibilities of accepting change than societies with less specialized and less solidary institutional orders (Parsons 1977; Eisenstadt 1978:61–63, 66; Alexander 1988:49–77; Alexander and Colomy 1990). If we are to move beyond the classification of static societies to study processes of social change, an understanding of variation in cultural and institutional order is of central interest. Our task, then, is to analyze historical processes of change and continuity in Native American cultural and institutional orders subject to changing political, economic, and cultural relations with colonizing societies.

"Conquest" and Change

When we speak of the conquest of indigenous cultures, are we talking about the destruction or adaptation of these cultures? Societies are not stagnant, as is well known; they have an inherent tendency toward change, although core cultural features may endure for centuries. Even if no European had ever set foot in the Americas, Native American societies would not be the same as they were five hundred years ago. Of course we do not know in what directions they would have changed. Certainly they would be different from contemporary Indian societies, which are survivors of intense political competitions and coercive cultural pressures.

Has there been wholesale destruction of Indian cultures and societies? In my view, institutional destruction of a society is a rare event, although there are precedents in world history. The destruction of a society occurs when all its members die or have internalized the norms and cultural orientations of another society and no longer participate in their original society. Although Indian societies have faced major threats to their survival, most continue in modified form under post-Columbian conditions.

Native Americans generally are conservative in their institutional orders. There are cultural reasons for their conservatism. As a rule, the mythologies of Native American cultures do not distinguish sharply between natural and supernatural orders or sacred and profane spheres. A mythical world view informs and defines the institutional order of society and informs individual action and normative order. In such cultures the institutional and normative orders become an immutable facet of the cosmic order, which has been foreordained in the creation myths (Campbell 1988:193, 1989; Weber 1964:268–269; Eisenstadt 1978:101). Hence transgression of or change in law or institutional order without divine sanction will cause disruption in the cosmic order. These disruptions result in this-worldly misfortune for the transgressing community or individual. Holy men must perform ceremonies to set the cosmic order in balance and restore order so that offended spirits will not cause military defeat, drought, or disease for the community or individual. The major societies of the American southeast and the Navajo are good examples of this type of world view (Campbell 1988:241–250; Beck and Walters 1977:3–36, 277–300).

Among the southeastern Chickasaw, an elder customarily addressed the community assembly near the end of the annual Green Corn Ceremony. The elder's speech illustrates the Chickasaw world view. He first addressed the warriors, recounting to them the positive and negative injunctions for keeping the sacred law. Then he turned to the women, advising them to follow strictly the ritual procedures of the Green Corn Ceremony and extinguish all the old fires in their cabins lest they carry impurities that might spoil their luck as individuals and that of the entire community in the forthcoming year. He warned that if the women gave impure food to the children, they would get worms and the community would suffer famine, disease, and other evils. If the people carefully adhered to the sacred law, the Great Spirit would grant the Chickasaw rainmakers and prophets power to bring bountiful harvests and would grant the Chickasaw victory over their enemies. Strict observance of the sacred law kept the ritual objects of the holy men pure. Blameless conduct kept open the channels of communication with the helpful upper-world spirits that ensured health and well-being among the Chickasaw. If, however, the Chickasaw broke the sacred laws and rituals, they would cause great calamities such as drought, disease, hunger, bouts with witches, and death at the hands of their enemies. Transgressions of the sacred law spoiled the purity and power of their sacred objects, impairing the power of the prophets and medicine men to prevent injurious events (Adair 1968:99–112). The Green Corn Ceremony was the central Chickasaw ceremonial event. Its purpose was the ritual purification and renewal of the Chickasaw nation. Individuals ritually purified their bodies, the women extinguished the old fires, and priests ignited a new fire that was placed in the hearths of the cabins. If performed correctly, the Green Corn Ceremony absolved the nation of past impurities. The new year began in a ritually purified state that, if maintained throughout the year, ensured health and prosperity for the nation (Adair 1968:99–111; Baird 1974:9).

Such a world view, as seen in the Chickasaw tradition, encourages acceptance of the institutional order as a given part of the cosmic order. While the specific religious doctrines of Native Americans vary greatly, they foster sacred views of the cosmic order. There is little separation of sacred and profane realms; institutions have divine or mythical origins. Indian religions emphasize ritual balance with the cosmic order. The Great Spirit dictated the sacred laws, which form part of the divine cosmic order. The sacred laws and the institutional order are not subject to change and negotiation during ordinary times (Campbell 1988, 1989; Weber 1964:268–269).

Despite their cultural conservatism many Native Americans have participated in significant changes in their societies. The changes depend on the external pressures and the form of the institutional order that the conservatives are defending. Those societies with more differentiated, or specialized, institutional configurations have been more capable of accepting change than societies whose conservatives defended decentralized and nondifferentiated institutional orders. Hence in some historical situations and with certain institutional arrangements, Indians have accepted change. A prime example of this pattern of resistance and the institutional order is the formation of democratic governments among the so-called five civilized tribes during the nineteenth century (Foreman 1934; Champagne 1989). Traditional Delaware society after 1760, for example, consisted of decentralized and mythically unified phratries—three groups of twelve lineages. As a group, the Delaware strongly resisted exchanging their religiously unified kin-based political order for a constitutional government. In the 1860s a group of U.S. government–supported Christian Delaware leaders tried to organize a constitutional government. Few Delaware, however, acquiesced. Most ignored the new government, and it failed to become a regular feature of Delaware society (Newcomb 1956:95–104; Ferguson 1972:166; Weslager 1972). Similarly, Iroquois conservatives still adhere to the rules and obligations of the confederate council, and many abide by the teachings of Handsome Lake, the Seneca prophet. The conservative Iroquois have steadfastly rejected U.S. culture and political institutions (Hauptman 1981:9, 179; Basic Call to Consciousness 1978:89, 92, 108).

With respect to social change, Indians are not passive receptacles of Western political, economic, and cultural domination. Within the range of opportunities and conditions available to them, Indians have acted upon their political, cultural, and economic interests. They have actively sought to preserve territory, political autonomy, and cultural autonomy; they have not always succeeded, for the forces arrayed against them often have been mighty (Cornell 1988).

Change in Native American societies is not reducible to assimilation or acculturation; it is a much more multidimensional and complex process. Change can occur simultaneously on several levels. Change may occur in economic relations, as during the fur trade, but not in religious or political relations. It is possible that changes occur differently in cultural, moral, political, and economic relations. Adoption of Western innovations can result in a strengthening of national resistance to political domination or can lead to individual Christianization. The complexity and variety of possible permutations of change should make researchers wary of one-dimensional assimilation or acculturation arguments that assume Indians have accepted Western culture wholesale and have rejected their own culture. Many Indian groups, however, have borrowed selectively from Western culture and usually not with the intention of assimilation. The borrowing of selective cultural, political, and economic features often strengthens the community's and the Indian nation's possibilities of political and cultural survival. This is often an unintended consequence of Christianization and assimilation policies, as Cherokee agricultural change and the adoption of a democratic government during the early 1800s suggest (McLoughlin 1986a, 1986b).

What is significant change? This is a question that needs definition and debate. I define significant social change as the institutionalization of increased differentiation within or among the major societal spheres or the institutionalization of increased centralization of social and political solidarity. The major societal spheres are culture, the polity, normative order, and the economy. By institutionalized change I mean that an innovation must gain support from major groups that are willing to provide material support and political and social commitments to the new institutional arrangement. Many proposed innovations may fail. In my view these failures are not of central importance since they have no long-term effects on future social action or institutional organization. The second Ghost Dance on the plains was a movement that failed to become a permanent part of all but a few societies; consequently, it did not become generally institutionalized. In contrast, during the same historical period the much less dramatic peyote cult was an alternative that has become an enduring feature of many Native American reservations; it has affected the lives of many individuals and eased the transition to reservation life in ways that the Ghost Dance could not (Campbell 1988:232–233, 250; Stewart 1987).

Thus, significant social change requires negotiation and change in the rules of cultural and institutional order. Great external forces have promoted change in Indian societies and these conditions have generated the myth of endemic factionalism within Native American societies. Much so-called factionalism is largely routine conflict. Since many Indian societies have decentralized social and political institutions, decision making depends on consensus among segmentary social, economic, and political groups, each having considerable leeway for independent action. The will of the majority is not binding on the dissenting groups; hence, in few instances have such societies united in collective action. Such independent political action is not factionalism, since there is agreement about the rules of social and political order and each group is exercising its own autonomy. As in a football game, this kind of conflict is contained within the normative rules of society.

Contemporary scholarship portrays internal political relations in Iroquois history before 1817 as highly factionalized. In my view, Iroquois political actions were largely routine conflicts played out within the rules of the decentralized and segmentary Iroquois political order. About 1700 the Iroquois ended the Beaver Wars (1649–1700) and adopted a new strategy to balance power between the British and French colonies, realizing that they had as much to fear from the British as the French since the former were settling the Mohawk Valley. The Iroquois proceeded to create trade agreements with many western Indian nations. In diplomatic meetings they informed the Europeans that they could muster nearly fifty nations of warriors. This boast was indeed a bluff. Historians have gone further to argue that Iroquois unity after 1700 was also a bluff (Haan 1980). In this view factionalism and continual bickering racked Iroquois society. Furthermore, immediately before the American Revolution the Iroquois nations and villages split their loyalties among the colonists, the British, and neutrality. As the war proceeded, Iroquois died on both sides of the conflict, while many tried to remain neutral. The issue here was not factionalism but rather the decentralized and particularistic kinship prerogatives of the Iroquois Confederacy. Each lineage made its political decisions independent of the rest. If there was no consensus, then the lineages, clans, and nations proceeded on their own. The behavior of the Iroquois during the American Revolution conformed to their constitutional guidelines. Since there was no consensus, the segmentary lineages, clans, villages, and nations independently decided their course of action in the conflict (Graymont 1972:47; Fenton 1949:238; Torok 1965:75). While the absence of consensus on the issue of alliance caused considerable disruption for the confederacy, the Iroquois followed their decentralized and segmentary rules of organization and decision making. The term "factionalism" applies more appropriately to the conflicts between Christian and pagan Iroquois after 1817. In this case the Iroquois had greater difficulties agreeing to a common political framework and common rules of political decision making; there were no common cultural assumptions of proper social or political order. The struggle was over whether Christian or pagan rules of cultural and institutional order were going to apply. Before 1817 the Iroquois had their confederacy, but its decentralized and segmentary organization did not function best when circumstances demanded sustained, unified collective action.

The term "factionalism" applies to situations in which the major groups of a society have basic disagreements over the fundamental rules of societal organization. Factionalism is likely to arise when groups cannot agree to adopt or reject institutional change. Unless they agree about institutional innovations, contending groups threaten to disrupt the entire social fabric. The Iroquois Christians versus the Iroquois pagans is one example. Another is reservations that have accepted an Indian Reorganization Act (IRA) government, while conservatives adhere to local chiefs. The latter kind of factionalism is evident within some Sioux reservations today. As Lacey (1985) observed, differing concepts of authority—modern and traditional—are contributing to Sioux tribal factionalism. Authority in IRA governments derives from position. In traditional Sioux views, authority refers to individuals and requires sustained consensus and support from the community:

This traditional concept of authority is very much alive today and has become, in some cases, a point of contention between recognized traditional leaders and elected constitutional officers. The takeover, occupation, and siege of Wounded Knee, South Dakota in 1973 is a good example of this traditional/nontraditional conflict . . . the Wounded Knee protesters entered the village to declare their separation from the constitution under which the Ogallala tribe operated. (Lacey 1985:137–38)

Traditional concepts of authority, the predominance of kinship groups in political relations, and the decentralized, segmentary character of the Sioux social order create difficulties for institutionalizing constitutional governments. The constitutional governments work better with more centralized forms of social and political solidarity and a social order in which policy is differentiated from religion and kinship groups (Schusky 1970:44–45; Champagne 1987:175–222).

Social Change within Native American Societies

Is it possible to make generalizations about social change within Native American societies? This is certainly a difficult task, but let me venture some arguments. Most Native American cultures foster conservative orientations toward institutional change. Indeed, societies that have conservative orientations, non-differentiated institutional orders, and decentralized institutions of social and political solidarity tend not to adopt institutional innovations or sustain collective actions. Among these societies revitalization movements often effected limited institutional change. Examples are the Delaware Prophet movement of the early 1760s and the Handsome Lake movement among the Iroquois early in the nineteenth century, which adjusted institutional relations to changing political and economic conditions (Wallace 1972; Champagne 1988). Many revitalization movements failed to become established, either because of repression by state and national governments or because they did not gain enduring commitments from followers. The Red Stick War (1813–14), the Shawnee Prophet movement (1806–11), the Winnebago Prophet movement (1831–32) and Black Hawk War, the Cherokee movement of 1811–12, and the two Ghost Dance movements did not create major, enduring institutional change among Indian nations. Most of these movements had traditionalistic orientations and opposed U.S. efforts to change Indian societies and assimilate Indians.

Christian concepts have had an important influence on some movements (the Winnebago Prophet movement and second Ghost Dance), but most movements have espoused traditional Indian world views that offered magical as well as realistic solutions to changing economic and political conditions (Champagne

1992). More enduring movements such as the Handsome Lake movement, the Shaker movement, the Kickapoo Prophet movement, the Delaware Prophet movement of 1760, and the Alaskan Native Brotherhood all accepted Christian-influenced teachings of personal salvation and strong cleavage between this world and the sacred world. The Indian prophets often combined Christian teachings with traditional ceremonies to validate change or group commitments to survival. Among the Iroquois and Kickapoo the new cultural orientations legitimated the transition of roles from hunter to farmer and supported individual moral reform. In different ways the adapted cultural views created political and social integration among the Delaware and the Tlingit of Alaska. As mentioned earlier, the Delaware revitalization movement led to political, social, and religious integration. The Christian influences among the Tlingit provided legitimation for individual participation in a politically oriented, voluntary association supported but not organized by Tlingit clan and moiety solidarity (Slagle and Weible-Orlando 1986:312–313; Trafzer 1986; Champagne 1988, 1989, 1990, 1992). Similarly the peyote cult has introduced Christian-influenced doctrine and emphasis on personal moral reform (La Barre 1969; Stewart 1987). At least within the U.S. political and cultural environment, movements that adopted Christian views of personal salvation produced more enduring and extensive change. Some groups such as the Cherokee Nighthawk Keetoowahs and a Sun Dance carried on in a special way by the new Northern Ute-Crow have endured, but their traditionalistic cultural orientations emphasize harmony, order, and balance. Their traditionalistic views do not emphasize or validate significant change in institutional differentiation or increased political solidarity (Jorgensen 1972:220–237; Hendrix 1983; IPH: vol. 9, 492–527).

Socially well-integrated Native American societies with conservative cultural orientations and relatively differentiated institutional orders are comparatively rare. Examples are the Cherokee during the nineteenth century, the Chickasaw between 1850 and 1907, and the Choctaw from 1860 to 1907. All these societies adopted constitutional governments and acquired self-sufficient agricultural economic bases (Champagne 1989).

Socially well-integrated societies have made quite remarkable responses to Western contact. In Cherokee society the mythically legitimated and ceremonially integrated clan system, in conjunction with a polity differentiated from religion and kinship, facilitated formation of a constitutional government and political nationality from 1809 to 1827. Two other examples are the Northern Arapaho and the Tlingit. Fowler argues that the Northern Arapaho have maintained their religiously integrated age-grade system and community solidarity over the past one hundred years of reservation life while accepting limited innovations in political organization. The Tlingit in Alaska retained their subsistence fishing base and ceremonially integrated clan-moiety system. This helped them preserve social cohesion and build the Alaskan Native Brotherhood as a response to declining political, economic, cultural, and demographic conditions at the beginning of the twentieth century (Fowler 1982; Champagne 1989, 1990).

Despite paying a heavy price in political subordination, economic marginalization, and cultural degradation, most Native American societies continue to survive five hundred years after the European discovery. Native Americans have not been passive. Given the political, economic, and cultural constraints of more powerful colonizing powers, Indians responded to Western contact in a variety of ways. These responses have included revitalization movements, creation of constitutional governments, traditionalistic resistance to change, and selective change while maintaining core cultural institutions and understandings. It is the task of social scientists to explore the ways in which Indian societies have responded with enduring forms of change and adaptation. To do this, they must study Indian cultures and institutional orders more systematically. Effective understanding of Indian historical action will come only when analyzed within its institutional and cultural context. Taking the point of view of the actor is not enough; historical action and history transpire within cultural and institutional contexts (among others). We cannot assume that all Indians behave alike. Each nation has its myths, culture, and institutional relations that are keys to their values, goals, and actions. Furthermore, Indians' historical action takes place within a context of colonial political competition, economic incorporation, and cultural exchange. Both transsocietal relations and Indian cultural and institutional context are necessary for understanding historical phenomena and the variation and duration of Indian institutional responses to Western contact. How Indian societies have survived and changed over the past five hundred years is of more than local interest. Their histories are microcosms of processes of social change and adaptation to changing political, economic, and cultural environments.

Note

I gratefully acknowledge research support from the Rockefeller Foundation, the Ford Foundation, the American Indian Studies Center at UCLA, the National Science Foundation (grant no. SES–853914), and the UCLA faculty senate.

References

Adair, James. 1968. *The History of the Indians of North America*. New York: Johnson Reprint Corp.

Alexander, Jeffrey C. 1988. *Action and Its Environments*. New York: Columbia University Press.

Alexander, Jeffrey C., and Paul Colomy, eds. 1990. *Differentiation Theory and Social Change: Comparative and Historical Perspectives*. New York: Columbia University Press.

Baird, W. David. 1974. *The Chickasaw People*. Phoenix, Ariz.: Indian Tribal Series.

Basic Call to Consciousness. 1978. New York: Mohawk Nation (Akwesasne Notes).

Beck, Peggy, and Ann L. Walters. 1977. *The Sacred: Ways of Knowledge, Sources of Life*. Tsaile, Ariz.: Navajo Community College Press.

Campbell, Joseph. 1988. *Mythologies of the Great Hunt*. Vol. 1, pts. 1 and 2; vol. 2, part 1. New York: Harper & Row.

————. 1989. *Mythologies of the Great Hunt*. Vol. 2, pts. 2 and 3. New York: Harper & Row.

Champagne, Duane. 1983. "Social Structure, Revitalization Movements, and State Building: Social Change in Four Native American Societies." *American Sociological Review* 48:754–763.

————. 1987. "American Bureaucratization and American Indian Tribal Governments: Problems of Institutionalization at the Community Level." Occasional Papers in Curriculum Series. Chicago: Newberry Library.

————. 1988. "The Delaware Revitalization Movement of the Early 1760s: A Suggested Reinterpretation." *American Indian Quarterly* 12, no. 2:107–126.

————. 1989. *American Indian Societies: Strategies and Conditions of Political and Cultural Survival*. Cambridge Mass.: Cultural Survival, Inc.

————. 1990. "Culture, Differentiation, and Environment: Social Change in Tlingit Society." In *Differentiation Theory and Social Change: Comparative and Historical Perspectives*, edited by Jeffrey C. Alexander and Paul Colomy, pp. 52–87. New York: Columbia University Press.

————. 1992. "Transsocietal Culture Exchange within the World Economic and Political System." In *The Dynamics of Social Systems,* edited by Paul Colomy, pp. 120–153. Sage Studies in International Sociology.

Corkran, David. 1957. "Cherokee Pre-History." *The North Carolina Historical Review* 34:363–364.

Cornell, Stephen. 1988. *The Return of the Native: American Indian Political Resurgence*. New York: Oxford University Press.

Durkheim, Emile. 1984. *The Division of Labor in Society*. New York: Free Press.

Eisenstadt, S. N. 1978. *Revolution and the Transformation of Societies: A Comparative Study of Civilization*. New York: Free Press.

Fenton, William A. 1949. "Collecting Materials for a Political History of the Six Nations." *Proceedings of the American Philosophical Society*, no. 93. American Philosophical Society: Philadelphia, Pa.

Ferguson, Roger. 1972. "The White River Delaware: An Ethnohistorical Synthesis, 1795–1867." Ph.D. diss., Ball State University.

Foreman, Grant. 1934. *The Five Civilized Tribes.* Norman: University of Oklahoma Press.

Fowler, Loretta. 1982. *Arapahoe Politics, 1851–1978: Symbols in Crises of Authority.* Lincoln: University of Nebraska Press.

Grant, C. L., ed. 1980. *Letters, Journals, and Writings of Benjamin Hawkins. Vol. 1, 1796–1801. Vol. 2, 1802–1816.* Savannah, Ga.: Belview Press.

Graymont, Barbara. 1972. *The Iroquois and the American Revolution.* Syracuse, N.Y.: Syracuse University Press.

Haan, Richard. 1980. "The Problem of Iroquois Neutrality: Suggestions for Revision." *Ethnohistory* 27:317–330.

Hauptman, Lawrence. 1981. *The Iroquois and the New Deal.* Syracuse, N.Y.: Syracuse University Press.

Hendrix, Janey B. 1983. "Redbird Smith and the Nighthawk Keetoowahs." *Journal of Cherokee Studies* 8:73–86.

Hewitt, J. N. B. 1939. "Notes on the Creek Indians." *Anthropological Papers,* edited by J. R. Swanton. Bureau of American Ethnology no. 123. Washington, D.C.: U.S. Government Printing Office.

Hudson, Charles. 1976. *The Southeastern Indians.* Nashville: University of Tennessee Press.

Indian Pioneer History of Oklahoma. n. d. [1934–35] *Indian Pioneer Papers,* edited by Grant Foreman. 120 vols. Oklahoma City: Oklahoma Historical Society.

Jorgensen, Joseph G. 1972. *The Sun Dance Religion.* Chicago: University of Chicago Press.

Lacey, Michael. 1985. "The United States and American Indians: Political Relations." In *American Indian Policy in the Twentieth Century,* edited by Vine Deloria, Jr., 83–104. Norman: University of Oklahoma Press.

La Barre, Weston. 1969. *The Peyote Cult.* New York: Schocken Books.

Lenski, Gerhard. 1969. *Power and Privilege: A Theory of Social Stratification.* New York: McGraw-Hill.

Longe, Alexander. 1969. "A Small Postscript on the Ways and Manners of the Indians Called Cherokee," edited by David Corkran. *Southern Indian Studies* 21:10–16.

McLoughlin, William G. 1986a. *The Cherokee Ghost Dance.* Macon, Ga.: Mercer University Press.

———. 1986b. *Cherokee Renascence in the New Republic.* Princeton, N.J.: Princeton University Press.

Morgan, Henry Lewis. 1877. *Ancient Society.* New York: Henry Holt & Company.

———. 1901. *The League of the Iroquois.* New York: Frank Burton.

Newcomb, William W. 1956. *The Culture and Acculturation of the Delaware Indians.* Anthropological Papers. Ann Arbor, Mich.: Museum of Anthropology.

Parsons, Talcott. 1977. *The Evolution of Societies,* edited by Jackson Toby. Englewood Cliffs, N.J.: Prentice-Hall.

Payne, John. n. d. [1820s]. *The John Payne Papers.* 13 vols. Microfilm. Chicago: Newberry Library.

Schusky, Ernest. 1970. *The Right to Be Indian.* San Francisco: American Indian Education Publishers.

Slagle, A. Logan, and Joan Weible-Orlando. 1986. "The Indian Shaker Church and Alcoholics Anonymous: Revitalistic Curing Cults." *Human Organization* 45:310–319.

Spencer, Herbert. 1971. *Structure, Function, and Evolution.* London: Michael Jospher.

Stewart, Omer C. 1987. *Peyote Religion: A History.* Norman: University of Oklahoma Press.

Swanton, John R. 1928. *Social Organization and Social Usages of the Indians of the Creek Confederacy.* Forty-Second Annual Report of the Bureau of Ethnology. Washington, D.C.: U.S. Government Printing Office.

Torok, C. H. 1965. "The Tyendinaga Mohawks." *Ontario History* 57:69–77.

Trafzer, Clifford E., ed. 1986. *American Indian Prophets.* Sacramento, Calif.: Sierra Oaks Publishing Co.

Wallace, Anthony F. C. 1972. *The Death and Rebirth of the Seneca.* New York: Vintage Books.

Weber, Max. 1964. *The Sociology of Religion.* Boston: Beacon Press.

Weslager, C. A. 1972. *The Delaware Indians.* New Brunswick, N.J.: Rutgers University Press.

Wilson, Edmund. 1960. *Apologies to the Iroquois.* New York: Farrar, Straus and Cudahy.

Definitional
Violence
and
Plains
Indian
Reservation
Life:
Ongoing
Challenges
to Survival

David Reed Miller

This essay concerns a special kind of violence and some of its repercussions in the long and varied history of European-Indian relations. The varied European assaults on the "discovered" indigenous peoples of North America have included encroachment, deracination, genocide, and subordination. Intentional enclavement and group isolation were forms of Indian resistance in the face of this invasion (Jennings 1975). Another form of resistance was negotiating the ambiguous applications of power and violence when confronted with the invader's systematic determination to rule. In an effort to control their territories and define the relationship with European Americans, some Indian groups responded in ways that even their enemies welcomed, at least temporarily (R. White 1991). For example, many groups used diplomatic mechanisms to suspend hostilities and prevent disruptions in trade relations (Blakeslee 1976; Wood 1980).

Interethnic cooperation and acceptance of new members into the group to achieve a numerical advantage over other groups often became an important strategy. Among northern Plains Indians, interethnic cooperation by the mid-nineteenth century included sharing similar military sodalities across tribal boundaries (Albers and Kay 1987; Sharrock 1974). Some groups added outsiders who were captives, slaves, orphans, outlaws, social outcasts, mixed-bloods, trading partners, or fictive kin (Sharrock 1974; Tanner 1978; R. White 1991).

Plains Indians' ideas about recruitment of outsiders and maintenance of their social and territorial boundaries came into conflict with European American views, resulting in definitional violence. This kind of violence against U.S. and Canadian Indian groups occurred especially during the nineteenth and twentieth centuries as they were being placed on reservations or reserves and allotted lands. Colonial and national governments imposed definitions and changing policies that were in direct conflict with indigenous identities and ideas of personhood. The reservation-reserve system was a means of social control over Plains Indians, who were subdued by political subordination, disease, new vices, and armed conflict (Carter 1990; Danziger 1974; Hoxie 1984; Iverson 1985; Prucha 1984; Takaki 1979; Trennert 1975).

The categories of identity imposed by non-Indians on indigenous groups were necessarily disparaging and did violence to many Indians' cultural autonomy and social systems. External notions of order and legitimacy were imposed to transform Indians into contributing citizens, reflecting the lifestyle and values of the national mainstream. Indoctrination by missionaries, suppression of Indian religions, and the imposed agrarian economic model of the nineteenth-century reservation and reserve administrations exemplified this definitional process. Bureaucrats, politicians, missionaries, traders, merchants, soldiers, and non-Indian settlers introduced their notions of what Indians should become (Beaver 1988; Burns 1988; Carlson 1981; Carter 1990; Dyck 1991; Price 1988). The subtle and complex nature of the conflicting, defining discourses about identity and the ways they affected behavior toward Indian peoples reverberated across generations.

Several northern Plains Indian groups that are today intertwined administratively, culturally, and biologically illustrate the results of definitional violence and strategies to counter the restrictions and other disruptions of colonial and national control with their own conceptions of self-definition and tribal membership. In this brief analysis the definitional violence done to Fort Peck Assiniboine and Sioux tribes, the Turtle Mountain Chippewa tribe, and the landless Chippewa-Cree Indians—and their resistance to it—will be discussed.[1]

New Associations and an Emerging Metis Population

In the mid-eighteenth century, as the Hudson's Bay Company extended its trading network for furs deeper into the interior of North America, many Assiniboine and Cree, who were allied against the Sioux, became trader middlemen. The Sioux, armed with guns by French traders, faced the Assiniboine and Cree in conflicts below the border lakes during the remainder of the eighteenth century (Anderson 1984). As the Ottawa and Chippewa expanded their own trading ventures west and southwest of Sault St. Marie and Lake Superior, warfare with the Sioux, who also wanted access to new markets, was inevitable (R. White 1991).

Increasing contacts among the Chippewa, Cree, Sioux, and Assiniboine lent new importance to temporary and long-term alliances. Trading partnerships were established through marriages or fictive kinship relations (DeMallie 1971, 1980b; B. White 1982, 1987). Metis (mixed-bloods), the offspring of Indians and non-Indian fur traders, might be incorporated into a particular Indian group. But if the fur post or other non-Indian settlement was where these mixed-blood children were socialized, acceptance within the Indian parent's group was bound to be incomplete. The difficulties must have seemed almost insurmountable for many Metis when they attempted to participate fully in the racially stratified non-Indian societies (J. Brown 1980; Ewers 1962; Foster 1976, 1978, 1986; Giraud 1986; Peterson and Brown 1985; Sprague 1988; Van Kirk 1983).[2]

The shifting economic pressures on these Indian groups to adapt to the widely diverse material and ideational cultures of non-Indians became particularly acute in the nineteenth century. Metis unattached to an Indian group were hit especially hard when the Northwest Company was absorbed into the Hudson's Bay Company, which took only a fraction of its labor force (Jackson 1988). Having to deal with the Hudson's Bay Company's reordering of the labor market for many of the trade's clients made the Missouri River country more attractive. The Assiniboine mingled with Cree and Chippewa (Saulteaux) who were engaged in hunting for the robe and provisions trade there (Ray 1974). Ranging between the Assiniboine River country and the valleys of the Souris and White Earth rivers, they anticipated an alternative marketplace in competition with Hudson's Bay Company posts when the American Fur Company built Fort Union in 1828 (see fig. 1).

The Metis, displaced from the receiving and transporting work of the trade in 1821, were thrown into competition with various Plains Indians as producers of the raw products that fueled the trade. Concentrated initially in the Red River settlements between Selkirk and Pembina, the Metis adjusted to a seasonal

NORTHERN PRAIRIE BORDERLANDS

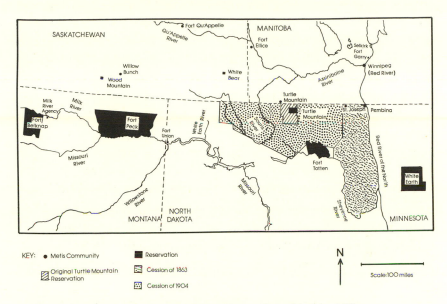

Figure 1. Map of the northern prairie borderlands. Susan Hopkins Miller.

round of activities—garden horticulture in the spring and fall, buffalo hunting on the prairies and plains to the west in the summer. Many of the Assiniboine, Plains Cree, western Sioux, Atsina Gros Ventre, and Blackfoot differed only in that they engaged in the chase year round. Many bands of Plains Indians also were deeply affected by epidemics (Ray 1975, 1976; Trimble 1987) and the credit system pressed on individual hunters by the traders (Swagerty 1988).

After 1828 the lower Assiniboine were unable to bottle up the upper Missouri River trade at Fort Union because much of the trade was coming downriver from the Yellowstone country and the Blackfoot country. As a result, they again concentrated on their skills as middlemen for their neighbors. In the same period a number of the Teton and Yanktonai Sioux bands attacked their traditional enemies on any pretense. Other kinds of pressures and confrontations among Plains Indians also increased (DeMallie 1986; R. White 1978).

Reservations, Resettlement, and the Indian-Metis Distinction

The non-Indian architects of U.S. policy for Indians in the mid-nineteenth century concluded that intertribal rivalries would have to be curtailed in the upper Missouri River country if all were to be under the control of a national "civilized" government in which tribes would respect one another's territories. This conclusion was based on the questionable premise that what tribes fought over was land, rather than a combination of resources and complex social interests. U.S. treaties with the Plains tribes in the 1850s provided non-Indians with additional influence among Indian groups by means of annuities—annual payments of goods to leaders for fixed periods. The annuities were redistributed as gifts throughout an Indian group, reinforcing the leaders' status and influence. They also carried the stipulation that Indians must cease the fighting that disrupted commerce and frontier settlements of the emerging nations of the United States and Canada.[3] In Canada, where the "numbered" treaties promising reserves came after confederation, Indian policy also intentionally isolated Indians, much as the reservations did during President Grant's peace policy.[4]

Pivotal to the treaty making of this period were territorial assignments to tribes and the assumption that the boundaries of observed occupancy in 1851 conformed to traditional territories. This attempt to define territories meant fixing the flexible interactions and fluid tribal boundaries of earlier times (Albers and Kay 1987).

Non-Indian civilization in its various manifestations brought European ideas of property, including systematic boundary surveys, deeds, and land as a commodity (Gibson 1984; Kaplan 1980). Plains Indians' notion of land as sacred, resource-rich spaces was gradually altered by interactions with non-Indians who treated land as fungible property (Albers and Kay 1987). The land-survey system of the Northwest Ordinance of 1787 was turned to marking and distributing the remaining open lands, referred to as the public domain (Gates 1976). From a European-American viewpoint, Indians were not using their lands in an efficient and civilized manner. European Americans felt that appropriation of these lands was justified, especially because the Indians did not practice permanent occupancy and lacked fenced property lines (Carlson 1981; Kaplan 1980; Sutton 1978).

The jurisdiction for Indian affairs and distribution of the Indian population shifted several times in what are now Montana and North and South Dakota (Janke 1988). Assiniboines took their annuities at Fort Union until the Milk River Agency was established in 1869. A portion of Sisseton and Wahpeton, who were eastern Sioux refugees under the leadership of the Sisseton headman Standing Buffalo, fled the Minnesota conflict in 1862 and eventually arrived at the Milk River. Yanktonai and Teton Sioux from the Grand River country also came in increasing numbers to live off the more plentiful resources there. By this time the seasonal hunting forays of the Metis hunters into the White Earth and Souris River country also had become common practice. In 1876 Sitting Bull dropped off many old men, women, and children as he moved his remaining force into Canada. After his surrender in 1881 part of these Hunkpapa stayed with the Yanktonai attached to the recently formed Fort Peck Agency (DeMallie 1986; Manzione 1991; Miller 1987).

Metis became an increasingly important part of Indian groups to the east. In the Dakota Territory a number of mixed-bloods spoke for the Pembina and Red Lake bands of Chippewa in the 1851 treaty councils over the cession of lands in the Red River Valley (the treaty was never ratified by the U.S. senate). In 1863 at the treaty councils at Old Crossing, of the 1,017 Chippewa living near Pembina and the Turtle Mountains, only 352 were defined as full-bloods. Without accepting any of their claims, the commissioners gave 464 mixed-bloods of the two groups scrip for 160 acres in the public domain (Folwell 1930:190–329; Wheeler-Voegelin and Hickerson 1974). By 1870 Metis men were an integral and dominant segment of the Indian communities in the Pembina–Turtle Mountains area (Murray 1984:19).

Initially, these Pembina Hills and Turtle Mountain Chippewa claimed much of the eastern part of north-central North Dakota, which they had occupied for hunting. They engaged in little agricultural activity compared with the Red River Valley mixed-blood communities north of the international border. To these Chippewa bands agriculture was not a significant, culturally defining activity. To the Dakota territorial and Minnesota state politicians who wanted their regions filled with yeoman farmers, however, permanent settlements and agriculture were a standard by which they measured the land rights of the Chippewa and their mixed-blood relatives (Lamar 1956:81–82; Pettigrew 1881, 1882). The more than 10 million acres claimed by the Chippewa bands, much of it prime potential farmland with interspersed lakes and stands of timber, became a contested prize. The politicians first refused to acknowledge the basis of the Pembina or Turtle Mountain Chippewa claim, contending that these Indians were not the "original inhabitants" of the region and suggesting that either Sioux or Assiniboine (who had been absent from this region for at least fifty years) had a more valid claim (Pettigrew 1882).

By the 1860s many immigrant farmers took up lands in the vicinity of Fort Garry, and in 1869 the Canadian government took over jurisdiction from the Hudson's Bay Company. When government officials began to survey new base lines near long-occupied Metis river lots, the members of Red River Metis communities interfered in defiance of the newly asserted authority. The survey symbolized to the Metis the rapidly growing mixed European and English population in the valley (in contrast with the French and native one), which the local Metis perceived as a threat to their autonomy (Murray 1984:20; Stanley 1960:44–66). In the Riel "rebellion" of 1870 many Metis and indirectly their Chippewa and Cree kin attempted to legitimate further their presence in the region and guarantee their political autonomy in the face of these encroaching interests. Although various guarantees were included in the Manitoba Act, the political reality was that Metis and Indians in the region were now outnumbered by European immigrants. Frustrated by the emergence of fully commercial farming in all parts of the Red River Valley and preferring to follow the buffalo rather than accept a sedentary existence regulated by others, many Metis quietly left (Murray 1984:20; Sprague 1988; Stanley 1960).

Two hundred Pembina Hills band members accepted lands on the White Earth Reservation in Minnesota in 1877, but few Turtle Mountain people wanted this arrangement. In 1876 Turtle Mountain band representatives petitioned Congress for approximately three thousand square miles, sixty miles west and fifty miles south of the edge of the Turtle Mountains. During this period many Turtle Mountain Chippewa and their mixed-blood kin spent at least several months a year hunting in the western Dakota Territory and deep within Montana; some even built cabins there and established seasonal villages.[5]

This transhumant lifestyle became an excuse for whites not to settle the claims of the Turtle Mountain band. The last of the buffalo were gone from Montana and the far northern plains by 1882, and railroads were expanding in North Dakota and westward in the late 1870s. Responding to increasingly militant statements by some Chippewa about so many settlers squatting on what they thought to be their reservation lands, President Chester A. Arthur on December 21, 1882, allocated these Indians an area of nearly twenty-two townships for their reservation in the northeastern Dakota Territory, which encompassed potentially excellent farmlands and most of the Turtle Mountains. In 1883 the U.S. Congress appropriated ten thousand dollars to relocate families onto lands within these boundaries and opened 9 million acres to homesteaders (Hesketh 1923:111–112; Murray 1984:23).

This should have been the turning point, but the U.S. Indian Office decided that only full-bloods were to have the reservation, very conservatively estimating these to be only three to four hundred persons (twenty-five families). The definition of Indianness became critical to the process of distinguishing Indian and non-Indian interests in the region. When Special Agent Cyrus Beede was sent to set up the reservation, he reported that the band consisted of only three hundred full-bloods and one thousand "half breeds," as he called them, and that there was little agreement about how everyone would occupy the assigned land. The full-bloods were opposed to dividing the reservation into individual tracts and wanted land held in common. Many of the Metis wanted individual tracts so they could make use of their previous, if limited, experience in seasonal farming and gardening (Hesketh 1923:113; Murray 1984:23).

Repeated complaints by the growing number of non-Indian squatters within the boundaries of the reservation resulted in an Executive Order on March 29, 1884, that reduced the reservation from twenty-two to two townships. Virtually all the best agricultural land was restored to public domain, and only 13,000 of the 46,080 acres in the reduced reserve were suitable for normal farm operations (Murray 1984:23). It was assumed that the three hundred less acculturated full-bloods could occupy 160-acre allotments, while the Metis members who acted more acculturated would remain or locate on public domain lands outside the new boundaries. This followed the logic of the earlier Red Lake–Pembina Treaty of 1863, in which treaty commissioners refused to recognize the Metis as parties to the treaty but promised them land in the form of scrip for future homesteads somewhere to the west (Camp 1990; Murray 1984:23).[6]

The Turtle Mountain Reservation was far from self-sufficient. Only one-fourth of the full-bloods were gardening, and the Metis lacked equipment and supplies of seeds.[7] The Commissioner of Indian Affairs' *Annual Report* for 1886 stated that 151 persons on the Turtle Mountain Reservation died of starvation during the winter of 1886–87 (Commissioner of Indian Affairs 1886). Severe weather added to the stress of "overcrowding, disunity, and friction" as members confronted non-Indians.[8] Another infusion of Chippewa and Metis refugees came southward to the Turtle Mountain Reservation and Montana after the failure of the second Riel "rebellion." This migration added greatly to the overcrowding, and soon there was further friction between full-bloods and established mixed-blood populations on one side and the newly arrived Metis on the other. Further resentment arose over the distinction between American-born Metis and Canadian-born Metis, which for many was difficult to prove if they had been born during their parents' participation in the communal summer hunts to the prairies earlier in the century. The Canadian-born Metis, in search of a place to subsist, had lost their land base in Manitoba and Assiniboia and were competing for new lands to the south (Delorme 1955; Ewers 1974; Murray 1984:24).

When North Dakota became a state in 1889, counties eager to increase their tax base placed homestead lands taken in the public domain on the tax rolls after proof of residence was established and entry fees were paid. Some of the Metis who became homesteaders soon lost their lands because of failure to pay their entry fees or property taxes. Most other Metis preferred to squat on lands rather than file a homestead claim and thus be liable to pay taxes. Many occupied lands within the original reservation's other twenty townships. Non-Indians in turn resented the Metis's refusal to become taxpayers, despite the fact that many were too poor to pay. Many non-Indians wanted the total removal of Indians and Metis farther west and the dismantling of the reservation, claiming that reservation lands were not being properly used (Murray 1984:24–25).

In 1890 a commission was appointed to negotiate the cession of land claimed by the Chippewa of North Dakota, persuade the Turtle Mountain full-bloods to relocate to Minnesota, and obtain permission from the Minnesota Chippewa for this relocation. The commission proposed to set aside a township on the White Earth Reservation for the relocation of the full-blood Pembina–Turtle Mountain Chippewa. Most did not wish to remove there and held out for further negotiations (Camp 1990; Meyer 1991:373). The leader, Little Shell (sometimes said to be from Moose Mountain in Canada), was particularly vocal, reminding the commissioners of the broken promises about the size of the initial reservation, restating his band's unwillingness to leave its homeland, and wanting to know why the non-Indian squatters could not be removed. Little Shell was willing to consider reasonable alternatives, but relocating from Turtle Mountain was unacceptable unless a very sizeable tract farther west was part of the agreement.

The 1890 commission failed to achieve a workable solution, so the Commissioner of Indian Affairs appointed a new commission in 1892. He suggested that the Turtle Mountain people might be relocated among the Assiniboine on the Fort Peck Reservation in Montana. This suggestion was based on his information that some Fort Peck residents were related to Turtle Mountain people and that the Fort Peck Reservation was in the immediate vicinity of the Milk River area visited by Chief Little Shell during the summer of 1891 (U.S. Senate Document 1900–1901:114–118).

Because resident non-Indians had become an influential political constituency in northeastern North Dakota, they would not be removed. The 1892 McCumber Commission proposed reducing the total number of tribal members, admitting that with such a reduced reservation there would not be enough land for allotment to all. This admission led to a new definition of the tribal roll that would conform to the reduced area of the reservation.

The Indian agents and the commission set up a tribal council composed of many representatives who under the new criteria would not be considered members of the Turtle Mountain tribe. Agent Waugh and Subagent Brenner selected sixteen American-born full-bloods and sixteen American-born Metis to advise in the creation of the roll. Such an advisory council affirmed the Indian Office's intention to deny enrollment to anyone born north of the international border. This council was instituted while Little Shell and many of his immediate followers were in Montana. In January 1892 Red Thunder, Little Shell's subordinate, submitted a document with three hundred signatures requesting that all mixed-blood descendants of the group be considered Indian and entitled to the same benefits as full-bloods. The roll finally produced by the McCumber Commission, with the aid of a five-member executive committee chosen from the newly constituted tribal council, excluded almost half the people who considered themselves Turtle Mountain Chippewa. Most notable among those excluded were Little Shell and his followers, who had steadfastly rejected a reservation smaller than the one initially promised, who had pressed for a just settlement of the 10 million-acre claim, and who had protested the exclusion of Metis born in Canada.

The local agents continued to separate the Indian and mixed-blood population into categories that reflected the clear distinctions they wanted. Non-Indian policy makers produced a roll that marginalized the tribal Metis by definition and effectively squeezed many of them out of the region. The reason given for the exclusion of Little Shell and others was that they resided away from the reservation most of the year. They and other families did so because of the growing non-Indian agricultural development of northeastern North Dakota and the diminishing resource base for hunting and gathering. Until his death in 1900 Little Shell continued to petition for a review of his followers' claims.

The McCumber Commission roll was reopened in 1904 for petitions from people who might have been incorrectly excluded in 1892. This was done in preparation for the allotment of lands to individuals on the already heavily settled reservation.[9] This roll became the basis for the initial payout of money and allotments to members. Here was another opportunity for Indian Office officials to manipulate the Turtle Mountain tribal council. One agent, Charles L. Davis, made specific recommendations on whether to enroll individual petitioners. Another special Indian agent, Edgar A. Allen, oversaw the land allotment process. Together, they effectively defined membership and land rights, distinguishing full-bloods from Metis biologically rather than culturally. The petitions were prepared in a formulaic manner—petitioners described their ancestry in the way they thought would best support a claim of membership in the Turtle Mountain tribe. Throughout the process the two agents applied their own criteria for membership with little or no additional information requested of potential enrollees, who could not appeal the agents' decision.

When the allotment was finalized in 1907, there was too little land for all enrolled members of the Turtle Mountain Reservation to receive an individual forty-acre parcel. Ironically, while in 1890, 1892, and 1904–1906 individuals were excluded from membership because their bands had been away from the defined reservation lands, after 1907 many members eventually were allotted lands far away from the reservation because of the increased numbers of enrolled members. During allotments in 1907 they were assigned lands hundreds of miles away in the public domain of western North Dakota and eastern Montana (Camp 1990; Carlson 1981:65–66). Just as all those who were not allowed membership were scattered in their search for survival, even some allotted tribal members in practice were expected to join the excluded Metis far to the west. Those denied enrollment came to be referred to as the landless Chippewa-Cree and were left to wander the Dakotas and Montana in search of a home (Burt 1986, 1987).

On the recently established Fort Peck Reservation in northwestern Montana, the first task assigned to the business committee by the Indian agent in 1891 was to pass judgment on enrollment petitions from the Assiniboine and Sioux. Enrollment meant access to rations, minimal medical services, opportunities for wage labor, and the promise of future land allotments. Many of the petitions were for adopted children, a culturally acceptable way of extending kinship among the Assiniboine and Sioux. Competition between these two tribes, however, made agreement on particular petitions virtually impossible. Meanwhile, some Chippewa and Metis were intermarrying with Assiniboine and Sioux members or were adopted and thereby enrolled. From 1908 to 1916 the Fort Peck Sioux and Assiniboine disputed each other's proposed adoptions for their respective tribal rolls (Miller 1987).

The boundaries of the Fort Peck Reservation in 1889 encompassed 2.1 million acres. On the basis of the formula of 160 acres per person, there was more than enough land for the Indians enrolled. Lands remaining after allotment (called by the government "surplus lands") were administered by the General Land Office and made available to homesteaders after 1913. The breakup of tribal lands on Fort Peck began in earnest in 1908 (Campbell 1988; Gates 1971; McDonnell 1991; Peffer 1951; Weil 1988).

The Past in the Present

The legacy of relocation and enrollment practices includes ongoing controversies in the vicinity of the Fort Peck Reservation. When land claim payments became available to various tribes in the twentieth century, special rolls often had to be prepared to determine "correct" descendants. This has never been a painless process. At Fort Peck few tribal members will claim openly to be descended from Turtle Mountain, landless Chippewa-Cree or Metis, but there are occasional complaints of Chippewa-Cree on the Assiniboine or Sioux rolls taking money that belongs to tribal members. Some of the richest oil and natural gas resources were found in the 1950s on adjacent off-reservation Turtle Mountain allotments, a development that also has caused resentment.

The presence of Turtle Mountain allottees, landless Chippewa-Cree, and other Indians who have become intertwined as kin remains a complication for Fort Peck Sioux and Assiniboine tribal members. The recent Supreme Court decision *Duro v. Reina* declared that tribal courts had no jurisdiction over nonmember Indians. The Bureau of Indian Affairs (BIA) advised all tribal governments that their jurisdiction was now limited to their own tribal members. At Fort Peck nonmember Indians who had been incarcerated by the tribal court were released from jail (Big Leggins 1990). The result was that relatives (especially those by marriage), culturally defined and integrated as relatives by the local communities, were further distinguished and separated by more federal definitions. In November 1991, after new federal legislation was signed into law, the U.S. government restored tribal courts' authority over all Indians within their reservation boundaries (Allrunner 1991).

The U.S. government has recently restricted services to Indians by enforcing its definition of Indian status. An example is the Indian Health Service's announcement in 1986 that it would enforce a one-quarter Indian blood requirement for most services. Grandmothers woke up one morning to discover that many of their grandchildren were no longer eligible for basic health care services (Eligibility for Health Care Services 1988). The BIA and related agencies also promote a one-quarter Indian blood standard, further infringing on the rights of tribes to establish their own membership criteria. The official notion of a full-blood Indian was fixed in a baseline enrollment of reservation-specific, tribe-specific membership at the time a reservation was established. Thus, if full-blood parents of different bands of the same tribe are not from the same reservation, their children are officially defined as less than full-bloods.

To counter such restrictions on membership some reservations of the same or related tribal heritage, including Fort Peck, are exploring joint enrollment. Blood quantum ratios would then be determined on the basis of tribal affiliations of parents and their genealogical history and not solely on the reservation of residence (Fort Peck Tribes 1988). To counter present practice the blood quantum determining degrees of Indianness would need to be redefined and recalculated for everyone enrolled on these cooperating reservations. Enrollment officers of tribal governments have been discussing changes to their enrollment procedures for several years, and several tribes have passed ordinances to proceed. The BIA is resisting this enormous bureaucratic task, with its implications for increased costs of expanded services and entitlements and the potential loss of regulatory control over the basic criteria for federal recognition of individual Indians within their member tribes.

Little Shell's band has remained landless to the present and is currently petitioning to become a federally recognized Indian tribe. Descendants of his band are not defined as Indian and thus are denied any rights accorded to the recognized tribal groups. In their petition the Little Shell claimants demonstrate that they still exist as a functioning group. In the 1988 Senate Select Committee on Indian Affairs hearing on the Federal Acknowledgment Process, there were 110 petitions under consideration, which included "Indian tribes or groups who for one reason or another lost their sovereign status . . . and Indian tribes or groups who have never been recognized by the Federal Government" (Federal Acknowledgment Process 1988:1). In defining a tribe, historical circumstances that prevented its formal recognition, genealogical continuity, and societal cohesion all become factors.[10]

Who defines tribal membership is a central question in power relations between Indians and government agencies. Those outside a social group cannot define the boundaries of association without doing violence to the ongoing practice of the group. One great criticism of John Collier's New Deal era for tribal governments was that the model constitutions legitimated by the Indian Reorganization Act did not give tribes full freedom to define their own memberships (Dobyns 1965; Taylor 1980; Washburn 1984). The law now requires petitioners to prove their right to membership solely with respect to the national government's criteria for membership. Securing government services and funding has become the source of much status and power within tribal governments. Leaders who secure resources from the government may share them with constituents in exchange for votes. Many tribal governments are without even the minimal tribal resources needed to deliver most basic services. Coupled with erratic government funding, this scarcity of capital is critical to the local economy. All these resources depend on meeting various definitions for qualification.[11] Indian and Inuit populations are growing much faster than the U.S. and Canadian national averages, while the resources spent on them per capita are falling.

Definitional violence continues in other ways, as do Indian responses (Burt 1982; Fixico 1986; Rosenthal 1985; Sutton 1985; Washburn 1985). The dogma of definition is embodied in volume 25 of the annually revised U.S. *Code of Federal Regulations* for the relationships of Indians to the United States. Under its provisions many tribal members who live off the reservation find that regulations and subsequent definitions exclude them and deprive them of rights and services. In 1985 the Reagan administration's special commission on reservation economies recommended another definitional solution for Indian reservations: economic enterprise zones. Unfortunately, more than another definition is needed (Commission on Reservation Economies 1985). Many tribes have set up comprehensive tax codes for utilities and issued development bonds for additional resources to meet infrastructural needs (Clow 1991). On several reservations gaming has been a valuable source of revenue for tribal government and social services. This practice has just recently been regulated by congressional legislation, giving more authority to state and federal authorities, but it is too early to estimate the effects of this additional intrusion. Real self-sufficiency means increasing the resources available for development of the infrastructure of Indian communities.

Much of the history of Indian education has been one of imposed assimilation and acculturation (Szasz and Ryan 1988). Many Indian children continue to suffer the definitional and frequently physical violence of imposed non-Indian values and language within the curricula of boarding schools and white-controlled public schools. There are not enough Indian teachers, and the Indian teacher corps training programs in the United States have lost their funding in the past decade. Negative self-images for Indians and racial misunderstandings are still fueled by schools teaching stereotypes of Indian history and cultures.

But in many cases educated Indians, who are still viewed with suspicion on some reservations, are charting the course of tribal economic development, devising methods to protect and preserve traditional sociologies of knowledge and creating tribally controlled institutions to serve evolving needs.[12] The colleges of the American Indian Higher Education Consortium (AIHEC) have enabled many Indians to control professionalization to meet local needs. More than 75 percent of the 1987–88 graduates of the AIHEC schools are employed and contributing to their communities and tribes.

The political agenda for many tribes is to decide how to participate fully in the decisions affecting their localities. Because so many reservations find their borders intersected by school board, county, and public utility jurisdictions, political participation must extend beyond tribal elections (Lopach, Brown, and Clow 1990; McCool 1985). The recent Crow voting rights decision demonstrates how threatened non-Indians can feel when Indian people decide to participate by delivering their votes in all the elections affecting them.

Indians have suffered a great deal in the power relationships with non-Indians, and they have been divided against one another in their relations with the U.S. government. But severing this established relationship would guarantee that these enclaves would become even more embattled. Tribal governments not having complete control over the definitions of their membership are necessarily faced with the continued threat of ethnocide. Biological inheritance, the basis of blood quantum definitions of Indianness, is only one consideration and must be weighed along with more complex circumstances of socialization and cultural orientations. These more complex circumstances are not taken into account in the enrollment regulations of the BIA. Tribes asserting increased stewardship of their own resources will need to attend to the definitions of membership and the means for their effective interpretation. Only by maintaining some measure of cultural autonomy and control over membership will Indians and other Aboriginals be able to reduce the violence done to them by externally imposed political definitions of who they are. Survival for many groups is minimally a resistance to external definitions that have contributed to relationships of perpetual accommodation to the larger society.

Notes

1. Space does not allow me to describe the further westward entanglements that resulted in the establishment of the Rocky Boy Reservation (Burt 1987; Dempsey 1984). The role of the Chippewa-Cree in the history of the Fort Belknap Assiniboine and Gros Ventre Reservation is discussed by Fowler (1987). The role of these fragmented populations in the demographic history of Montana's four other reservations remains undescribed.

2. The French term, *Metis*, refers to mixed-blood offspring of French, Scottish, and English fur traders in Canada (Foster 1986; Peterson and Brown 1985:3–8). The term has been extended to mixed-blood individuals and groups generally. The term "mixed- blood" also is widely used. Pannekoek (1991) argues a societal distinction, both externally defined and self-subscribed, between English "half-breed" and French Metis orientations. The primary focus of this essay is on relations concerning Indian groups and degrees of identification with native heritages. The terms "mixed-blood" and "half-breed" also prevail.

3. DeMallie has described the representational aspects of the treaty process among most Plains Indians and what constituted their participation in these events (1977, 1980a). Translation into different languages at the councils was a serious obstacle to mutual understanding, and "touching the pen" came to represent agreement with the treaty process on some level. The entire exchange was further complicated by different concepts of land ownership in relationship to use and political authority.

4. Eleven treaties, each bearing a number and designating a region, were negotiated for the lands of central and western Canada. The treaties, numbered one to eleven, are often referred to as the numbered treaties (Surtees 1988a, 1988b).

5. The locations in Montana extended as far west as the Teton, Sun, Marias, Judith, Deerhorn, Yellowstone, and Milk rivers country (Dusenberry 1958).

6. This reinforced the pattern of pushing mixed-bloods out with promises of land allotments farther west. Distributing scrip for future land allotments began as early as the 1840s in Michigan and Wisconsin (Folwell 1930:vol. 4, 190–329; Peterson 1978).

7. According to Murray (1984:24) "183 full-bloods, 731 Metis with United States citizenship, and 400 persons described as Canadian Metis lived on the reservation. By 1887 the number of full-bloods had increased by 100 and combined Metis groups by 230."

8. The weather on the northern plains between 1880 and 1892 was very erratic, with severe winter storms and summer droughts. It caused problems for all farmers there. Those toiling on the Turtle Mountain Reservation also were under stress.

9. The Ten-Cent Treaty was the agreement negotiated by the Commission of 1892 chaired by Sen. Porter McCumber of North Dakota. It was finally ratified by the U.S. Senate in 1904. The ratified agreement stipulated that tribal members' claim to the region of northeastern North Dakota was extinguished when they accepted allotments and a payout sum of fifty dollars each in 1905 and 1906 (Murray 1984:31–32).

10. The term "tribe" was coined by earlier travelers and used by later ethnologists to refer to a particular type of social organization. It has come to be accepted as a concept in a larger discourse, used even by Indians to describe their unique societies and make them recognizable to non-Indians (Isaacs 1975; Kuper 1988).

    There are many critics of the federal recognition process, precisely because of the definitional violence represented in such scrutiny and its ethnocentric and Eurocentric biases (see Barsh, Fogelson, Jorgenson, and Suttles testimony in Federal Acknowledgment Process 1988; Barsh 1988).

11. A number of scholars have examined the underdevelopment and infrastructural weaknesses facing most reserves, reservations, Alaskan Native corporations, and other organized communities (Bee 1982; Bee and Gingerich 1977; Berger 1985; Dyck 1992; Hall 1987; Jorgensen 1971, 1978, 1984; Jorgensen et al. 1985; Satzewich and Wotherspoon 1992; Snipp 1986).

12. The Fort Peck Reservation is served by two institutions of higher education that are tribally controlled: Fort Peck Community College, established in 1974, and Native American Educational Services College–Fort Peck Site, established in 1970. The Turtle Mountain Reservation is served by Turtle Mountain Community College, established in 1972. Twenty-nine tribally controlled colleges now belong to the Ameri-

can Indian Higher Education Consortium. In Canada there is one Indian-controlled university college and thirteen community colleges–technical institutes. The majority of these institutions have been established in the northern plains region during the past two decades (Boyer 1989).

References

Allrunner, Iris. 1991. "Duro Decision Reversed, Tribal Jurisdiction Intact (Passage of PL 102–137)." *Wotanin Wowapi* 22, no. 44:1.

Albers, Patricia, and Jeanne Kay. 1987. "Sharing the Land: A Study in American Indian Territoriality." In *A Cultural Geography of North American Indians*, edited by Thomas E. Ross and Tyrel G. Moore, 47–91. Boulder: Westview.

Anderson, Gary Clayton. 1984. *Kinsmen of Another Kind: Dakota-White Relations in the Upper Mississippi Valley, 1650–1862*. Lincoln: University of Nebraska Press.

Barsh, Russel Lawrence. 1988. "Dialogue on Federal Acknowledgment of Indian Tribes: A Challenge for Anthropologists." *Practicing Anthropology* 10, no. 2:2, 20.

Beaver, R. Pierce. 1988. "Protestant Churches and the Indians." In *History of Indian-White Relations*, Vol. 4, *Handbook of North American Indians*, edited by Wilcomb E. Washburn, 430–458. Washington, D.C.: Smithsonian Institution Press.

Bee, Robert L. 1982. *The Politics of American Indian Policy*. Cambridge, Mass.: Schenkman Publishing Co.

Bee, Robert L., and Ronald Gingerich. 1977. "Colonialism, Classes, and Ethnic Identity: Native Americans and the National Political Economy." *Studies in Comparative International Development* 12:70–93.

Berger, Thomas R. 1985. *Village Journey: The Report of the Alaskan Native Review Commission*. New York: Hill and Wang.

Big Leggins, Garrett. 1990. "Tribes Lose Criminal Jurisdiction over Non-Indian Members, Supreme Court Deals the Blow." *Wotanin Wowapi* 21, no. 22:1.

Blakeslee, Donald J. 1976. "The Plains Interband Trade System: An Ethnohistoric and Archaeological Investigation." Ph.D. diss., University of Wisconsin-Milwaukee.

Boyer, Paul. 1989. *Tribal Colleges: Shaping the Future of Native America*. Princeton, N.J.: Carnegie Center for the Advancement of Teaching.

Brown, Jennifer S. H. 1980. *Strangers in Blood: Fur Trade Company Families in Indian Country*. Vancouver: University of British Columbia Press.

Burns, Robert I. 1988. "Roman Catholic Missions in the Northwest." In *History of Indian-White Relations*, Vol. 4, *Handbook of North American Indians*, edited by Wilcomb E. Washburn, 494–500. Washington, D.C.: Smithsonian Institution Press.

Burt, Larry W. 1982. *Tribalism in Crisis: Federal Indian Policy, 1953–1961*. Albuquerque: University of New Mexico Press.

————. 1987. "Nowhere Left to Go: Montana's Crees, Metis, and Chippewas and the Creation of Rocky Boy's Reservation." *Great Plains Quarterly* 7:195–209.

Camp, Gregory S. 1990. "Working Out Their Won Salvation: The Allotment of Land in

Severalty and the Turtle Mountain Chippewa Band, 1870–1920." *American Indian Culture and Research Journal* 14, no. 2:19–38.

Campbell, Susan D. 1988. "Reservations: The Surplus Lands Acts and the Question of Reservation Disestablishment." *American Indian Law Review* 12, no. 1:57–99.

Carlson, Leonard A. 1981. *Indians, Bureaucrats, and Land: The Dawes Act and the Decline of Indian Farming*. Westport, Conn.: Greenwood Press.

Carter, Sarah. 1990. *Lost Harvests: Prairie Indian Reserve Farmers and Government Policy*. Montreal and Kingston: McGill-Queen's University Press.

Clow, Richmond L. 1991. "Taxation and the Presentation of Tribal Political and Geographical Autonomy." *American Indian Culture and Research Journal* 15, no. 2:37–62.

Commission on Reservation Economies. 1985. *Report of the Presidential Commission on Reservation Economies*. Washington, D.C.: Government Printing Office.

Commissioner of Indian Affairs. 1886. *Annual Report*. Congressional Serial Set no. 2467.

Danziger, Edmund J. 1974. *Indians and Bureaucrats: Administering the Reservation Policy During the Civil War*. Urbana: University of Illinois Press.

Delorme, David P. 1955. "History of the Turtle Mountain Band of Chippewa Indians." *North Dakota History* 22, no. 3:121–134.

DeMallie, Raymond J. 1977. "American Indian Treaty Making: Motives and Meanings." *American Indian Journal* 3, no. 1:2–10.

————. 1980a. " 'Touching the Pen': Plains Indian Treaty Councils in Ethnohistoric Perspective." In *Ethnicity on the Great Plains*, edited by Frederick Luebke, 38–53. Lincoln: University of Nebraska Press.

————. 1980b. "Change in American Indian Kinship Systems: The Dakota." In *Currents in Anthropology: Essays in Honor of Sol Tax*, edited by Robert Henshaw, 221–241. The Hague: Mouton.

————. 1986. "The Sioux in Dakota and Montana Territories: Cultural and Historical Background of the Ogden B. Read Collection." In *Vestiges of a Proud People: Ogden B. Read Collection of Western Art*, edited by Raymond J. DeMallie and Royal B. Hassrick, 19–69. Burlington, Vt.: Robert Hull Fleming Museum.

Dempsey, Hugh. 1984. *Big Bear, the End of Freedom*. Lincoln: University of Nebraska Press.

Dobyns, Henry F. 1965. "Therapeutic Experience of Responsible Democracy." In *The American Indian Today*, edited by Stuart Levine and Nancy O. Lurie, 268–291. Baltimore: Penguin Books.

Dusenberry, Verne. 1958. "Waiting for a Day That Never Comes." *Montana, The Magazine of Western History* 8, no. 2:23–31.

Dyck, Noel. 1991. *What Is the Indian "Problem"?: Tutelage and Resistance in Canadian Indian Administration*. Social and Economic Studies, no. 46. St. John's: Institute of Social and Economic Research, Memorial University of Newfoundland.

Eligibility for Health Care Services Provided by the Indian Health Service. 1988. Hearing before the Selection Committee on Indian Affairs, U.S. Senate, 100th Cong., 2d sess., June 30, 1988, Sacramento, Calif. Washington, D.C.: Government Printing Office.

Ewers, John C. 1962. "The Mothers of the Mixed Bloods: The Marginal Women in the

History of the Upper Missouri." In *Probing the American West: Papers from the Santa Fe Conference*, edited by K. Ross Toole et al., 62–70. Santa Fe: Museum of New Mexico Press.

————. 1974. "Ethnological Report on the Chippewa Cree Tribe of the Rocky Boy Reservation, Montana, and the Little Shell Band of Indians." In *Chippewa Indians*, Vol. 6. American Indian Ethnohistory series, edited by David Agee Horr. New York: Garland Publishing Co.

"Federal Acknowledgment Process." 1988. Hearing before the Select Committee on Indian Affairs, U.S. Senate, 100th Cong., 2d sess., Oversight Hearing on Federal Acknowledgment Process, May 26, 1988, Washington, D.C.: Government Printing Office.

Fixico, Donald L. 1986. *Termination and Relocation: Federal Indian Policy, 1945–1960*. Albuquerque: University of New Mexico Press.

Folwell, William W. 1930. *A History of Minnesota*. 4 vols. St. Paul: Minnesota Historical Society Press.

Fort Peck Tribes. 1988. Enrollment Ordinance, passed in special election, May 7, 1988.

Foster, John E. 1986. "The Plains Metis." In *Native Peoples: The Canadian Experience*, edited by Bruce Morrison and R. C. Wilson, 375–403. Toronto: McClelland and Stewart.

Fowler, Loretta. 1987. *Shared Symbols, Contested Meanings: Gros Ventre Culture and History, 1778–1984*. Ithaca, N.Y.: Cornell University Press.

Gates, Paul W. 1971. "Indian Allotments Preceding the Dawes Act." In *The Frontier Challenge: Responses to the Trans-Mississippi West*, edited by John G. Clark, 141–170. Lawrence: University of Kansas Press.

————. 1976. "An Overview of American Land Policy." *Agricultural History* 50, no. 1:213–229.

Gibson, Arrel M. 1984. "Philosophical, Legal, and Social Rationales for Appropriating the Tribal Estate, 1607 to 1980." *American Indian Law Review* 12:3–37.

Giraud, Marcel. 1986. *The Metis in the Canadian West*. 2 vols. Lincoln: University of Nebraska Press.

Hall, Thomas D. 1987. "Native Americans and Incorporation: Patterns and Problems." *American Indian Culture and Research Journal* 11, no. 2:1–30.

Hesketh, John. 1923. "History of the Turtle Mountain Chippewa." *Collections of the North Dakota State Historical Society* 5:85–154.

Hoxie, Frederick E. 1984. *A Final Promise: The Campaign to Assimilate the Indians, 1880–1920*. Lincoln: University of Nebraska Press.

Isaacs, Harold R. 1975. *Idols of the Tribe: Group Identity and Political Change*. Cambridge, Mass.: Harvard University Press.

Iverson, Peter, ed. 1985. *The Plains Indians of the Twentieth Century*. Norman: University of Oklahoma Press.

Jackson, John C. 1988. "Old Traders in a New Corporation: The Hudson's Bay Company Retreats North in 1822." *North Dakota History* 55, no. 3:23–38.

Janke, Ronald A. 1988. "The Loss of Indian Lands in Wisconsin, Montana, and Arizona." In *A Cultural Geography of North American Indians*, edited by Thomas E. Ross and Tyrel G. Moore, 127–148. Boulder, Colo.: Westview.

Jarvenpa, Robert. 1985. "The Political Economy and Political Ethnicity of American Indian Adaptations and Identities." *Ethnic and Racial Studies* 8, no. 1:29–48.

Jennings, Francis. 1975. *The Invasion of America: Indians, Colonialism, and the Cant of Conquest.* Chapel Hill: University of North Carolina Press.

Jorgensen, Joseph G. 1971. "Indians and the Metropolis." In *The American Indian in Urban Society,* edited by Jack O. Waddell and O. Michael Watson, 66–113. Boston: Little, Brown.

————. 1978. "A Century of Political and Economic Effects on American Indian Society, 1880–1980." *Journal of Ethnic Studies* 6, no. 3:1–82.

————. 1984. "Land Is Cultural, So Is a Commodity: The Locus of Differences among Indians, Cowboys, Sodbusters, and Environmentalists." *Journal of Ethnic Studies* 12, no. 3:1–22.

————. 1990. *Oil Age Eskimos.* Berkeley: University of California Press.

Jorgensen, Joseph G., Richard McClearly, and Steven McNabb. 1985. "Social Indicators in Native Village Alaska." *Human Organization* 44, no. 1:2–17.

Kaplan, Michael J. 1980. "Issues in Land Claims: Aboriginal Title." In *Irredeemable America: The Indians' Estate and Land Claims,* edited by Imre Sutton, 71–86. Albuquerque: University of New Mexico Press.

Kuper, Adam. 1988. *The Invention of Primitive Society: Transformations of an Illusion.* London: Routledge.

Lamar, Howard. 1956. *Dakota Territory, 1861–1889: A Study of Frontier Politics.* New Haven: Yale University Press.

Lopach, James J., Margery H. Brown, and Richard L. Clow. 1990. *Tribal Government Today: Politics on Montana Indian Reservations.* Boulder, Colo.: Westview.

McCool, Daniel. 1985. "Indian Voting." In *American Indian Policy in the Twentieth Century,* edited by Vine Deloria, Jr., 105–134. Norman: University of Oklahoma Press.

McDonnell, Janet A. 1991. *The Dispossession of the American Indian, 1887–1934.* Bloomington: Indiana University Press.

Manzione, Joseph. 1991. *"I Am Looking to the North for My Life": Sitting Bull, 1876–1881.* Salt Lake City: University of Utah Press.

Meyer, Melissa L. 1991. " 'We Can Not Get a Living as We Used To': Dispossession and the White Earth Anishinaabeg, 1889–1920." *American Historical Review* 96, no. 2:368–394.

Miller, David R. 1987. "Montana Assiniboine Identity: A Cultural Account of an American Indian Ethnicity." Ph.D. diss., Indiana University.

Murray, Stanley N. 1984. "The Turtle Mountain Chippewa, 1882–1905." *North Dakota History* 51, no. 1:14–37.

Pannekoek, Frits. 1991. *A Snug Little Flock: The Social Origins of the Riel Resistance, 1869–1870.* Winnipeg: Watson and Dwyer Publishing.

Peffer, E. Louise. 1951. *The Closing of the Public Domain: Disposal and Reservation Policies, 1900–1950.* Palo Alto, Calif.: Stanford University Press.

Peterson, Jacqueline. 1978. "Prelude to Red River: A Social Portrait of the Great Lakes Metis." *Ethnohistory* 25, no. 1:41–67.

Peterson, Jacqueline, and Jennifer S. H. Brown, eds. 1985. *The New Peoples: Being and Becoming Metis in North America*. Lincoln: University of Nebraska Press.

Pettigrew, Richard. 1881. Letter to Commissioner of Indian Affairs, May 2, 1881, no. 7519–1881, Special Case 110 Turtle Mountain, RG75 National Archives, Washington, D.C.

———. 1882. Letter to Henry M. Teller, Secretary of the Interior, May 1, 1882, no. 8078–1882, Special Case 110 Turtle Mountain, RG75 National Archives, Washington, D.C.

Price, John A. 1988. "Mormon Missions to Indians." In *History of Indian-White Relations*, Vol. 4, *Handbook of North American Indians*, edited by Wilcomb E. Washburn, 459–463. Washington, D.C.: Smithsonian Institution Press.

Prucha, Francis P. 1984. *The Great Father: The United States Government and the American Indians*. 2 vols. Lincoln: University of Nebraska Press.

Ray, Arthur. 1974. *Indians in the Fur Trade: Their Role as Hunters, Trappers, and Middlemen in the Lands Southwest of the Hudson Bay, 1660–1870*. Toronto: University of Toronto Press.

———. 1975. "Smallpox: The Epidemic of 1837–1838." *Beaver* 306, no. 2:8–13.

———. 1976. "Diffusion of Diseases in the Western Interior of Canada, 1830–1850." *Geographical Review* 55:139–157.

Rosenthal, Harvey D. 1985. "Indian Claims and the American Conscience: A Brief History of the Indian Claims Commission." In *Irredeemable America: The Indians' Estate and Land Claims*, edited by Imre Sutton, 35–70. Albuquerque: University of New Mexico Press.

Satzewich, Vic, and Terry Wotherspoon. 1993. *First Nations: Race, Class, and Gender Relations*. Scarborough, Ont.: Nelson Canada.

Sharrock, Susan. 1974. "Crees, Cree-Assiniboines, and Assiniboines: Interethnic Social Organization on the Far Northern Plains." *Ethnohistory* 21:95–122.

Snipp, C. M. 1986. "The Changing Political and Economic Status of the American Indians: From Captive Nations to Internal Colonies." *American Journal of Economics and Sociology* 45, no. 2:145–157.

Sprague, D. N. 1988. *Canada and the Metis, 1869–1885*. Waterloo, Ont.: Wilfred Laurier University Press.

Stanley, George F. G. 1960. *The Birth of Western Canada: A History of the Riel Rebellions*. Toronto: University of Toronto Press.

Surtees, Robert J. 1988a. "Canadian Indian Policies." In *History of Indian-White Relations*, Vol. 4, *Handbook of North American Indians*, edited by Wilcomb E. Washburn, 81–95. Washington, D.C.: Smithsonian Institution Press.

———. 1988b. "Canadian Indian Treaties." In *History of Indian-White Relations*, Vol. 4, *Handbook of North American Indians*, edited by Wilcomb E. Washburn, 202–210. Washington, D.C.: Smithsonian Institution Press.

Sutton, Imre. 1978. "Sovereign States and the Changing Definition of the Indian Reservation." *The Geographic Review* 66, no. 3:281–295.

———. 1985. "Configurations of Land Claims: Toward a Model." In *Irredeemable*

America: *The Indians' Estate and Land Claims*, edited by Imre Sutton, 111–132. Albuquerque: University of New Mexico Press.

Swagerty, William R. 1988. "Indian Trade in the Trans-Mississippi West to 1870." In *History of Indian-White Relations*, Vol. 4, *Handbook of North American Indians*, edited by Wilcomb E. Washburn, 351–374. Washington, D.C.: Smithsonian Institution Press.

Szasz, Margaret Connell, and Carmelita Ryan. 1988. "American Indian Education." In *History of Indian-White Relations*, Vol. 4, *Handbook of North American Indians*, edited by Wilcomb E. Washburn, 284–300. Washington, D.C.: Smithsonian Institution Press.

Takaki, Ronald T. 1979. *Iron Cages*: *Race and Culture in Nineteenth-Century America*. Seattle: University of Washington Press.

Tanner, Helen H. 1978. "The Glaize in 1792: A Composite Indian Community." *Ethnohistory* 25, no. 1:15–39.

Taylor, Graham D. 1980. *The New Deal and American Indian Tribalism*: *The Administration of the Indian Reorganization Act, 1934–1945*. Lincoln: University of Nebraska Press.

Trennert, Robert A., Jr. 1975. *Alternative to Extinction*: *Federal Indian Policy and the Beginnings of the Reservation System, 1846–1851*. Philadelphia: Temple University Press.

Trimble, Michael K. 1987. *An Ethnohistorical Interpretation of the Spread of Smallpox in the Northern Plains Utilizing Concepts of Disease Ecology*. Lincoln: J&L Reprint.

U.S. Congress. Senate. 1900–1901. *Paper in Agreement with Turtle Mountain Band of Chippewa Indians in North Dakota*. 56th Cong., 1st sess. S. Doc. 444. Serial 3878.

Van Kirk, Sylvia. 1983. *Many Tender Ties*: *Women in Fur-Trade Society, 1670–1870*. Norman: University of Oklahoma Press.

Washburn, Wilcomb E. 1984. "A Fifty-Year Perspective on the Indian Reorganization Act." *American Anthropologist* 86:279–289.

———. 1985. "Land Claims in the Mainstream of Indian-White Land History." In *Irredeemable America*: *The Indians' Estate and Land Claims*, edited by Imre Sutton, 21–33. Albuquerque: University of New Mexico Press.

Weil, Richard H. 1988. "The Loss of Land inside Indian Reservations." In *A Cultural Geography of North American Indians*, edited by Thomas E. Ross and Tyrel G. Moore, 149–171. Boulder, Colo.: Westview.

Wheeler-Voegelin, Ermine, and Harold Hickerson. 1974. "The Red Lake and Pembina Chippewa." In *Chippewa Indians*, Vol. 1. American Indian Ethnohistory series, edited by David Agee Horr. New York: Garland Publishing Co.

White, Bruce. 1982. " 'Give Us a Little Milk': The Social and Cultural Meanings of Gift Giving in the Lake Superior Fur Trade." *Minnesota History* 48, no. 2:60–71.

———. 1987. "A Skilled Game of Exchange: Ojibway Fur Trade Protocol." *Minnesota History* 50, no. 2:229–343.

White, Richard. 1978. "The Winning of the West: The Expansion of the Western Sioux in the Eighteenth and Nineteenth Centuries." *Journal of American History* 65, no. 2:319–343.

————. 1991. *The Middle Ground: Indians, Empires, and Republics in the Great Lakes Region, 1650–1815*. Cambridge: Cambridge University Press.

Wood, W. Raymond. 1980. "Plains Trade in Prehistoric and Protohistoric Intertribal Relations." In *Anthropology on the Great Plains*, edited by W. Raymond Wood and Margot Liberty, 98–111. Lincoln: University of Nebraska Press.

Gender and Culture: American Indian Women in Urban Societies

Jennie R. Joe

In the 1950s the federal government through the Bureau of Indian Affairs (BIA) embarked on a massive relocation of American Indians and Alaska Natives from reservations and villages to various major cities. Although the relocation program was promoted as a way to curb unemployment on the reservations and enhance job skills for the relocatees, this government endeavor has frequently been described by Indian leaders as another attempt by the federal government to assimilate the American Indians and Alaska Natives (Fixico 1986; Thornton 1987).

The government-sponsored relocation program caught the research interest of a number of social scientists, primarily anthropologists. For a decade or so one major research interest was the problems encountered by these individuals or families as they attempted to adapt to the urban environment (Peterson 1972; Synder 1971; Ablon 1964). From this body of research and government programs came the much-abused and generic label "urban Indian," a term still used today to distinguish Indians living in the cities from the "reservation Indians."

Unfortunately, much of the research on urban Indians did not pay close attention to tribal or gender differences, something that might be attributed to the fact that a majority of researchers were male. Thus the urban Indian world described in these reports tended to reflect the male world, leaving the Indian women more or less as part of the backdrop. The oversight meant that Indian women in the city remained invisible in most of these studies, although some lip service was paid to the idea that women were important in the continuity of culture and tribalism (Parsons 1919; Landes 1971; Downs 1972; Hilger 1952; Lurie 1961; Bennett 1968).

The purpose of this essay is to explore some of the ethnic boundaries and social structures of urban American Indian women from two tribes, the Tohono O'odham and the Yaquis, who live in the city of Tucson but whose tribal reservations are either within the city boundaries or within a few miles of the city boundaries. Despite many years of urban living, most of these women have maintained a strong tribal identity. And because they are close to their reservation, some of their urban experience is different from that of Indian women in other cities who are farther removed from their reservation. These Tohono O'odham and Yaqui women in Tucson, however, face many of the same problems confronting Indian women in other cities who must try to rear their children in a bicultural world dominated by non-Indians and in an impersonal urban environment that often refuses to acknowledge their ethnicity or tribal roots.

The Making of the Urban Indian

Although the label "urban Indian" did not emerge until rather recently, efforts to mainstream the Indian population date to the colonial period. Since that time, the federal government has periodically attempted to hasten the assimilation of American Indians into mainstream society. Initially, the assimilation attempts began with a combined program that included conversion to Christianity and formal education. To own land and gain citizenship Indians had to renounce their tribal heritage. This choice generally was illustrated by baptism and the ability to read and write. While this approach worked for some Indians, the majority preferred to maintain their culture and traditions. And for a number of decades the reservations themselves helped prevent or slow the assimilation efforts.

With the advent of industrialization more jobs became available in the cities, and before long urbanization emerged as the next convenient mechanism for assimilating American Indians into mainstream society. Although today there are third- and fourth-generation urban Indians, the extent to which the urban-ized American Indian is willing to embrace wholesale membership in main-stream society still remains unclear. There is, however, considerable evidence that substantial numbers of the younger generation in the cities are still not will-ing to give up their ethnic identity or their linkages with their tribal reserva-tions. While some of this resistance may not be visible, cultural values and at-titudes indicating loyalty to the tribal heritage continue to surface. The urban community at large, on the other hand, is satisfied with lumping all tribes to-gether; in their eyes Indians are Indians. At this level there are no differences between urban and reservation Indians.

While the federally sponsored relocation program of the 1950s and 1960s is often viewed as the major urbanization experience for Indian people, urban-ization was not a new phenomenon for some tribes, especially those who were among the first to be dispossessed of their land or those whose ancestral home-land served as sites for a number of major urban growth centers. In retrospect, a number of large urban centers in the Americas existed before the European contact (Fixico 1986; Thornton 1987).

It has been noted that urbanization has also posed problems for Indian fam-ilies living in the city before the policy of relocation. As a matter of fact, the problems of Indians residing in cities were described in the 1928 Meriam Re-port, which detailed for Congress a variety of difficulties faced by urban and reservation-based American Indians throughout the United States. The prob-lems raised by those living in the city mirrored many of the concerns expressed by those living on the reservation—the need for decent housing, affordable health care, and more employment opportunities (Meriam 1928). Despite a num-ber of improvements, many of the problems underlined in the Meriam Report still haunt Indian families living in the cities today.

During the two decades that the relocation program was in operation, the BIA relocated approximately 120,000 American Indians and Alaska Natives to urban areas (Burt 1986). This movement coincided with other major efforts of the fed-eral government to relinquish its responsibility to Indian tribes. For example, the BIA was asked to identify tribes that could be removed from trustee status, and some tribes were subsequently removed (Prucha 1984). Also, the BIA's health service responsibility was transferred to the U.S. Public Health Service. Part of the termination of the federal responsibility to Indian tribes therefore in-cluded the dismantling of a number of the programs under the federal govern-ment, including the relocation of Indians to the cities. Undoubtedly because the relocation program was part of this new government initiative, it was seen by tribes as a way to sever the bonds that tied most Indians to their tribes or reservations. Relocatees were often resettled in different sections of the city, presumably so that they would not be tempted to socialize with other Indians and rapid integration would be ensured. In addition, to discourage their unauthorized return to the reservation, relocatees were offered only one-way transportation to the city (Waddell and Watson 1971).

Within a few months after relocation, many relocatees became disenchanted with the program, primarily because the urban experience fell short of the expectations promoted by the BIA staff who recruited the young families for relocation. The problems that surfaced quickly for many Indian families were unemployment, poverty, and alcoholism. These problems were compounded by the isolation and loneliness that came with living in the more unhealthy enclaves of the urban ghetto society. Employment expectations, in particular, were not fulfilled. Most jobs obtained for the relocatees were low-paying and tended to be the type of work shunned by non-Indians. Thus instead of sharing the idealized American lifestyle, most of the Indian families found themselves social outcasts. Faced with poverty, prejudice, and isolation in the urban ghettos, 30 to 70 percent of the relocatees eventually returned home to their reservations (Ablon 1964; Fixico 1986; Graves and Van Arsdale 1965). Once back on the reservation, however, the returnees faced the same economic problems, causing some families to try the cities once more but this time without the financial support of the federal government. For some, migrating between the reservation and the city has become a normal pattern. Thus, despite the unattractiveness of the urban ghettos and low socioeconomic lifestyle associated with inner-city living, some Indian families do find it an improvement over the Third World–like conditions of reservation life.

Not all Indians who moved to the city were confined to the ghettos. Some urban families have worked their way into jobs with financial security and have invested in homes in the suburbs. Some have had careers or jobs that afforded them a place in the middle or higher socioeconomic strata. Clearly, the more acculturated an Indian was before relocation, the greater his or her chances of succeeding in adjusting to relocation (Burt 1986; Miller et al., 1975; McFee 1968). For these families the government-financed relocation experience was a positive outcome in some respects, but it did not lead them to choose assimilation.

Although relocation in the city offered some economic improvements over the poor job prospects and living conditions on the reservations, many relocated

Indians during these early years retained strong social and cultural ties to their reservation homelands and used various adaptive strategies to help cope with the loneliness and the separation from their extended family and kin living on the reservation. Despite different tribal backgrounds, a sense of an Indian community emerged, fostered by the formation of tribal clubs and other social events such as pow-wows, picnics, sport events, and monthly pot-luck dinners. Some of these events were organized by the YMCA or various church groups. Out of these interactions grew more formal institutions such as urban Indian centers. This intertribal blending and the subsequent emergence of a new generic American Indian inspired scholars to describe this development with the more abstract term "pan-Indianism" (Robert K. Thomas, personal conversation, April 2, 1989). Today, these programs for urban Indians continue to serve as a focal point for Indian families in the city as well as for other agencies that wish to have access to this population. This is not to say that informal institutions such as the neighborhood bar no longer exist. The role of the Indian centers, however, has changed over the years; they no longer provide only social activities. The Indian centers in urban areas now provide education, family social services, foster homes, and a variety of other service activities.

While urban life has fostered pan-Indianism, some Indians are still reluctant to join the movement or take advantage of the urban Indian agencies. In some instances these families may elect to distance themselves from the pan-Indian network but do so because their own tribal or family networks are strong. This strength serves to insulate them against the assimilation pressures of urban life (Mayer 1962). Frequently those who elect to insulate themselves are more likely to be those who are less acculturated and thereby are more dependent on their own kinship system for assistance and continuity of ethnic identity (Sorkin 1978; Krutz 1973; Miller et al. 1975). Indian families that choose to migrate to cities near their reservations often fall into this category.

Another important factor that affects ethnic identity today is the pressure to be among those tribes recognized by the federal government as American Indians or Alaska Natives. Members of such tribes have tribal enrollment numbers and meet a certain blood quantum. Therefore, there is a growing concern about who is "legally" Indian and, therefore, eligible for programs for federally recognized Indians. Such eligibility criteria are becoming increasingly important among Indians in the city as well as on the reservation. Verification of one's tribal enrollment is now required for many programs and serves as a way to separate Indians from non-Indians. This question of federal recognition and percentage of Indian blood, for example, has surfaced on a number of agendas among congressional groups and tribal councils. Within some of these discussions strong concerns have been expressed by tribal leaders about the effects of urbanization and modernization on the erosion of traditional tribal cultures, values, and identity.

These concerns are backed by a number of facts. According to the 1990 census, more than half of 1.9 million American Indians and Alaska Natives now live in off-reservation communities, with approximately 49 percent residing in urban areas (Bureau of the Census 1991). Many of these urban dwellers are descendants of the individuals and families relocated by the federal government between 1950 and 1970. Substantial numbers of the population represent those born and reared in the city who consequently view the city as their permanent home. Their ties to the city are further evidenced by the increasing numbers of their children who marry into non-Indian families. One American Indian demographer has recently predicted that by the year 2080 the percentage of urbanized American Indians with 50 percent or more Indian blood will decrease from the present 87 percent to 8 percent (Thornton 1987:237). Apparently by 2080 there will be very few Indians in the city who will claim to be full-blooded. In 1970 the percentage of all American Indians married to non-Indians was 33 percent. By 1980 this percentage had increased to 50 percent, an increase of 17 percent (Thornton 1987:236). Partly because of this "melting" and because of the increase in the number of children from mixed marriages (intertribal and between Indians and non-Indians) who claim membership in three or more tribes, the self-identification among urbanized Indians has become more generic over time—that is, these individuals are more likely than those living on the reservation to identify themselves generically as American Indians rather than as members of specific tribes.

This dilution of tribal identification is further evidenced by the gradual loss of the tribal language. In contrast to those living on the reservation, Indians living in the cities are less likely to know or speak their tribal language. Although there are no specific national data for all Indians in the 1980 census, in 1970 Thornton (1987:238) found that 26 percent of urbanized Indians and 32 percent of reservation Indians reported a tribal language as their first language. Also on the basis of the 1980 census, the Ethnic Studies Centers at the University of California at Los Angeles (1987) found that 23 percent of the 54,569 American Indians and Alaska Natives living in Los Angeles County reported that English was their second language. If this urbanized Indian population in Los Angeles County is viewed as a reflection of the larger urban Indian population in the country, then one can predict a decreasing trend in the number of urbanized Indians who know or speak their tribal language.

Women in the City

Although their status and presence in the contemporary Indian world are not always acknowledged, native North American women have been part of the frontier picture and history of the United States. Most Native American scholars today agree that the frontier picture of Indian women—as either princesses or denigrated beasts of burden known as "squaws"—continues to cast its stereotypical shadow. In a review of some of the early literature and descriptions of Indian women, Green (1980:249) notes: "Native American women have neither been neglected nor forgotten. They have captured hearts and minds, but, as studies of other women have demonstrated, the level and substance of most passion for them has been selective, stereotyped, and damaging." In the more balanced views Indian women may actually be said to play a significant role in the continuity of tribal cultures, both on the reservations and in the cities (Zak 1985; Bennett 1968; Landes 1971; Lincoln 1983).

Long before the massive federal relocation program in the 1950s, young Indian women were pushed toward becoming someone else's version of an ideal American woman. New England missionaries in the eighteenth century, for example, recommended that Indian girls be formally trained in housekeeping, and the government supported this idea in the hope that such training would help their Indian spouses become assimilated—it was thought that these young girls would learn to appreciate the labor-saving conveniences found in non-Indian homes, thereby forcing their spouses to provide the same as well as houses like those of the families for whom they worked (Trennert 1988; Prucha 1984). School officials also were convinced that by accepting and educating Indian girls they were rescuing them from a life of drudgery—that is, tanning hides and tending the gardens.

In retrospect, life in boarding schools was hard for most Indian students, for the girls were kept busy providing free labor. They were assigned to do the cooking, washing, cleaning, and sewing, and during the summer months or weekends they were rewarded with further on-the-job training by being placed with white families. School officials defended these outings as opportunities for the Indian girls to further refine their housekeeping skills (Trennert 1988). Well into the 1950s, female students from such institutions as the Phoenix Indian School were in high demand because they were a source of cheap domestic help. Unfortunately, upon graduation these housekeeping skills were not always applicable in Indian homes on the reservation. Most of the domestic skills learned were inappropriate because Indian homes, which usually had dirt floors and no indoor plumbing, were not equipped with washing machines or carpets.

Another formal push toward migration to the city for Indian women occurred as a result of the manpower shortage associated with World War II. Although it is not clear how many were women, about 40,000 Indians were recruited to towns and cities to assist with the war effort. With few employment opportunities available back on the reservations, some Indian women remained in the cities after the end of the war and continued to work in a variety of blue-collar jobs (Burt 1986; Metcalf 1976, 1982). Others remained in the city because they met and married someone, usually a non-Indian.

Under the federal relocation program implemented in the 1950s, Indian women either accompanied their spouses to the cities or came independently for job training or other educational programs. While in most instances such relocation was designed to resettle the relocatees hundreds of miles away from the reservation, some moved to the cities without the aid of the federal government. Most of the latter generally resided within only a few miles of their tribal homeland. The Tohono O'odham and Yaqui women who live in the city of Tucson or Phoenix represent such a group.

Tohono O'odham and Yaqui Women of Tucson

Tucson is the second largest urban center in Arizona and is home to 6,868 American Indians, mostly members of the Tohono O'odham and Yaqui tribes who live near or within the city's boundaries (Tucson Planning Department 1989). Unlike Indians living in the urban centers of San Francisco, Los Angeles, and other major U.S. cities, Indians residing in or near Tucson are for the most part not far from their historical homeland (Spicer 1940).

There are two Yaqui villages (Old Pascua and New Pascua) in Tucson. Tohono O'odham San Xavier reservation is located just outside the city limits of South Tucson. Thus with close proximity to the city, these two tribal groups constitute close to 89 percent of all the Indians living in the city (Evaneshko 1988).

Compared with the Tohono O'odham, the Yaquis are newcomers to Tucson. They fled from northern Mexico in the late nineteenth and early twentieth centuries and settled in a number of small villages and enclaves between Tucson and Phoenix. Historically and culturally, the Yaquis have remained distinct from their neighbors of northern Mexico and from their new neighbors, the Tohono O'odham (Chaudhuri 1974). After years of work and countless negotiations, the Yaquis were officially granted federal recognition as an American Indian tribe in 1978 (Locust 1987:4). Although not all Yaquis are enrolled as members of this newly recognized tribe, there is nevertheless a strong sense of community, and the new 894-acre reservation of New Pascua serves as headquarters for the Yaqui tribal government. The Tohono O'odham, on the other hand, were residing in southern Arizona when the Spanish explorers first entered the region and view the valley of Tucson as part of their ancestral homeland.

In 1988 the Native American Research and Training Center (NARTC) of the University of Arizona assessed the health needs of Indian families served by an urban-based Indian health program in Tucson. From a sample of 300 families, 60 were selected for an in-depth interview (Joe, Miller, and Narum 1988). From these a subsample of 33 is the subject of this paper. Twenty-three of these women were members of the Tohono O'odham nation; 10 were Yaquis. Table 1 gives a brief profile of these women:

Table 1. Profile

Tribe	Average Age	Average Education (years)	Number of Children
Tohono O'odham	34.7	9.6	2.7
Yaqui	45.4	6.9	2.3

In general, most of the Yaqui women interviewed were older than the Tohono O'odham women. Thirty percent of these women from both tribes were the head of their households, a somewhat higher number than the 23 percent found among the Indian households in Los Angeles County (UCLA Ethnic Studies Centers 1987). Unlike many Indians residing in Los Angeles County, all the Yaqui women were born and reared in Tucson. Only 30 percent of the Tohono O'odham women report similar backgrounds.

Not unexpectedly, a majority of the women from both tribes are members of the Catholic church. In addition, women from both tribes agreed that marriage in the Catholic church was desirable, especially for the first marriage. Most of the women, however, were flexible in their views about divorce and remarriage. Because most of them want to maintain their standing in the Indian community and the Catholic church, a number of the remarriages occur outside the church as a result of common-law arrangements. In fact, slightly more than 30 percent indicated that they had been married more than once. Having a marital partner or a man in the house is important for most of these women. Although 44 percent declared themselves single on public documents, most were sharing a home with a mate who may or may not be the father of their children.

The ethnicity of the spouse also is important for these women. Most want to marry Indians. Of the women who are married or living with someone, 53 percent of these men are Indian. Of the 18 percent who are married to or living with a non-Indian, the mate is likely to be a Hispanic. Overall, the number of out-marriages (marriages to non-Indians) is not significantly different between the two groups of women.

A majority of these women and their families fall within the lower rungs of the socioeconomic ladder, with the Tohono O'odham families facing more severe problems than the Yaqui families. Sixty percent of the Yaqui women cite wages as the primary family income, compared with 26 percent of the Tohono O'odham women. Table 2 summarizes some of the economic as well as social problems:

Table 2. Economic and Social Problems

Problems	Yaqui No.	Yaqui %	O'odham No.	O'odham %	Total No.	Total %
On welfare	5	50	17	75	22	67
Single parent	4	40	15	65	19	58
Alcohol and drug problems	3	30	5	22	8	24
Children with school problems	4	40	7	30	11	33

Chronic or frequent unemployment forces more than half the Tohono O'odham women to rely on public assistance. In this regard the Tohono O'odham women and their families are similar to the reservation population; the situation for the Yaquis appears to parallel what has been reported for Indian families living in Los Angeles County during this same period (Lenore Stiffarm-Noriega, personal conversation, November 8, 1989). Sixty-five percent of the Indian families living in Los Angeles County have one or more members employed.

Alcohol and drugs are a significant problem for a number of these women and their adolescent children. The children's performance in school is affected; a number of the mothers report that one or more of their children have left school. Although most of the single mothers do not attribute their children's problems to the lack of an adult male in the house, most feel that the schools have failed their children or that the children became involved with the "wrong kids" at school.

The Yaqui women point to their culture and distrust of public institutions as reasons why fewer of them receive or apply for welfare. One woman remarked: "We were raised to value work." Another said, "The reason why some families do not apply for welfare is because we do not want to get reported to immigration officials or to have to answer all kinds of embarrassing questions when the welfare worker interviews you." One Tohono O'odham woman explained that she was forced to go on welfare when her husband was laid off work and they could not qualify for other assistance. She said, "At first, I hated asking for welfare, but when your children are hungry and there is no food, you have no choice." Both she and her husband have less than a ninth-grade education and therefore have a difficult time in the job market.

Because the Yaqui families are less likely to be on public assistance, they are more likely to be home buyers. In this sample 60 percent of the Yaqui families were buying their homes in the city while only 31 percent of the Tohono O'odham were. Where the family has adequate income, home ownership is a good indicator of an Indian family's commitment to establishing permanent roots in the city. Most families with low incomes or unpredictable work situations generally rent. Most Indian families in Los Angeles are more likely to rent; in a study conducted in 1979, only 38 percent owned their own homes. Buying a home is also important to the Yaqui families because the Yaquis were not always a federally recognized tribe. Such stability was a point in their favor when they sought citizenship or membership on the tribal rolls (Connie Gomez, personal conversation, December 10, 1989). On the other hand, purchasing a home was not a priority for most of the Tohono O'odham women interviewed. The most frequent reasons given are their economic situation and the reluctance to make a long-term commitment such as a thirty-year mortgage for a home not built on the reservation.

The ability to speak the tribal language also is viewed by these women as an important indicator of cultural continuity. Sometimes this becomes confusing for the Yaqui families, many of whom say that Spanish and not Yaqui is their primary language in the home. Because of the overlay of the Hispanic culture among the Yaquis, many of the Tohono O'odham women view themselves and their families as more "traditionally Indian" than do their Yaqui neighbors. Tohono O'odham women point to the fact that they can speak their tribal language as one of the primary indicators of their Indianness. In fact, most of the 43 percent of the women in the sample who said they spoke their tribal language were Tohono O'odham.

For the Yaqui women, however, the ability to speak Yaqui is not as important an indicator of one's Indianness or tribalism as self-identity, especially if that self-identification can be further supported with legal enrollment papers or confirmed by the right physical appearance. As one woman replied: "I do not speak the language, but I am Yaqui—and my children are Yaqui."

Self-identification, in addition to speaking the language, is also important to the Tohono O'odham women. One woman, for example, commented, "To me I am O'odham—I may be an American Indian to someone else, but I am O'odham." The women from both tribes use their tribal self-identification unless they are introducing themselves to non-Indians. There is an assumption that most non-Indians do not care about making tribal distinctions. Some Yaqui women say that instead of explaining that they are Yaqui, they just let the non-Indians assume that they are Hispanic.

The tribal identification of these women, however, is important and is underscored by the actions of each tribe. In their battle to obtain federal recognition as an Indian tribe, for example, the Yaquis kept reemphasizing that despite the overshadowing Hispanic influence, they were nevertheless Yaqui, an Indian tribe. Similarly, the Tohono O'odham fought to have their tribal name changed from Papago to Tohono O'odham (the Desert People), their historical name.

Despite the strong attachment to tribal identification, these women also see themselves as products of acculturation. When asked how they would describe their families' cultural orientation, the women replied with the responses given in table 3.

Perhaps because the Yaquis have had more intensive exposure to the Hispanic culture than the O'odham, they have often been described as tricultural, and many still continue to blend the three cultures. And because the Spanish language is more functional in dealing with the outside world, many of the Yaqui children have learned Spanish instead of Yaqui (Chilcott et al. 1979). Over the last eight to ten years, however, the Yaqui community has aggressively supported a Yaqui-English bilingual education program for their children.

The Tohono O'odham schoolchildren in the city, however, learn their native language in the home, where they are taught by their parents and grandparents.

Table 3. Cultural Orientation

	Tohono O'odham	Yaqui
Mostly Indian	40%	30%
Bicultural	43%	40%
Mostly non-Indian	17%	30%
	100%	100%

Sometimes parents of the Tohono O'odham children place them in boarding schools on the reservation so that they might be with other O'odham children and retain or learn more of the language. The Tucson public schools hire a number of Indian bilingual teachers to work with the Indian children. Programs such as Title IV Indian Education, which coordinates some of these bicultural educational activities, are usually conducted under an Indian parent committee composed mostly of mothers.

Legal proof of Indian blood is extremely important for Indian families in the city. The Yaqui mothers are particularly sensitive to this issue because not all Yaquis are enrolled members of the tribe. Most mothers, therefore, indicate that they carefully guard birth certificates and other records so that their children will not be counted by the schools as non-Indian or miss out on the chance to be enrolled if there is another opportunity for the Yaqui tribe to reopen enrollment. The need for documentation of Indian blood is not as urgent for the Tohono O'odham mothers, many of whom have their babies registered with the tribe because they usually deliver in Indian Health Service hospitals or receive their prenatal care in IHS clinics. As a result, most Tohono O'odham mothers report that their children are enrolled in the tribe. The tribe recognizes those with one-quarter or more Indian blood as eligible for enrollment in the tribe.

In addition to taking legal steps to ensure tribal identification, a number of the Tohono O'odham women also said they pass on the tribal culture by giving their children Indian names, allowing their children to live with their grandmothers or other relatives on the reservation, taking their children to native healers, teaching their children some of the stories and customs of the tribe, and teaching them to appreciate Indian food and Indian music. Most believe that to instill cultural values in their children the children must be surrounded by people who share the same culture. Some of the mothers who work hire other Indian women to care for their young children so that the child rearing is done by those from the same tribe.

The need to ensure in-culture child rearing also leads many of these women to volunteer for a number of community projects. These projects and activities are usually Indian-oriented. In addition, women head many of the visible Indian programs in the city. The directors of the Tucson Indian Center and the urban Indian health program are both women. Furthermore, a majority of the women working in these facilities are Indian women. Elsewhere in Tucson, Indian women are well represented on various cultural enrichment programs in the schools funded by federal funds under the Johnson-O'Mally Act and Title IV Indian Education. In these programs for Indian children the staff hired to tutor or assist are predominately Indian women. Similarly, the key work force behind the Tucson program for the elderly are Indian women.

The visible role of urban Indian women in various leadership programs is also seen in other cities such as Phoenix and Los Angeles. Here, too, most of the key human service agencies providing services to Indian families in the city are headed by Indian women. In addition, in most of these cities the Indian women help organize the pow-wows and special outings for elders and youth and serve on committees advising various agencies on how best to serve the Indians in the city. They also help popularize Indian arts and crafts by buying or selling arts and crafts.

Most of the Indian women described here are married to Indians and continue, consciously or unconsciously, to be the tribal culture bearers. Indian women who are married to non-Indians, on the other hand, are less likely to be actively involved in these types of activities, although they may support the culture survival activities in other ways—for example, by attending fund-raising functions. Because they often keep themselves marginal to the world of the other Indian women, most remain invisible to the Indian network unless their children, on finding that they have Indian heritage, begin to participate in Indian activities or programs in the city.

Indian women represent a critical barrier to assimilation under prolonged urbanization. Certainly this description of Yaqui and Tohono O'odham women and mothers demonstrates that these women have helped foster cultural continuity and tribal identity not only for themselves but also for their children. From day to day, however, most of these women worry more about losing their men and their children to the ravages of alcoholism and drugs than to losing them to mainstream society. As long as they themselves identify with their tribal heritage, they not only align themselves with a marriage partner who is from the same tribe but also find ways to manage the home and social environment as much as possible to ensure that their children do not forget who they are. They may not speak the language or share all the beliefs and teachings of the tribe, but these mothers do instill in their children information and identification with their tribal roots. Thus the goals of the two groups of women are similar in many ways, but there are some differences as well.

The Yaqui women find themselves coping with three cultures—Yaqui, Mexican, and Anglo—but with each generation these women and their families are losing ground to the influences of the European American culture. The development of the Yaqui reservation has slowed the process of acculturation, but not all Yaqui families that want to live on the reservation are able or eligible to do so. And because most Yaqui families have not been included in federal Indian programs, most of them have relied on themselves for economic survival. More Yaqui women report members of their family working or investing in a house in the city; thus, in addition to being born in Tucson, most have fostered their ties to the city by encouraging members of their family to invest in a home and a career there.

The Tohono O'odham women, on the other hand, are more likely to view their presence in the city as temporary or as an adjunct to their more "permanent" home on the reservation. Thus, few see the need to buy a home in the city unless it is a mobile home that can be moved to the reservation. For many of these women the reservation serves as a refuge and a place to reaffirm their Indianness; the reservation environment allows them the freedom to be Indian. Although they can take many elements of their culture into the city with them, they do not always feel free to express or carry on some of these cultural practices and values.

The development of a reservation home base for some of the Yaqui families has opened similar opportunities, but many tribal customs and religious activities pivot around Catholicism or Mexican traditions. This integration, however, is central to the Yaqui culture of today.

As students of American Indian life, we must take note of the contributions of the Indian women—not only the strategies they use to foster tribalism and Indianness but also the ways in which they help redefine these important concepts of tribal identity. We also must take another look at the increasing numbers of people who are discovering that they are Indian and who are thus enlarging the American Indian and Alaska Native population statistics. And finally we must ask the all-important question: What does this mean for our ideas of pan-Indianism and Indianness?

References

Ablon, Joan. 1964. "Relocated American Indians in the San Francisco Bay Area." *Human Organization* 23:296–304.

Bennett, Kay. 1968. *Kaibah: Recollection of a Navajo Girlhood.* Los Angeles: Western Lore Press.

Bureau of the Census (1991). *Place and County Population Counts for American Indians, Eskimos, and Aleuts.* Washington, D.C.: U.S. Department of Commerce.

Burt, Larry. 1986. "Roots of the Native American Urban Experience: Relocation Policy in the 1950s." *The American Indian Quarterly* 10, no. 2:85–100.

Chaudhuri, Joystpaul. 1974. *Urban Indians of Arizona: Phoenix, Tucson, and Flagstaff.* Tucson: University of Arizona, Institute of Government Studies.

Chilcott, John, Barbara Buchanan, Felipe Molina, and James Jones. 1979. *An Education-Related Ethnographic Study of a Yaqui Community.* Department of Anthropology Monograph. Tucson: Department of Anthropology, University of Arizona Press.

Downs, James. 1972. "The Cowboy and the Lady: Models as Determinants of the Rate of Acculturation of the Pinon Navajos." In *Native Americans Today: Sociological Perspective*, edited by Howard Bahr, Bruce Chadwick, and Robert Day, 275–290. New York: Harper and Row.

Evaneshko, Veronica. 1988. "Demographics of Native Americans in the Traditional Indian Alliance Catchment Area" (unpublished manuscript). Tucson: University of Arizona, College of Nursing.

Fixico, Donald L. 1986. *Termination and Relocation: Federal Indian Policy, 1945–1960.* Albuquerque: University of New Mexico Press.

Graves, Theodore D., and M. Van Arsdale. 1965. "Values, Expectations, and Relocation: The Navajo Migrant to Denver." *Human Organization* 25, no. 4:300–307.

Green, Rayna. 1980. "Native American Women." *Signs* (Winter):248–266.

Hilger, M. Inez. 1952. *Chippewa Child Life and Its Cultural Background.* U.S. Bureau of American Ethnology Bulletin, no. 146. Washington, D.C.: U.S. Government Printing Office.

Joe, Jennie R., Dorothy Miller, and Trudie Narum. 1988. *Traditional Indian Alliance: Delivery of Health Care Services to American Indians in Tucson.* NARTC Monograph Series, no. 4. Tucson: Native American Research and Training Center, University of Arizona.

Krutz, Gordon. 1973. "Transplanting and Revitalizing of Indian Culture in the City." In *American Indian Urbanization*, edited by Jack O. Waddell and O. M. Watson, 130–139. Lafayette, Ind.: Purdue Research Foundation.

Landes, Ruth. 1971. *The Ojibwa Woman.* New York: W. W. Norton and Co.

Lincoln, Kenneth. 1983. *Native American Renaissance.* Berkeley: University of California Press.

Locust, Carol. 1987. *Yaqui Indian Beliefs about Health and Handicaps.* NARTC Monograph Series, no. 12. Tucson: Native American Research and Training Center, University of Arizona.

Lurie, Nancy. 1961. *Mountain Wolf Woman: Sister of Crashing Thunder, A Winnebago Indian.* Ann Arbor: University of Michigan Press.

Mayer, Phillip. 1962. *Townsmen or Tribesmen.* London: Oxford University Press.

McFee, Malcolm. 1968. "The 150 Percent Man: A Product of the Blackfeet Acculturation." *American Anthropologist* 70:1,096–1,107.

Meriam, Lewis. 1928. *The Problem of Indian Administration.* Baltimore: Johns Hopkins University Press.

Metcalf, Ann. 1976. "From School Girl to Mother: The Effects of Education on Navajo Women." *Social Problems* 23:534–544.

————. 1982. "Navajo Women in the City: Lesson from a Quarter of a Century of Relocation." *American Indian Quarterly* 6, nos. 1–2:71–89.

Miller, Dorothy, Beulah Bowman, Walter Carlin, Anthony García, Chris Maybee, and Peggy Sierras. 1975. *American Indian Families in the City.* San Francisco: Institute for Scientific Analysis.

Parsons, Elsie C. 1919. "Mothers and Children of Zuni." *Man* 19:168–173.

Peterson, John. 1972. "Assimilation, Separation, and Out-Migration in an American Indian Group." *American Anthropologist* 74:1,286–1,295.

Prucha, Francis P. 1984. *The Great White Father: The United States Government and the American Indians.* Lincoln: University of Nebraska Press.

Sorkin, Alan L. 1978. *The Urban American Indian.* Lexington, Ky.: Lexington Books.

Spicer, Edward H. 1940. *Pascua, A Yaqui Village in Arizona.* Chicago: University of Chicago Press.

Synder, Peter. 1971. "The Social Environment of the Urban Indians." In *The American Indians in Urban Society*, edited by Jack O. Waddell and O. M. Watson, 206–243. Boston: Little, Brown, and Co.

Thornton, Russell. 1987. *American Indian Holocaust and Survival: A Population History since 1492.* Norman: University of Oklahoma Press.

Trennert, Robert A. 1988. *The Phoenix Indian School: Forced Assimilation in Arizona, 1891–1935.* Norman: University of Oklahoma Press.

Tucson Planning Department. 1989. Computer Printout of Tucson Census Data.

UCLA Ethnic Studies Center. 1987. *Ethnic Groups in Los Angeles: Quality of Life Indicators.* Los Angeles: UCLA.

Waddell, Jack O., and O. M. Watson, eds. 1971. *The American Indian in Urban Society.* Boston: Little, Brown, and Co.

Zak, Nancy. 1985. "Sacred and Legendary Women of Native America." *Wildfire* 1, no. 1:12–15.

Coda:
Context
as
Montage
▲ ▲ ▲

Violence
and
Resistance
in the
Americas:
The
Legacy
of
Conquest

Michael Taussig

For those of us who spend time wondering if not worrying about the social impact of ceremonial and the reproduction of dominant discourses, codes, and images by means of civic ritual, the Columbus Quincentenary provides much to think about—especially if you are part of the knowledge industry and even more especially if you are participating, as I am, in a Quincentennial rite. One of the first things such participation alerts us to, so I believe, is that the truth and knowledge produced by the immense apparatus of college teaching, research, scholarship, and funding thereof are inevitably ritualistic and anchored in remembrance, no matter how scientific, in the Enlightenment sense of that term, such teaching and research may be. Therefore, far from being a special problem, my preoccupation with the way to represent the phenomenon called Columbus is merely a heightened version of the tension involved in this confusing yet ubiquitous mixture of truth with ritual and ritual with remembrance.

A formative influence on the precise constitution of this mixture and its ten-

sion is paranoia, as if the makeup of knowledge, the Self, and the very princi-
ple of identity itself cannot exist without the fantasmic presence of a feared
Other. Today, in this Columbus Quincentenary in the Smithsonian, one of the
First World's great temples of Othering, the Other to be exorcised in this process
of self-fashioning is that adulation of the admiral as the Great Discoverer, an
adulation that poetically sustains European imperialism in the very notion of
the newness of the New World.

Against this version of Columbus, our being here today perpetuates a different image of the New World's meaning for the Old, namely the well-known
Black Legend, so dear to the Protestant Dutch and English critics of Spanish
cruelty and devastation in the Indies. And while it is almost too easy to point
out that this Black Legend conveniently served the economic interests of those
burgeoning mercantile powers, Britain and Holland, covering over the oppression their own overseas endeavors entailed, it is a necessary reminder because
in focusing on violence and resistance in the Americas we do too easily project
onto others unproblematic notions of violence and resistance that rightfully
begin with us. Thus I want to ask what it means to turn the question away from
Others, especially poor and powerless Others, to ourselves and our own quite
violent practices whereby we figure ourselves through the creation of objects
of study. Instead of making more knowledge industries about violence and resistance, what about the politics of violence and resistance in the way we construct legacies and thereby generate power from the great gamut of stories, official and unofficial, of the violent American past?

The Heights of Machu Picchu

In 1983 I traveled for close to two months with an elderly Ingano medicine man
named Santiago Mutumajoy from the forested lowlands of the Putumayo district of southwest Colombia through the highlands of Ecuador and Peru. With
herbs and medicines, ready to take on patients, we hoped to compare notes with
other healers in other localities so that we might better understand the ways by
which the image of the shaman of the lowland forests served to further or abate
misfortune. After many adventures and misadventures we found ourselves in
the ancient Incan capital of Cuzco, and the day before we caught the train to
visit the ruins of Machu Picchu the papers were full of the news that archaeol-
ogists had at long last discovered the Incan secret by which the massive stones
were so precisely fashioned and held together. But hadn't I seen exactly this

story when I first visited Cuzco in 1971, twelve years earlier? I started to realize that this constant puzzling by the authoritative voices of society about purported secrets of monumental and large-scale Incan construction was itself a sort of ritual, an obsession, a way of defining a sense of mystery about the meaning of the pre-European Indian past so as to control the life of the present. What makes this defining mystery powerful is that it is part of a virtually unconscious way of constituting an alleged essence and originary point in sacred time of the nation-state and thus a particularly enduring notion of America, defined and perpetuated in the legacy of massive monumentalization of Indian ruins, nowhere more so than in the iconicity of Machu Picchu itself.

I was stunned by Machu Picchu, its sublime grandeur, the warm sunlight on the brooding quiet of the ruins. Of course I had seen it before, not only on a visit but in images adorning glossy magazines the world over. But they were only copies. This was the real thing. I leaned over to my Indian companion from the woods of the Putumayo—like me, so far from home—and asked him what he thought of it all. "Only the rich." he said phlegmatically. "There weren't any poor people here. These houses were for the rich." He paused. "I've seen it before," he casually added. "These mountains. These stones. Exactly the same. Several times."

"What on earth do you mean?" I was not only incredulous but disappointed. Hadn't I gone to extraordinary lengths to bring him to this extraordinary place discovered if not by Columbus then at least by Hiram Bingham and immortalized by the great poets such as Pablo Neruda with his epic poem, *Alturas de Macchu Picchu*? Of course discovery is a rather self-serving concept here, recalling O'Gorman's (1961) displacement of that term by the concept of the invention rather than the discovery of America. After all there were people tilling the fields of Machu Picchu when Bingham was guided there in 1911. What the "discovery" of Machu Picchu amounted to was that local knowledge was exploited, providing the stepping stone to its erasure within a universalizing narrative constructing America, a narrative in which the ruins would achieve not merely significance but magnificence. One can hardly imagine poor Indians cultivating corn and potatoes on the terraces of Machu Picchu today! Yet as testimony to the precious and fleeting moment in which invention becomes discovery, Bingham's book captures just that instant when real live Indians worked the soil of Machu Picchu, converting its terraces to their immediate needs. Among a dozen or so photographs depicting the discovery, Bingham has an arresting shot of two Indian women he met living there. They have been

posed standing barefoot on the spindly grass against great polygonal blocks of white granite of what he called the Memorial Temple of the Three Windows. In their rough woolen clothes, their gaze respectful yet quizzical, these women seem no less rugged and timeless than the stones of memory themselves but completely dwarfed by them.

"Yes, when I was healing with yagé," the old Indian man from the Putumayo was saying, "I saw it all before, all these cliffs, all these stones."

I was taken aback. Yagé is the most important medicine in the Putumayo. It comes from a vine in the forest and with the visionary capacity it stimulates, the healer, as well as the sick person who drinks it, can obtain insight into the cause of serious misfortune and power to overcome it. Such power, however, does not necessarily come from seeing the causes of misfortune but instead can come from having a particular image, a *pinta* or painting, as it is referred to commonly, and one of the ways of becoming a healer is to buy such *pinta*. Thus when the old healer said that he had seen Machu Picchu in his yagé-induced vision, this means something more than merely seeing something; it is potentially an empowering and even a curing image.

How wonderful, I thought, that in his very remoteness of the lowland forests the old man was able to see this incredible place by means of mystical insights given to the guardians of ancient American shamanic lore. It made me curious. I wanted to better ascertain his connection to this Machu Picchu place high in the sun and the cold wind, so ponderously still in the muteness of its massive stones. Like a flash it occurred to me. "Look at the size of those stones," I said. "How was it ever possible to build like that?" I was echoing the newspaper, evoking national discursive formations much bigger than my own limited imaginings.

"That's easy to explain," he replied without so much as a blink. "The Spanish built all this." And he waved his arm in a peremptory gesture encompassing the great vista.

"What do you mean?" I feebly responded. I felt cheated.

"It was with whips," he said in a distinctly disinterested tone. "The Spanish threatened the Indians with the whip and that's how they carried these stones and set them in place."

As far as he was concerned this was a thoroughly unremarkable event, just as Machu Picchu itself was unremarkable. "That's exactly what the Spanish did to my father-in-law," he added. "An Indian went and told them that he was a sorcerer and so they punished him by making him carry stones to build their church. They said they'd whip him if he didn't do what they ordered. His wife and children followed him along the path also carrying stones."

For my old Indian friend, at least, there was no mystical secret of ancient Indian technology. To the contrary, the mysticism lay with the need the wider world has to monumentalize the pre-European Indian past. For him these glorified ruins were monuments to racism and the colonial authority to wield the whip. And in so far as his yagé-inspired dream-image of the ruins was a curing image—as it most definitely is for the world at large—it is probably because of a deep-seated complicity on his part with that authority, using rather than simply resisting it. Here, at this point where meanings collide and thought is arrested, we should seize the opportunity to sort out our ideas about violence, resistance, and the legacy of conquest.

Dream-Work

The old man's perception certainly caught me off balance, and I would assume it is unsettling for most of you, too. There is more than a touch of blasphemy here, so reverentially has the mighty Machu Picchu been impressed into our hearts.

> Come up with me, American love.
>
> Kiss these secret stones with me.
> The torrential silver of the Urubamba
> makes the pollen fly to its golden cup.
> The hollow of the bindweed's maze,
> The petrified plant, the inflexible garland,
> soar above the silence of these mountain coffers.

Thus, the poem of the esteemed Neruda, his finest work, according to his translator, Nathaniel Tarn, images the epic of all America in the stones of Machu Picchu, the city of the dead,

> . . . raised like a chalice
> in all those hands: live, dead, and stilled,
> aloft with so much death, a wall, with so much life,
> struck with flint petals: the everlasting rose, our home,
> this reef on the Andes, its glacial territories.

And it is with pain and remorse for the suffering occasioned by the construction of Machu Picchu that the poet shall bring his poem to an end,

> and leave me cry: hours, days, and years,
> blind ages, stellar centuries.
> And give me silence, give me water, hope.
> Give me the struggle, the iron, the volcanoes.
> Let bodies cling like magnets to my body.
> Come quickly to my veins and to my mouth.
> Speak through my speech, and through my blood

Yet the Indian healer from the Putumayo forests resists this mighty nostalgia that converts the tears occasioned by self-castigation into a life-stream of blood and words presumed to make common cause through the ruins with the travail of the Indian past, sentiments that had such an impact on the Peruvian government that it decorated Neruda in person. "My poem, *Alturas de Macchu Picchu*," writes Neruda in his *Memoirs*, "had gone on to become part of Peruvian life; perhaps in those lines I had expressed sentiments that had lain dormant like the stones of that remarkable structure" (1976:324). Not only capitalist governments warmed to those sentiments. Che Guevara was also a great admirer of the poem. Neruda tells us that Che would read the *Canto General*, of which the *Alturas de Macchu Picchu* is a significant part, to his guerrillas at night in the Sierra Maestra in eastern Cuba. Years later, after Che's death at the hands of the Bolivian government and the Central Intelligence Agency, Neruda was told that in his campaign in Bolivia Che carried but two books—a math book and the *Canto General* (1976:323).

The question arises, however, as to what sort of identity is being forged through such a representation of Machu Picchu—and on behalf of whom? For is not Neruda's a distinctly European—let us say, a Columbus-derived—vision of the New World's rawness vis-à-vis civilization as a mixture of mathematics and epic verse? If so, one might want to ask what it then means to reawaken, as Neruda in his 1974 Nobel Prize acceptance speech defined the poet's task, the old dreams that sleep in statues of stone in the ruined ancient monuments, in the wide-stretching silence in planetary plains, in dense primeval forests, in rivers that roar like thunder? For might it not turn out that these were all along the colonist's dreams? In which case the further question might be fairly put as to what other discourse is there, anyway, that is not hopelessly rigged by those dreams and the history such dreams underlay? Can the subaltern speak? Can we speak, let alone weep, for the subaltern? Or does our task lie elsewhere? Here indeed lies the issue of resistance.

This is why I think the old man's flash of memory and interpretation of the meaning of Machu Picchu is particularly relevant to the themes of violence and resistance in the legacy of the conquest of America. A mere fragment, whole in its partiality, unheroic yet capacious, coolly bloodless and tearless, drastically unmystical yet dependent on shamanic flights of vision and dreaming, his is the marginal discourse that eludes essentialization in the outrageously carefree way it snakes through the semantic mills of colonial subject-positioning—at the cost, of course, of the ambiguities of indeterminancy, the charge of ignorance as to true history, and the political isolation that absorbs marginal discourse. As the object of colonial knowledge making and representation, which in fact gives him, just like Machu Picchu itself, much of his shamanic power, this particular Indian stands deafer than any stone to these heartfelt appeals to the Indian past for a contemporary national if not continental identity on the part of states or revolutionary projects. He turns our expectations upside down, no matter how sophisticated or cynical we might be, and, what is more, he seems to do this in a relaxed and even unthinking sort of way, not trying to shock or consciously resist the frames into which history and our expectations would hold him as fast as the massive stones of Machu Picchu itself. And in this unintentionality of his, I take his cryptic style of montage to be of paramount importance for its pointed effect on us.

The Meaning of Context: Mediation and Montage

As such the old man's style cannot be separated from its context, a context that merely begins with the magnificent heights of Machu Picchu and extends, through me, the conveyor of this story, to this other, quite different magnificence, of the Smithsonian, with which it is today, by virtue of this Quincentenary, indissolubly, instrumentally and symbolically connected. I want to stress context not as a secure epistemic nest in which our knowledge-eggs are to be safely hatched but as this other sort of connectedness incongruously spanning times and juxtaposing spaces so far apart and so different from each other. I want to stress this because I believe that for a long time now the notion of contextualization has been mystified, turned into some sort of talisman to the point that by "contextualizing" social relationships and history, as the common appeal would have it, significant mastery over society and history is guaranteed—as if our understandings of social relations and history, understandings that constitute the fabric of such context, were not themselves fragile intellectual constructs posing as robust realities obvious to our contextualizing gaze. Thus the very fabric of the context into which things are to be inserted and hence explained turns out to be that which most needs understanding. This seems to me the first mistake necessary for faith in contextualization. The second one is that the notion of context is so narrow. In anthropology and history appeals to contextualize invariably mean that the social relationships and history of the Other are to form this talisman called the context, which shall open up as much as it pins down truth and meaning.

I say, to the contrary, that contextualization is a deeply mystifying political practice in the guise of objectivism and that first and foremost the procedure should be one that very consciously admits of our presence, our scrutinizing gaze, our social relationships, and our enormously confused understandings of history and what is meant by history.

This is not autobiography. This is not narcissistic self-indulgence. It is neither of these things because, first, it opens up a science of mediations—neither Self nor Other but their mutual co-implicatedness—and, second, it opens up the colonial nature of the intellectual relationship to which the contextualized Other has for so long been subjected.

It is also montage—the juxtaposition of dissimilars such that old habits of mind can be jolted into new perceptions of the obvious. In fact, we have been surreptitiously practicing montage all along in our historical and anthropological practices, but so deeply immersed have we been in tying one link in a chain to the next, creating as with rosary beads a religion of cause and effect bound to a narrative ordering of reality, that we never saw what we were doing, so spellbound were we by our narrativizing—and thus we repressed one of the very weapons that could resist, if not destroy, intellectual colonization and violence.

Therefore, if it is the institution of anthropology in the context of this Columbus Quincentenary ritual that allows me to act as the conveyor of an old man's perception of monumentalized ruins and thus cut and splice space and time, abutting context with context, Machu Picchu with the Smithsonian, then this has now to be seen as its own style of neocolonial montage—a non-Euclidean ordering of space and time that we took so for granted that we didn't even see it. All ethnographic practice is blindly dependent on this cutting and splicing, abutting context to context, them to us. The task now is to bring this to conscious awareness, which I choose to do by thinking about the old man's style of montage—part of my point being that I think we will not easily accept it.

For surely it is interesting, if not bewildering and paradoxical, how wrong he is as regards space and time, yet how unsettling he is with regards to the truth-effect of his statements? He must be mightily wrong when he says he has seen Machu Picchu in his yagé-stimulated dreams and visions. Although we can accompany the poet and the ethnographic textual representation, for some reason we cannot accompany the healer from the forest on such vast southbound flights of the eye in an instant of time across hundreds of miles of Andean cloud forest. And as regards time, he is decidedly anachronistic in his notion of the Spanish and the timing and nature of what we call the Conquest. The Spaniards he is referring to are the Capuchin fathers from Igualada, close to Barcelona, Spain, who served as missionaries in the Putumayo district from 1900 onward and whom the Indians referred to as "los Españoles." Thus, owing to particularities and coincidences of a local history, the old man has collapsed three centuries of what figures as American history into a flashing instant of time, a monad, in which the ruins are emblematic of recurrent neocolonial violence practiced on Indian labor, Indian land, and on the very concept and image of what it means to be designated as Indian. What, I feel compelled to ask, might this sort of historiography—for it is certainly history in the graphic mode—teach us?

Monuments create public dream-space in which, through informal and often private rituals, the particularities of one's life makes patterns of meaning. These patterns are neither necessarily conscious nor totalizing but instead contain oddly empty spaces capable of obtuse and contradictory meanings swirling side by side with meaning reified in objects such as the famous stones of Machu Picchu set into the sublime landscape of the Andes. What we daydream about in places like these may well include images and strands of images that are a good deal more ideologically potent than what we get directly in school or from the church and political doctrine. At the same time this very capacity of the monumentalizing daydream to deepen and strengthen ideology rests upon the existence of strategic vacuities and switch-points that can radically subvert ideology and the authority sustained. A site like Machu Picchu is a sacred site in a civic religion in which daydreaming naturalizes history and historicizes nature. Think back for a moment to the first photographs of Machu Picchu as frame-frozen images of this dual process—the photograph, for instance, of the Indian women dwarfed by the great granite block, rugged yet precisely worked and thus poised between nature and culture, on the threshold of history where invention becomes discovery itself. The compelling narrations that make nations, no less than worlds like the New World, use this daydreaming capacity to naturalize history as in stones and Indians and conversely to historicize nature as in reading a history into those stones and those Indians. Hence the heartfelt rhetoric to make the stones of history and the Indians speak and, in lieu of that, speak for them and channel the daydream into waking consciousness. In this regard Machu Picchu is one of the New World's great sites, perhaps its greatest, for rendering the collective dream-work that naturalizes America and holds the American project in creative tension with the primitivism it requires and daily reproduces.

And this is why the old Indian healer's yagé dream-vision perception of the ruins of history is important. Not only because it so easily shrugs aside that primitivism and hence the Great American Project. Nor because in so doing it creates a discourse counter to the official voices and authorized versions and representations of the past. Surely all of that. But more important still is that his dream-vision so disturbingly engages with our daydreaming precisely where we have been mobilized as subjects—indeed, professional anthropologizing subjects—for the American project. For in my very attempt to use him as a true Indian voice, he disarmingly dislodges that essentialization. That is the crucial point. His dreaming catches and tugs precisely where the strategic vacuities and switch-points exist in the understructure of our dominant discourses and in doing so has the effect of all good montage, which is to shock patterns of connections into quite different patterning, capturing what Stanley Mitchell calls in this regard the infinite, sudden, or subterranean connections of dissimilars, catching our breath, so to speak. All of which is to ask, What then? Where will this breath go? What song will we go on to sing if not the *Canto General*?

The Mothers of the Disappeared: Dialectic at a Standstill

At this point I want to move from the all-too-eloquent silence to which the dead of the ruins of Machu Picchu have been subjected to consider the role of the mothers of the disappeared vis-à-vis the violent silencing enacted by state terror in much of Latin America during the past decade.

First, what is extremely important in their activity is that they contest the state's attempt to channel the tremendous moral and indeed magical power that the dead hold over the living, especially those who die (or disappear) under violent or mysterious circumstances—those whom Hertz in 1907 called the souls of the "unquiet dead" forever impinging on the land of the living. As I see it, in assassinating people and causing others to disappear and then denying and enshrouding the disappearance in a cloud of confusion, the state (or rather its armed and policing forces) does not aim at destroying memory. Far from it. What the state aims at is *the relocation and refunctioning of collective memory*. This point is of fundamental importance. The state's interest is in keeping alive memory of public political protest and memory of the sadistic and cruel violence unleashed against it. (Foucault's notion of control through norm, through normalization, could not be more irrelevant. Combining violence with law, the state in Latin America rules through the strategic art of abnormalizing. It is Kafka and Bataille who are relevant here.) The memory of protest and the violence enacted against it by the state best serves the official forces of repression when its collective nature of that memory is broken, when it is fragmented and located not in the public sphere but in the private fastness of the individual self or of the family. There it feeds fear. There it feeds nightmares crippling the capacity for public protest and spirited intelligent opposition. And that is why the actions of the mothers of the disappeared strike me as so important. For they create a new public ritual whose aim is to contest this privatization of fearful memory, whose aim is to allow the tremendous moral and magical power of the unquiet dead to flow into the public sphere, empower individuals, and challenge the would-be guardians of the nation-state, of its dead as well as its living, of its meaning and its destiny. This recognition of moral power lies behind Benjamin's injunction in his "Theses on the Philosophy of History" (1969) that "even the dead will not be safe from the enemy if he wins. And this enemy has not ceased to be victorious."

I think that Benjamin would have conceived this resurrection of the dead from the privatized interior of the Self into the public sphere as a movement creating a shock, the dialectic at a standstill. At other times he referred to this same movement as a messianic cessation of time, equivalent to what he called "a revolutionary chance in the fight for the oppressed past." One can sense the awesome potential of this shock in the dialectic of reality and illusion occurring within the isolated fastness of the dreaming self as one listens to Fabiola Lalinde, for instance, speaking of her son last seen being boarded by the Colombian army onto a truck in October 1984. Now he returns to her in her dreams. Just as he's about to answer her question, "Where have you been?" she wakes up. "It's so real," she says, "that at the very moment of awakening I have no idea what's happening or where I am, and to return to reality is sad and cruel after having him in front of me." The true picture of the past flits by and is gone. Other nights she dreams of running through bush and ravines, searching piles of cadavers. What is more, her son returns in dreams to her friends and neighbors, too.

As I scan this thread connecting the purgatorial space of the disappeared with the recuperation of collective memory by the mothers of the disappeared in various Latin American countries, I see the way by which an essentialist view of woman has been radically refunctioned by women in relation to the state, parallel to the way the old Indian healer from the Putumayo refunctioned Machu Picchuism. Such refunctioning of assumed essences is part of the struggle for the definition of the past when it flashes forth involuntarily in an image at a moment of danger. As I understand this refunctioning with reference to the mothers of the disappeared and current state terror in Latin America, these women are wresting from the state its use of woman to embody not only the nation and the people in a moment of intense political crisis but also memory itself at that precise moment when it is the aim of the state to bury collective memory in the frightened fastness of the individual soul. This can be seen by juxtaposing in the form of a dialectical image two uncannily similar yet radically different photographs—the one from Hiram Bingham's book on the discovery of Machu Picchu, portraying two Indian women posed in front of an immense granite slab said to belong to the temple of memory, and for comparison one from Hernan Vidal's book, *Dar la vida por la vida*, depicting two women who, on April 18, 1979, together with fifty-seven other people, mainly women, chained themselves to a national monument, namely the Chilean Congress.

In the former photograph Indian women have been posed to register, so it seems to me, not merely the discovery of the ruins by the man from the First World but also a powerful sense of almost natural connectedness of the present to antiquity. In the Chilean image, however, the constellation of women, memory, and the eternalization of the present in the past has been radically broken apart and reconstellated through a courageous and inventive ritualization of monumentalized public space, the space that Vidal defines as the most heavily charged with Chilean constitutional history. Bearing photographs of the disappeared, these women (and a few men) have placed their very bodies as symbols of a people enchained against that which would try its utmost to use the sym-

bols of women and family to sustain the patriarchal state and capitalism and thus justify state terror. The interweaving of individual and collective memory created by this counterritualization of public monuments can unleash feelings of self-confidence, which in turn inspire visions and joy, as we hear in the words of one of the participants.

With all the nervousness of the night before, I dreamt of my disappeared husband. I dreamt that there was knocking at the door and then he entered. I felt indescribable joy and knelt in thanks at seeing him. He looked just the same as when he was arrested on the 29th of April, with his blue clothes, just as he was, with his grey hair going bald, with his smile, his small teeth. I felt him in the bed. I felt him in my arms. And when I awoke, with my arm like this, embracing my loved one, I saw that there was nothing by my side. I quickly said to myself, "He's gone to the bathroom." But then reality brusquely returned and I realized that everything I had experienced that night was just a dream. I arose early and happy. In all the actions, not only this one, I have a vision. That the day following, in a quarter of the city, a married couple will wake to see in the newspaper a photo of us in a hunger strike or chained, and they will feel good, they will be joyful because someone is showing the face of the people, someone is keeping the fight going. (Vidal 1982:132)

Our Move

At this point I feel it fair to ask about us scholars. What do we do from this point on? Carry out more studies of other people's resistance? Surely not. For while it is crucial that the whole world be informed of injustice when it occurs and make that injustice its concern, surely part of that concern should now be with the whole Western project of self-fashioning through constructing the Third-World Other as an object of study? Surely this project has to be radically rethought and refunctioned? To deny the authority once invested in the memory of Columbus in favor of a project to consider violence (always elsewhere) and resistance (always by the poor and powerless) strikes me as running the risk of continuing the early colonial project but under a liberal guise made all the more deceitful by the rhetoric of Enlightenment science as in the appeals for an ethnographic practice that strives to grasp the natives' world and point of view—for their own good, of course!

In place of such grasping I think our new focus on Columbus can serve as the time to begin the long overdue task of refunctioning anthropology as a First-World pursuit—just as the old healer refunctioned the meaning of the past monumentalized by its ruins, just as the mothers release the power of the spirits of the disappeared so as to wrest tradition away from a conformism that is about to overpower it.

Such a refunctioning of anthropology would have to turn its resolute gaze away from the poor and the powerless to the rich and the powerful—to current military strategies of low-intensity warfare as much as to the role of memory in the cultural constitution of the authority of the modern state. After all, who benefits from studies of the poor, especially from their resistance? The objects of study or the CIA? And surely there is more than an uncomfortable grain of truth in the assertion that in studying other people's resistance, heroic or Brechtian, one is substituting for one's own sense of inadequacy. For all the talk of giving voice to the forgotten of history, to the oppressed and the marginal, it is of course painfully obvious that the screen onto which these voices are projected is already fixed—and it is this screen, not the voices, wherein the greatest resistance lies, which is why something more is required than the injunction to study up instead of down or to study the political economy of the world system rather than local meanings. For what such simplistic injunctions overlook is precisely our profound entanglement and indeed self-constituting implication in the screen of interpretation that in itself is the great arena where world history, in its violence as in its easy harmonies, in its sexualities and national-state formations, folds into rules of customary sense.

Yet I do not think, just as Hegel in his parable of the master and the slave did not think, that such scrutiny can be undertaken alone. To assume it could would be to fly in the face of what I take to be axiomatic as to the dependence of being on others. What is more, there are too many ghosts to be settled, too much violent history to be reworked, which is why I have felt impelled to invoke two powerful images of constructed Others whose place in fashioning universal history has been profound beyond words—namely, the woman as mother, embodiment of memory and the people, and the Indian as healer of the American project. In invoking their presence I have not tried to speak for them, whatever that might mean. Nor have I made it my goal to carry out what in anthropology and history is called contextualization and thereby "explain" them, whatever that might mean. I have tried to allow their voices to create in the context of our hearing contradictory images, dialectical images I will call them, in which their attempts to redress the use of themselves as mnemonics for the vast projects of building other selves, white male selves, nation-states, and America itself bring our own expectations and understandings to a momentary standstill—and thereby present us with the opportunity if not the necessity to commence the long overdue discovery—rather than invention—of the New World.

Note

I would like to thank Rachel Moore and Adam Ashforth for their comments on an earlier draft of this paper. I want also to thank Santiago Mutumajoy for his perceptions on Machu Picchuism and the late Walter Benjamin, to whose theories on the philosophy of history I am deeply indebted.

References

Benjamin, Walter. 1969. "Theses on the Philosophy of History." In *Illuminations*, edited by Hannah Arendt, 253–264. New York: Schocken.

Bingham, Hiram. 1948. *Lost City of the Incas: The Story of Machu Picchu and Its Builders*. New York: Duell, Sloan and Pearce.

Franco, Jean. 1986. "Death Camp Confessions and Resistance to Violence in Latin America." *Socialism and Democracy* 2 (Spring-Summer).

Hertz, Robert. [1907] 1960. "A Contribution to the Study of the Collective Representation of Death." In *Death and the Right Hand*, translated by Rodney and Claudia Needham, 27–86. Aberdeen: Cohen and West.

Mitchell, Stanley. 1973. Introduction to *Understanding Brecht*, by Walter Benjamin, vii–xix. London: New Left Books.

Neruda, Pablo. 1966. *The Heights of Macchu Picchu*. Translated by Nathaniel Tarn. New York: Farrar, Straus & Giroux.

———. 1976. *Memoirs*. New York: Farrar, Straus & Giroux.

O'Gorman, Edmundo. 1961. *The Invention of America*. Bloomington: Indiana University Press.

Vidal, Hernán. 1982. *Dar la vida por la vida: La agrupación chilena de familiares de detenidos desaparecidos (ensayo de antropología simbólica)*. Minneapolis: Institute for the Study of Ideologies and Literature.

Contributors

Rolena Adorno teaches Spanish and Spanish American literature at Princeton University and writes about Spanish American literary and cultural history of the sixteenth and seventeenth centuries.

Duane Champagne is associate professor of sociology at the University of California at Los Angeles. He has received postdoctoral fellowships from the Ford Foundation and the Rockefeller Foundation. His interests include macrosociological theory, social change, and social movements, especially social change in American Indian societies. He is the author of *American Indian Societies: Strategies and Conditions of Political and Cultural Survival.*

Jennie R. Joe directs the Native American Research and Training Center at the University of Arizona and is on the faculty of the department of family and community medicine. She previously taught in the department of anthropology at the University of California at Los Angeles. Her recent publications include *Traditional Indian Alliance*: *Delivery of Health Care Services to American Indians in Tucson*, with D. Miller and T. Narum (NARTC Monograph Series, 1988).

Alice B. Kehoe is professor of anthropology at Marquette University. Among her publications are the widely used textbook *North American Indians*: *A Comprehensive Account* (Prentice-Hall, 1981) and *The Ghost Dance*: *Ethnohistory and Revitalization* (Holt, Rinehart and Winston: 1989). A recent article of special interest to readers of this volume is "Primal Gaia: Primitivism and Plast Medicine Men," in *The Invented Indian*, edited by J. A. Clifton (Transaction Books, 1990). Her current academic interests include American Indians and history of archaeology.

William L. Merrill is curator of anthropology at the National Museum of Natural History, Smithsonian Institution. He attended the University of North Carolina and the University of Michigan. Since 1977 he has conducted research on the culture and history of the Rarámuri (Tarahumara) Indians of Chihuahua, Mexico. His publications include *Rarámuri Souls: Knowledge and Social Process in Northern Mexico* (Smithsonian Institution Press, 1988). Currently he is completing a cultural and social history of northern Mexico.

David Reed Miller is assistant professor and head of the department of Indian studies, Saskatchewan Indian Federated College–University of Regina. He was a postdoctoral fellow in the department of anthropology at the Smithsonian Institution during 1988–89 and is currently writing a cultural history of the Assiniboine and Sioux tribes of the Fort Peck Reservation of northeast Montana.

José Luis Mirafuentes Galván, a graduate in history from the Ecole des Hautes Etudes en Sciences Sociales, Paris, is a researcher in the Instituto de Investigaciones Históricas of the Universidad Nacional Autónoma de México (UNAM) and professor in UNAM's philosophy and literature faculty. He is the author of several papers on Indian resistance in northern Mexico during the colonial period and is preparing a book on Spanish colonization and Indian resistance in Sonora during the eighteenth century.

Franklin Pease G. Y. is professor of history at the Pontificia Universidad

Católica del Perú, where he has served as a trustee and dean of literature and social sciences. He held the directorship of the National Library of Peru from 1983 to 1986 and a Guggenheim Fellowship for the year 1982–83. His many publications on Andean history and anthropology include *Atahualpa* (1964), *Los últimos incas del Cuzco* (1972), *Perú: Una aproximación bibliográfica* (1979), and *Los mitos en la región andina* (1985). His current book project concerns Andean chroniclers of the sixteenth and seventeenth centuries.

José Rabasa is associate professor of Spanish at the University of Maryland, College Park. He has published articles on colonial discourse in Mercator's *Atlas*, Cortés's representation of Tenochtitlan and indigenous counterdiscourse, utopian ethnology in Las Casas, and the scriptural economy in Columbus's writings, and is the author of *Inventing America: An Essay on Sixteenth-Century Spanish-American Historiography and the Formation of Eurocentrism*. He is currently studying colonial representations of the farthest northern frontier of New Spain.

Michael Taussig was born in Sydney, Australia, where he graduated from medical school, and went on to study sociology at the London School of Economics, beginning fieldwork in rural Colombia in late 1969, a country he has returned to many times since. He has researched and written about the abolition of African slavery, peasant economics, commodity fetishism, terror, and the impact of colonialism on Indian healing. His most recent book is *Shamanism, Colonialism, and the Wild Man: A Study in Terror and Healing* (1986). At present he teaches in the department of performance studies of New York University.

William B. Taylor, professor of history at Southern Methodist University, writes on colonial Latin America and Anglo-American representations of modern Mexico. His books include *Landlord and Peasant in Colonial Oaxaca* (Stanford, 1972) and *Drinking, Homicide, and Rebellion in Colonial Mexican Villages* (Stanford, 1979). *Magistrates of the Sacred: Priests in Their Parishes in Eighteenth-Century Mexico* is nearing completion.

Index